PELICAN BOO[K]

THE PELICAN HISTORY OF EU[ROPE]
Advisory Editor: J. H. Plumb

THE AWAKENING OF EUROPE

Philippe Wolff was born in Montmorency, near Paris, in 1913. He studied in Rennes and later at the Sorbonne, where he was a pupil of Ferdinand Lot and Marc Bloch. From 1938 to 1939 he did research at London University, and at the outbreak of war he became a liaison officer with the British Expeditionary Force in France. He taught in the United States, in 1955 at the University of Chicago, in 1958 at the University of Texas – also participating in the Second International Congress of Historians of the United States and Mexico – and in 1966 at Harvard summer school. From 1945 until 1974 he was Professor of History at Toulouse University, and Emeritus Professor since 1974.

His other publications include *Histoire de Toulouse* (1958), *Les origines linquistiques de l'Europe* (1971) *Ongles bleus, Jacques et Ciompi,* (with Michel Mollat) *Les révolutions populaires en Europe au XIVe et XVe siècles* (1970) and *Les Toulousiens dans l'histoire.*

THE PELICAN HISTORY
OF EUROPEAN THOUGHT
VOLUME 1

The Awakening of Europe

PENGUIN BOOKS

Penguin Books Ltd, Harmondsworth, Middlesex, England
Viking Penguin Inc., 40 West 23rd Street, New York, New York 10010, U.S.A.
Penguin Books Australia Ltd, Ringwood, Victoria, Australia
Penguin Books Canada Limited, 2801 John Street, Markham, Ontario, Canada L3R 1B4
Penguin Books (N.Z.) Ltd, 182–190 Wairau Road, Auckland 10, New Zealand

First published 1968
Reprinted 1985, 1987

Printed and bound in Great Britain by
Cox & Wyman Ltd, Reading
Set in Monotype Bembo

To the Memory of
Eileen Power

CONTENTS

CONTENTS

MAPS

INTRODUCTION

This book is not a history of literature, or of ideas, or even a complete history of European culture from the ninth century to the twelfth – the period to which its birth may be confidently assigned. Its object is more modest, though still over-ambitious.

I have set myself, first of all, the task of examining the relationship between history in general and the growth of culture. This involves at least a brief glance at the historical background, particularly the development of social and economic conditions, showing the progressive build-up of what may be called the cultural foundations of Europe, and at the same time how this general development produced a parallel development in culture and gave it a particular direction. And exactly when and how did this intellectual stirring cease to be academic and somewhat artificial, and become an integral part of everyday life, concerned with real problems, attempting to find solutions for them, thus affecting the course of history as a whole?

Secondly, I have examined the psychological process whereby the work of those who were intellectually the most gifted, and living in the most favourable social environment, resulted in the gradual upward curve that indicates the intellectual rise of Europe. To do this properly I would have to be a psychologist, which I am not. The present work is therefore no more than a rough sketch which may attract the attention of psychologists with an inclination to regard the past as a suitable field for study.

The problems set today by the spread of culture to the underdeveloped or – to put it more optimistically – the developing countries, seem to offer an incentive for such a study. The Europe of Charlemagne was incontestably under-developed, and it too acquired a great deal of its culture from without, as a legacy from a splendid past which had to be more or less rediscovered. Of course, historical conditions do not repeat themselves exactly, and comparative history must be approached with the utmost circumspection. Even so, it can provide no simple answers, and it probably only serves to emphasize the complex problems raised at any period by the implementation and development of a particular culture. Even this, however, is a valuable service.

Since the most that can be done in a book of this length is to point out a few possible paths without actually pursuing any of them very far, I have tried to avoid making it too laborious. In the four centuries or so under consideration I have selected the three periods, each of about fifty years, which seem to have produced the greatest density of innovation. To each of these periods I have given the name of one outstandingly important individual and made him the central figure, while leaving myself free to stress anything which does not fit into the general picture rather than throw a false light on it. Biographical details, where these help to provide real insight into the historical background, have also been allowed to play a part.

The book is therefore riddled with gaps, a fact for which I accept full responsibility. I must mention one omission which I deeply regret, but which was forced on me by my ignorance of the subject concerned: this is in the history of artistic development. What I should very much like to see is a similar investigation into the vast field of art, which could point to conjunctions, parallels and compensations. My own teacher, Marc Bloch, once wrote of the eleventh and twelfth centuries:

The remarkable artistic flowering of the feudal era ... was ... very often a refuge, as it were, for values which could find no outlet elsewhere. The gravity so lacking in the epic must be sought in romanesque architecture. The intellectual precision which lawyers failed to attain in their documents came out in the work of the men who built arches.

Ultimately the history of man's intellectual development is a single whole. All I have done here is to bring to it my own humble contribution.

PART ONE

The Time of Alcuin

Chapter 1

THE HISTORICAL BACKGROUND

ONE day in the winter of 780–81 the head of the episcopal school and library at York, a man of nearly fifty, famous for his piety and learning, took ship across the Channel. His name was Alcuin and he was on his way to Rome as the emissary of the newly installed archbishop of York, Eanbald, to receive from the Pope on his behalf the *pallium*, a woollen vestment adorned with the sign of the cross, which was the emblem of his high office. It was not Alcuin's first visit to the Continent. He had already made the journey to Rome in the company of the former archbishop, his revered master Aelbert. On another occasion he had travelled up the Rhine, visiting the most famous cities and monasteries on the way, and had met the young Frankish king Charles, the future Charlemagne, whose reign had already seen such an auspicious beginning.

We can picture his journey: the small company travelling as fast as possible at that time of year, urging their tired horses over the few, indifferent roads and compelled to call an early halt at nightfall. At that time the chief port in Gaul was Quentovic at the mouth of the Canche, not far from the small, present-day town of Étaples. It was a thoroughfare for the clerks, pilgrims and merchants from England who had embarked somewhere in the region of Hastings and were familiar guests in the monasteries of northern Gaul. Beyond, their routes diverged.

Alcuin arrived in Rome at last and remained there for several weeks, taking part in ecclesiastical debates and, of course, attending a great many religious services all designed to enhance the prestige of the Holy See. Then, armed with Eanbald's *pallium*, he set out for home. At Parma, in the middle of March 781, his path crossed that of Charlemagne, who was himself on his way to celebrate Easter in Rome. It was then that the king asked him, when he had completed his mission, to return and help him in the task of educating and reforming his court and the clergy of his realm. It may be thought that Alcuin would have hesitated before committing himself to a life which, for all its splendid prospects, was utterly new to him. However, the death of his beloved master Aelbert and the wars which for some years past had ravaged Northumbria, of which York was the capital, had already weakened his ties with his native land, and he accepted the offer.

It was a decisive step for the history of European culture. Alcuin's was the moving spirit behind what we now know as the 'Carolingian Renaissance'.

Our first impression of Charlemagne is of a conqueror. Each spring, as soon as there was sufficient new growth to ensure adequate provision for men and horses, the army would gather on the '*champ de Mai*'. This was the occasion for presenting all major political decisions by the sovereign. Then the troops set out under his command to spend the summer campaigning. They returned in the autumn, somewhat fewer in numbers, and dispersed to rest for the winter. Such, with little variation, was the pattern for forty-seven years of a reign which knew hardly any real time of peace. This incessant activity enabled Charlemagne to push back on all sides the boundaries of the already well-established Frankish kingdom he inherited from his father, Pepin the Short.

In Italy, Charlemagne conquered the Lombard kingdom which covered the whole northern part of the peninsula and placed on his own head the iron crown of the Lombard kings. He also extended a more or less irksome protectorate over the Roman States which Pepin had granted to the papacy and, farther south, over the two hitherto independent Lombard duchies of Spoleto and Benevento.

But it was Germany on which he chiefly concentrated. In more than thirty years of bitter fighting, punctuated by fearful reprisals, he subdued the pagan Saxons who inhabited the north, from the Ems to the Elbe. Bavaria, too, which had shown signs of wriggling free of a dependence hitherto more theoretical than real, was sharply brought to heel. Thus the old Roman dream, in pursuit of which the legions of Varus had perished, of a Germany fully integrated into the civilized world, had come true at last, even if it was a Frank, and consequently a German, who actually brought it about.

Charlemagne was not always equally successful. True, in the south-east he was lucky enough to carry the fortified Ring of the Avars and bring under his dominion the remnants of this once-great Asiatic people, scattered over a large part of what is now Hungary. But Muslim Spain had some rude shocks in store for him. When in May 777 a somewhat bewildered Arab delegation arrived at Paderborn, in the heart of Saxony, to solicit his aid against the emir of this Muslim province, he may have had visions of liberating the entire Iberian peninsula from the Crescent. Under the walls of Saragossa, which closed its gates to him, he had bitter proof of the fragility of the support on which he had counted. Moreover, at Roncesvaux, on the return journey across the Pyrenees, his army suffered a defeat of which contemporary sources cannot entirely conceal the gravity – although it was later to be glorified in the *Chanson de Roland*. Charlemagne was obliged to be content with creating a defensive barrier between the Ebro and the Pyrenees, which was to remain under the threat of Muslim armies for a further two hundred years or more.

With the exception of the British Isles, which Charlemagne could never hope to conquer – although he maintained consistent relations with the most powerful ruler, King Offa of Mercia – the Frankish king now controlled nearly the whole of western Christendom. The official titles which appear at the head of his acts show the extent and variety of his powers: 'Charles by the grace of God, king of the Franks and Lombards, and Roman patrician'. He might also have added: 'liberator of Gothia (present-day Catalonia and Bas Languedoc)'. This quasi-universal power did seem to bear a striking resemblance to that of the Roman emperors to whose title no 'barbarian' had as yet dared lay claim. In fact, the imperial throne in Constantinople was occupied at the time by a woman, Irene, who because of 'the fragility and inconstancy of mind of that sex' could not be considered a true emperor. On Christmas night 800, when Charlemagne attended the Mass of the Nativity in the church of St Peter in Rome, the Pope placed a golden crown on his head and all those present acclaimed him. 'To Charles, augustus, crowned of God, great and peaceful Emperor of the Romans, life and victory!'

To attempt to revive in the West, and for a Frank at that, the glorious rank held by Augustus, Trajan, Marcus Aurelius and Constantine was undoubtedly a new and audacious move. The Byzantines chose either to ignore it or to scoff. The chronicler Theophanes mockingly described Charlemagne being 'anointed with oil from head to foot' by the Pope. What is more doubtful is whether Charlemagne himself fully understood all that the idea had once stood for. He tried in his own way – the heavy handed way – to play the part of a Christian emperor as it had been envisaged since Constantine, but he was unable to divest himself of the Frankish custom of dividing up his inheritance, and distributed his possessions among his sons as if he were dealing with a family estate rather than the *res publica*. In the end it was pure chance that only one of his sons survived him, and Louis the Pious inherited the whole. Louis, though better educated, was weaker and afflicted besides with sons who were tenacious of life, and he perpetuated this mistake. The ensuing squabbles and divisions were one cause of the Carolingian decline.

Charlemagne is not generally ranged among the great captains of history. His personal courage, the powerful organization of his armies and the weakness and isolation of his enemies do more to explain his successes than any particular strategical genius. An examination of his campaigns reveals, moreover, that he suffered more than one defeat. Even before his death his strength, which was rooted almost entirely in the land, had shown itself quite ineffective in the face of those new, sea-borne enemies, the Normans and the Saracens. After his death the struggle against them exhausted the already divided resources of the Empire.

Even so, the achievements of these few decades of victory and good fortune were remarkably significant. If we look for a moment at the map of the Carolingian Empire we find that it calls to mind another picture, one infinitely closer to our own times. With only a few minor differences on its eastern frontiers, the picture is that of Europe of the Common Market, to which, despite a great variety of obstacles, Great Britain is drawing ever closer, while Spain's position is not yet clear. It cannot be altogether accidental that the old structures built up since the middle ages on Carolingian foundations should have emerged again in the mid-twentieth century as a practicable base on which to build a new Europe. This is the connexion we have to establish in the field of culture.

But before we come to describe this Carolingian culture which owed so much to the work of Alcuin, a word or two must be said about the physical, economic and social conditions under which it developed.

The glory of Charlemagne should not make us forget that these conditions were exceedingly primitive. Scholars have long argued, and will no doubt continue to argue for a long time to come, as to whether the time of Charlemagne was an era of economic progress or not. There is certainly evidence that the king and a few great abbeys showed a new interest in the working of their estates (it is this interest we have to thank for most of our documentary information about rural life of the period), just as there is evidence that military conquest, especially in Saxony, was the first step towards the cultivation of hitherto untamed areas, and the bad roads of the Empire were busy with the traffic of goods and victuals wanted by the court and the armies. But the important fact is that in a world where agricultural techniques remained so primitive none of this could go very far.

In the very limited extent to which we can assess them, harvests seem to have been incredibly poor. By a piece of rare good luck an inventory has been preserved which was made of the royal domain of Annapes, on the borders of Flanders and Artois. The grain crop it records is less than double the amount sown. This may have been a particularly bad year, but the few other indications we possess also suggest an average somewhere in the region of two to one. Moreover corn had to be sown very sparingly and the land left periodically to lie fallow. On the rich, better-cultivated soil of a region such as the Paris basin, given good weather conditions, one year's fallow might be enough to balance two years of crops, one of cereal sown in the autumn (wheat, which was the most sought after for human consumption, spelt and rye), and the other of spring corn (oats for horses, and barley). When conditions were less favourable, and elsewhere at all times, the fallow periods had to be more frequent. Lastly, in all regions the habit of a temporary, nomadic system of cultivation existed and often predominated, very much as it does in underdeveloped countries today. A patch would be cleared and enclosed, produce one or two crops and then be left to lie fallow again for years on end.

From what we know of the agricultural methods of the time, this poor yield is quite understandable. Comparatively few cattle meant little manure, and this was generally kept for the gardens which were under continuous cultivation around the poorer dwellings. There were as yet few metal tools. The entire domain of Annapes, which must have been extremely large since it supported nearly two hundred head of cattle, boasted altogether only two scythes, two sickles and two spades. The peasants of Charlemagne's time snatched their miserable livelihood from the soil with the aid of wooden tools the operative parts of which had been hardened in the fire.

Clearly such implements could only be of use where the soil was particularly suitable, well-drained and sufficiently friable to be dug without too much effort. Such soil was not to be found everywhere. In other places, only sturdy wheeled ploughs equipped with shares and mould boards could have defeated the moist, heavy ground and dense natural vegetation, and probably very few of these were yet in existence. So, although these were the richest lands, they lay idle for want of the proper tools. Even where cultivation was possible it demanded plenty of labour. Think of the manpower required to hoe the fields by hand, to complete the work of the swing-plough by periodically digging with a spade, enclose the cultivated ground and carry the harvest home.

There is nothing at all surprising therefore in the picture of the overall distribution of population reflected by the all too rare documents of the time. An inventory of his domains compiled in about 820 for the abbot of St Germain des Prés, on the outskirts of Paris, included eight villages in the region of Paris, the number of whose inhabitants was already very close to that estimated for the same area in the mid-eighteenth century. The most heavily cultivated areas were also the most densely populated to meet the demand for labour in the fields. But there were many more regions, in England, Germany and even in Gaul itself, which were virtually uninhabited. And life was equally precarious in both, although for different reasons: too many people in one place, and insufficient cultivation in another.

These vast areas of waste land, all more or less heavily forested, were still indispensable to man, who found in them a subsidy for his meagre diet and provision for a wide variety of needs. In the forests people could gather a multitude of berries and the fruit of trees which at a later date would be grown specifically in orchards. They could let their animals, especially their pigs, loose to roam there almost at will. They could hunt and fish, find wood for their houses, fires and tools, as well as resin for torches and bracken for their beds. All cultivated land must have been surrounded by these deep fringes of wild country without which it would not have been able to support the inhabitants.

In this landscape still almost untouched by man – and even that at the cost of tremendous effort and with such pathetic results – there could not be many towns. Indeed, there was not much use for them. Outside the Mediterranean area, where a more highly-developed system of agriculture and relatively intensive trade had encouraged urban development, real towns only developed where there was a political and military need, for example along the Rhine frontier of the Roman Empire.

But the towns no longer fulfilled the administrative and civilizing functions which Rome had given them, and they were no longer sustained by the busy traffic of the Roman world. Even in southern Europe, from the third century, they had declined beyond redemption under the protracted strain of invasions. Rome, her aqueducts ruined in the course of various sieges, was now no more than a shadow of herself. But these ghost cities with their ruined monuments still retained a certain grandeur beside the miserable overgrown villages which constituted the so-called episcopal 'cities' elsewhere, and were the only centres of any importance. Alcuin, at the end of his life, found the city of Tours with its 'smoky roofs small and contemptible' but at least the bishop was able to supply from his vast domains the provision necessary for the several hundred servants and artisans who made up its population.

Apart, therefore, from legal complications raised by certain statutes, Carolingian society seems to have been simple enough. At its base was the immense, toiling mass of people who worked the land and lived constantly on the verge of starvation. Among them, and probably more numerous than the documents suggest, were small, theoretically independent landowners subject only to the taxes that were demanded of them by Church and State. But there were also many tenants dwelling on the great domains, paying various dues to their masters and providing vital labour for the running of the main farm, on which, in addition, a number of slaves were still kept.

Above these was a tiny minority of overlords concerned with the more exalted tasks of prayer, warfare and administration. They were few because, however undernourished the mass of the peasantry might be, there was still very little over, and if they were to survive at all, especially on the lavish scale befitting their station, they had to accumulate fantastic amounts of land. The secular domain of Leeuw-Saint-Pierre in Brabant covered more than eighteen thousand hectares (some 45,000 acres). The abbey of St Germain des Prés owned at least thirty-three thousand, while St Martin at Tours controlled not only the estates directly round about but also lands scattered all over Austrasia, Aquitaine and Provence. On his acquisition of the Lombard kingdom in 774, Charlemagne even added the gift of the Isle of Sirmio on Lake Garda and of the whole of Camonica valley. Of course, not all estates were as large as this, although Charlemagne's victories allowed him to bestow lavish gifts, increasing the wealth of his followers and adding somewhat to the number of Church foundations. Even so, the 'Carolingian Renaissance' can have affected only a very few people.

Chapter 2

THE DECLINE IN
CLASSICAL CULTURE

THE belief that a renaissance of learning and culture did actually occur in the Carolingian era – and the majority of historians do believe this – implies the previous existence of a more or less lengthy period when culture of any kind was dead or at least dormant. The ruin of the once vast and mighty Roman Empire is one of those astounding phenomena which have never ceased to exercise the minds of historians. Even confined to only one aspect, the problem still retains all its interrogative force. How could this decline of ancient culture come about and what caused it?

But the belief in a Carolingian renaissance does not mean that it happened all at once. There is no need to exalt Charlemagne by blackening the picture of what he found when he came to the throne. On the contrary, we should study these previous events in some detail if we are to discover what lay behind the Carolingian achievement – an immense project that must be confined to the bare essentials.

EDUCATION IN ANCIENT ROME

The first subject deserves particular attention because the nature, form and omissions of the system of education built up little by little in ancient Rome were to have a lasting effect on our European culture.

Once the first rudiments of reading, writing and arithmetic had been acquired by means of a private tutor or local school, the young Roman studied under a grammarian, but his lessons were not confined to learning his own language correctly. Textbooks commonly propounded systems of rules from grammar, spelling and prosody. Moreover, by way of example, these studies included the analysis of many verse and prose texts which gave the pupil a fairly wide literary knowledge. The next step was the school of rhetoric where the future lawyer or magistrate learned the art of speechmaking. Theoretical studies were rounded off by practical exercises, involving more or less slavish copies of classical examples, and also by a fairly brief analysis of the rules of logical reasoning known as dialectic.

The most original aspect of Roman education was the study of law, which Virgil actually regarded as the real vocation of Rome: 'It is your peculiar art to make laws for peace among the nations ...' The schools also functioned as legal chambers and besides a knowledge of the law and its processes were able to give their pupils a thorough grounding in legal science and its practical application to actual cases.

Above all, then, this was the kind of literary and practical education designed to turn out the citizens, lawyers and administrators Rome needed. Access to a wider culture necessitated the study of Greek, as this was the language of the philosophical and scientific works current in the Hellenistic East. Here it was customary to recognize four principal branches of learning: arithmetic, geometry, astronomy and music (by which was meant theory of music). To these must be added specialized sciences such as medicine, which were not included in the general education. With the three branches of literature already mentioned – grammar, rhetoric and dialectic – this made up a total of seven subjects, which came to be known very early on as the Liberal Arts – a heading perpetuated in our own time by such titles as Bachelor of Arts.

Even before the Roman Empire had been overrun by invasion this programme had become greatly impoverished. In the west a knowledge of Greek had become extremely rare and all that remained of the remarkable scientific heritage of the Hellenistic world were a few collections of curious anecdotes and some elementary notions derived from Pliny the elder and men like Solinus who imitated him. Pliny was a glutton for work, but utterly lacking in discrimination. He amassed a vast collection of quotations drawn at random from Greek authors of widely unequal value, and many bizarre legends about animals and outlandish medical prescriptions common throughout the Middle Ages can be traced back to him. Only in a few technical spheres, such as agronomy, land surveying, and civil and military architecture does the legacy of Rome seem to have been of any real use.

Christianity, as a religion based on written Revelation and sacred texts, demanded a minimum of education if these were to be preserved and understood. The Roman educational system was clearly not designed with a view to such understanding, while the mythology and immorality which were widespread in the texts studied for grammar might also, and with good reason, prove shocking to a Christian. However, the Roman converts were still so accustomed to classical methods of education that it did not occur to them to modify them either wholly or in part. The medieval monks who were so thrilled by the mythology of Virgil and the love poems of Ovid were only following this dangerous example. Only St Augustine, who before his conversion had received a very thorough education, conceived and expounded in his work, *Of Christian Doctrine*, a programme of education that was specifically Christian and designed for a better understanding of the Scriptures. Rhetoric was relegated to a humbler place, while history and geography made their appearance. But the Roman Empire was already beginning to crumble before the barbarian assaults and the time was not propitious for innovations.

INVASIONS AND DECADENCE

The great invasions and, in the West, the growth of 'barbarian kingdoms' with a cruder administration on the ruins of the Roman Empire, together with a general decline of cities, combined to bring about a complete breakdown in education and culture. Little by little, throughout the old Roman world, swiftly in one place, and more slowly in another, the schools disappeared, leaving the future channels of culture drastically reduced. Education was not much more than a small comfort amidst the evils of the time, a way of making one's mark in society. Sidonius Apollinaris, who belonged to a senatorial family from Auvergne in the fifth century, maintained that: 'Now that the degrees of honour which made it possible to distinguish the social classes from the humblest to the highest, no longer exist, the only gauge of nobility will henceforth be that of literacy.'

Like a plant deprived of its roots, Roman culture could only shrivel and die. A glance at the poetical works of Sidonius Apollinaris himself is enough to show the affectation, the quest for obscurity and the artificial preciosity to which it descended. In fact Sidonius has been described by his principal biographer as a 'dark-age précieux'; the phrase, however paradoxical, expresses all too well the fragility of a culture unloved by Christians and barbarians alike.

A few celebrated instances have suggested too readily that the barbarian kings and their followers who settled in what had once been *Romania* wanted nothing better than to assimilate the Roman culture which was so far beyond the traditions of their own people. It is a fact that Latin supplanted the germanic dialects, though not without being in some degree affected by them. The kings imitated the Romans in writing down the oral customs of their people which did not escape some infiltration of Roman law. Some adopted the Roman dress and way of life, and accepted the calculated flattery dealt out to them by Latin poets. Some even prided themselves on an ability to write in Latin. But on the whole the 'barbarian' aristocracy remained foreign to this artificial culture and continued to give its sons an education based on military training and epic poems exalting the memory of their national heroes. Occasionally even Roman families drifted into adopting the same attitudes. In this way there grew up 'a new aristocracy ... more war-like and less cultured, the ancestor of the medieval nobility' (P. Riché).

The Christian attitude to classical culture varied a good deal. Many bishops (Sidonius Apollinaris was one of them) recruited from among the senatorial families remained loyal to it in a way which others found shocking. Cassian, who founded monasteries at Marseilles at the beginning of the fifth century, expressed this opposition vigorously:

I have been deeply impregnated with literature. My spirit is so infected with the work of poets that the frivolous fables and vulgar stories imbued in me from my earliest childhood occupy me even in the hour of prayer. While these phantoms play with me my soul is no longer free to aspire to the contemplation of heavenly things.

In the sixth century, following the example of, among others, the monastery of Lérins on the Provençal coast, the monks in an ever-increasing number of monasteries were given an education based on the Bible and from which all profane culture had been excised. But this was still very rudimentary.

There were, however, some notable Christians who regarded this ancient culture in a more favourable light, deplored its decline and tried to save it. They were to be found particularly among the aristocratic Roman families who were determined to collaborate with the Ostrogoths, as they were urged to do by their ruler, Theodoric, who was then master of Italy. Boethius translated and wrote commentaries on a number of Aristotle's philosophical works, and compiled a handbook on each of the four 'sciences' incorporating all the best of the Hellenic contribution. A crisis in relations between Theodoric and the Roman Emperor at Constantinople led to Boethius being thrown into prison, where he was executed at the age of forty-four. Before he died he wrote the *Consolation of Philosophy*, a work more Stoical than Christian, which was to earn him greater fame than anything he had written before. Cassiodorus, Theodoric's Chancellor, survived him, only to be caught up in the troubles brought about by the Byzantine attempt to re-conquer Italy. He was forced to take refuge on his estate of *Vivarium* in Calabria, where he founded a monastery and endowed it with a library rich in translations of Greek works. Cassiodorus was the forerunner of a type of learned monk which later became widespread, and the remains of his library provided a fund of information for later centuries. But at the time few people understood or followed him.

A little later, in Visigothic Spain, a member of another great Roman family, Isidore, Bishop of Seville, gathered into one vast encyclopedia the 'Twenty Books of Etymology', an immense variety of information drawn from the Scriptures and the Fathers of the Church, as well as from profane writers. It contained all kinds of subjects, from God and the Church to different races and languages, man, animals, the geography of the world, and food and clothing. Following St Augustine, Isidore declared that 'the learning of grammarians may be profitable to our lives, if it be taken in so as to make the better use of it'. The fame of Isidore's work in later centuries is in striking contrast to its lukewarm reception in his own time. Isidore himself describes the mockery poured on his efforts to re-establish a more accurate Latin pronunciation by the clergy of Seville.

Such men lived either too late or too early: too late to revive an already exhausted and moribund culture in a troubled age, and too early to enjoy the ultimate success of their endeavours.

THE FIRST SIGNS OF AWAKENING

Supposing it were absolutely necessary to set a precise date for the beginning of that slow revival which paved the way for the Carolingian renaissance, the year 590 would probably be the most acceptable. In about 590, Columban, accompanied by a dozen Irish monks, founded an establishment on the continent at Luxeuil in the Vosges. In 590, Gregory (afterwards called

Gregory the Great) ascended the throne of St Peter, shed fresh lustre on the Papacy and embarked on the conversion of the Anglo-Saxons. It was this collaboration between Rome and the regions situated at the furthest limits of the Roman world which was to provide the decisive impulse.

The growth of religious and intellectual life in Ireland from the sixth century onwards is one of those facts before which the inadequacy of all historical explanations becomes rapidly obvious. That the Christian religion, carried to that country by St Patrick, should have flourished there, and that in this rural setting the Church should have been centred on monasteries such as Clonard, Bangor, Derry and Iona, practicing a keen and rigorous asceticism, is readily understood. What is less easy to understand is that these monasteries should also have taken the trouble to master Latin, which was to them an unfamiliar language, and that they should have been able, at the cost of arduous grammatical labours, to learn it directly in its literary form, without reference to the halting, vulgar Latin. Still more surprisingly, they also read profane authors, including works which have now been lost; some apparently acquired rudiments of Greek and wrote in a complex style reflecting the mannerism of the Hellenistic East. Who were the first teachers of the Irish monks, and how the Latin manuscripts on which they worked first reached them, are unanswerable questions. The driving force which led so many missionaries from that country (of whom even Columban was not the first) to travel to the Continent in order to awaken or propagate the Christian faith can only be explained by reference to some innate disposition in the Irish national temperament.

There is a well-known though no doubt legendary story of how Augustine came to be sent to England. Walking in Rome one day, Pope Gregory is supposed to have seen a number of Angles offered for sale as slaves. Attracted probably by the appearance of the tall, blond, fair-skinned youths, he asked where they came from. When he was told, he replied: 'Not

Angles but Angels', 'Non Angli sed potius Angeli'. This gave him the idea of converting their people. Early in the seventh century Christianity took root in Kent and from there it gradually spread. From then on England became the scene of competition between Roman and Irish influences. The latter trickled down from the north, by way of the monasteries established on the island of Lindisfarne and Whitby. Young Anglo-Saxons were also sent over to spend short periods in Irish monasteries. The Irish and the Romans were fiercely divided on matters of liturgy, particularly the date for the celebration of Easter, although an agreement was reached at last.

One thing must be stressed: these movements were limited to the religious and moral spheres. Columban was only interested in establishing missions to convert the pagans of Germany – a task which did not demand extensive learning. His rule gave little room to scholarship. In the same way the studies which Augustine instituted in his Kentish foundations remained fairly elementary. All that resulted from these endeavours was the propagation of the Faith, an awakening of religious awareness, especially among laymen. But new cultural demands follow fairly rapidly on the heels of such religious revivals. The monasteries established or revived at this period, after eking out a precarious existence for a few years, soon began to look about them for fresh possibilities.

A particularly fertile link of communication passed from the British Isles through Northern Gaul to Italy and Germany, growing stronger throughout the seventh and eighth centuries and foreshadowing the shape of the Carolingian renaissance. From Rome came men like Theodore, a Greek hailing originally from Tarsus, who occupied the see of Canterbury in 679 and gave it a new brilliance. Rome was also rich in manuscripts, and pilgrims brought back treasures to enhance the libraries of monasteries such as Wearmouth and Jarrow (founded in 674 and 685 respectively), where the Venerable Bede was educated.

The Italian monasteries – such as that founded at Bobbio by Columban – served as posting houses along this route and helped to convert the Lombards, barbarians who had settled in Italy but, like the Anglo-Saxons, long remained apart from Roman culture.

Christian influences converged on Germany from all directions. Bavaria and Lombardy were closely linked. But it was largely Irish and Anglo-Saxon monks who filled the new monasteries of Fulda, Reichenau and St Gall, while the Anglo-Saxons Willibrord and Boniface courageously penetrated into the refractory regions at the mouth of the Rhine and in central Germany.

Lastly, the monasteries of Neustria – among them Corbie, St Riquier and St Amand – which provided halts for pilgrims and missionaries on their travels, and enriched their own lives by the contacts which developed between them, encouraged the growth of richer, more open minds. It is somehow symbolic that the manuscript of the first five books of Livy's *Fifth Decade* – all that we possess today – should have been written down in Italy, probably in the fifth century, then carried to England in the seventh or eighth, and taken from there by a preacher or missionary to the region of Utrecht, whence it finally passed into the possession of the abbey of Lorsch (which owned lands in the same area), where a humanist found it in the sixteenth century.

Another good effect of these contacts was that they encouraged the spread of the Benedictine Rule, which had not yet been adopted by most European monasteries. Columban's monks themselves helped to propagate this spread. Part of its success is due to the wisdom with which it had been laid down, the moderation by which the trials of monastic asceticism were adapted to the capacities of individuals, and the balance it established between the various occupations of the day. St Benedict of Nursia, an educated man but extremely suspicious of classical culture, had not remotely intended to make his community a centre of intellectual life; however,

Chapter 48 of his Rule did set aside several hours a day for reading and study.

> Leisure is the enemy of the soul; consequently the brothers should busy themselves at certain times with manual work and at other set hours with the reading of divine matters. For this reason we think it needful to arrange the time devoted to these two kinds of labour according to the following disposition: from Easter until the 14th September, the brothers shall go out early in the morning and give themselves up to necessary toil, from the first hour [five o'clock to us] until the fourth [about half past eight]. But from this time until about the sixth hour [eleven] they shall devote to reading. Then after the sixth hour when they have risen from table, they shall rest on their beds in perfect silence; at that time any who wish to read may do so in private so as not to trouble anyone else. The office of nones will be advanced somewhat towards the middle of the eighth hour [two thirty] after which they will resume their necessary toils until vespers. But should local conditions or policy demand that the brothers themselves should see to the crops and harvests, let them not be melancholy, because it is then they are truly monks, living by the work of their hands as our Fathers did and the Apostles. However, let all be done in moderation on account of the weak.

Moreover, the six or seven hours a day laid down for manual work might well be used in copying out the manuscripts needed for this reading. The library and writing room were normal parts of a Benedictine monastery. Everything would depend on the practical instructions written into their constitutions.

These were the conditions that formed the background against which the proper schools developed. They were monastic schools for the most part, although there were some episcopal schools, of which York offers the finest example. A succession of cultivated bishops, several of them pupils of Bede, had built up a library and a tradition of education which in the eighth century must have been more or less unique in western Europe. Some of the schools were for women – which leads us to another important point: as the Anglo-Saxon princes and aristocracy became aware of the need for Christian culture they took care to hand it on to their children, not in the classical way by private tutors, but by sending them for some years into the monasteries themselves.

The culture of the seventh and eighth centuries derived very little from the methods of classical education. Grammar – Latin grammar – was studied assiduously, especially in places where Latin was not the spoken language – in England, Ireland and Germany; most of the texts were taken from Christian authors. Rhetoric and dialectic were regarded with suspicion. Isidore of Seville's encyclopedia was still very much neglected. The Venerable Bede made little attempt to use his scientific knowledge to explain the Bible. Such scientific teaching as there was concentrated chiefly on computation, which was needed for fixing religious festivals, and was based on astronomy, cosmography and arithmetic – all fields in which Bede excelled. Being an islander, he described the workings of the tide with great precision and felicity. All the same it is not surprising that, as far as we can tell, texts of the profane authors of classical antiquity appear to have been comparatively few in monastic libraries before the end of the eighth century.

Few, also, as yet, were the centres of learning. Even in such monasteries as then deserved the title, educated clerks were probably still in the minority. The Frankish kingdom, where the Pepinid dynasty were patiently setting about the task of political reconstruction, was particularly lacking in such centres. Compared with the progress of monastic life, the secular clergy as a whole seem to have been distressingly second-rate; lay men were ignorant and boorish. But few individuals were at all aware of this, and their efforts could have only a local bearing. Chrodegang, bishop of Metz, for example, endeavoured under Pepin the Short to organize the clergy of his cathedral church into some kind of monastic order and train them in the singing of plainsong. In 772 Duke Tassilon of Bavaria promulgated measures through the Bavarian bishops to set up schools which already foreshadowed the acts of Charlemagne.

What had to be done next was to multiply and enrich the centres of learning, extend the scope of their teaching, and use them systematically to improve the cultural level of clergy and laymen alike. Charlemagne's great achievement was to undertake this task. This acknowledgement in no way diminishes the achievement but simply makes it a little easier to understand.

Chapter 3

CHARLEMAGNE
AND HIS FOLLOWERS

THE RULER AND HIS MOTIVES

He talked with ease and fluency and was able to express whatever he wanted to say with great clarity. Not satisfied with his native tongue he applied himself to the study of foreign languages and learned Latin so well that it was all one if he expressed himself in that or in his mother tongue. This was not so with Greek which he understood better than he could speak it. Moreover he had a flow of speech verging almost on prolixity. He cultivated the liberal arts with passion, and filled with veneration for those who taught them, he loaded them with honours. He also essayed writing and was accustomed to place tablets and sheets of parchment beneath the pillows of his bed in order to profit from his moments of leisure to practise tracing the letters; but he took it up too late and the results were not a success.

In a celebrated passage from chapter 25 of his *Life of Charlemagne*, Einhard draws this intellectual portrait of his royal protector. Walafrid Strabo, in a preface which he added to the same work asserted for his own part that

of all Kings, this was the most eager to seek out learned men and provide them with the means to philosophize at their ease, by which he was able to foster a new flowering of all knowledge, much of it hitherto unknown in this barbarous world.

Discounting flattery and hyperbole, these extracts still convey the impression Charlemagne produced on his followers. The second shows that some of these scholars did have a distinct sense of living in a period of renewal, in fact in precisely what we call the Carolingian renaissance. The first also obliges us to ask certain questions, such as precisely what degree of education had the man generally considered as the author of this renaissance, and what were the motives which inspired him?

Einhard took as his model a classical work, Suetonius' *Lives of the Twelve Caesars,* and followed it closely. Suetonius always pointed out the ease or lack of it with which the Roman emperors spoke Greek. Following this example, Einhard may have exaggerated Charlemagne's fluency in Latin; certainly the Frankish king cannot have known more than a few words of Greek. It is also clear from this passage that Charlemagne learned to write only late in life. His initiation into the liberal arts was equally belated: according to Einhard his teachers were Peter of Pisa and Alcuin, who are known not to have entered his service until he was past thirty. Unfortunately nothing is known of his childhood and the education he received. Charles Martel had followed the example of Anglo-Saxon princes and sent his sons Pepin and Carloman to the monastery of Saint-Denis near Paris. It is quite possible that Pepin the Short may have done the same for Charlemagne, but even so the education meted out was probably elementary, to say the least. Charlemagne, was, to a great extent, self-taught.

There can be no doubt that Charlemagne in his efforts to educate himself as well as in all he did to raise the general standard of learning in his domains, was inspired by a Christian belief in his duties as a ruler. He was often told that his power had been entrusted to him by God in order to protect the Church and order the morals of his subjects. He must not merely offer them the spectacle of an exemplary life, but watch over their growth in the Faith, and extend its dominion. Consequently, one of his first tasks was to ensure that the clergy itself was well versed in this faith and capable of teaching it to the people in their preaching. This, although a modest enough requirement, was actually far from being the case.

In Charlemagne this object was undoubtedly coupled with an idea of unity. To combat the surviving remnants of paganism among an ignorant population, and the infiltration of heresies (of which there were a number in Charlemagne's time), the clergy had to have books written with some degree of uniformity. The correcting and collating of sacred works provides a spiritual parallel to Charlemagne's evident ambition in the temporal sphere to bring the whole of his domains under the control of a single authority.

In addition, in every aspect of his administration it was Charlemagne's deliberate policy to encourage the use of written records. The customs of some races which had hitherto been handed down by word of mouth were now put in writing. Palace scribes wrote out 'Capitularies' to do with laws, instructions for the inspectors sent into the various kingdoms, and agendas of meetings. The overseers of the royal estates had likewise to produce inventories, reports and accounts. This insistence was highly novel and reflected the conviction that unless such things were written down there could be no order, stability or justice in the state. But it also presupposed the existence of a certain number of educated men, able to read and write these documents, understand them correctly and get them copied. There were, we know, too few such men in the reign of Charlemagne. Understandably, the king was anxious to increase their number by fostering education.

THE BASIC TEXTS

The origins of the Carolingian renaissance must therefore be sought in Charlemagne's sense of his own duty and the dignity which piety inspired in this sovereign, who for all his own belated education was in love with order and unity, as well as being in a position of exceptional power. The documents in which these aims are made clear are few, and nearly all of them express the same preoccupations.

The 'General Exhortation' (*Admonitio generalis*) of 798 is particularly concerned with the qualities and degree of learning proper to parish priests. They should know the truths of the

Faith, the form of the sacraments, the prayers of the Mass and the psalms, and they should show some aptitude for preaching. 'And let there be schools to teach the children to read. Let the psalms and their tunes, singing, computation and grammar be taught in each bishopric and every monastery and let them have books which have been scrupulously corrected.'

A letter to Baugulf, abbot of Fulda – the famous *Epistola de Litteris colendis* – probably written between 794 and 797, while Charlemagne was suppressing revolts among the Saxons and organizing the spread of Christianity in their lands – reveals similar preoccupations. This document is so important that it is worth quoting a few paragraphs of it.

Be it known to your Devotion, which is pleasing to God, that we together with our faithful have deemed it expedient that the bishoprics and monasteries entrusted by Christ's favour to our government, in addition to the observance of monastic discipline and the practice of the religious life, should vouchsafe instruction also in the exercise of letters to those who with God's help are able to learn, each according to his capacity; seeing that, even as the monastic rule directs purity of conduct, so practice in teaching and learning directs and orders the composition of words, to the end that those who strive to please God by right living may not omit to please Him also by right speaking. For it is written (Matth. xii, 37), 'either by thy words thou shalt be justified or by thy words thou shalt be condemned'; and though it is better to do what is right than to know it, yet knowledge must precede action. ... Since in these years there were often sent to us from divers monasteries letters in which was set forth the zeal on our behalf in holy and pious prayers of the brethren dwelling there, we have observed in very many of the aforesaid writings of the same persons right sentiments and uncouth language, because that which pious devotion faithfully dictated inwardly, outwardly, owing to neglect of learning, the untutored tongue could not express without faultiness. Whence it came that we began to fear lest, as skill in writing was less, wisdom to understand the Sacred Scriptures might be far less than it ought rightly to be. And we all know that, though verbal errors are dangerous, errors in interpretation are far more dangerous. Wherefore we exhort you not only not to neglect the study of letters but even with the most humble God-approved earnestness to vie in learning, so that you may prevail more easily and rightly in penetrating the mysteries of sacred literature. But, inasmuch as in the sacred pages are found embedded figures and tropes and other like forms of speech, no one can doubt that every one in reading those the more quickly understands [what he reads] in a spiritual sense the more fully if he has before been instructed in the discipline of literature. Let then such men be chosen for this task as have willingness, ability to learn, and the desire to teach others. And let this be done with zeal as great as the earnestness with which we exhort you ...

The instructions given to inspectors of the Empire, the so-called *missi dominici,* in 805, emphasize the persistence of these aims which the imperial title had only made yet more dear to Charlemagne's heart: 'Reading. Singing. Scribes, so that they shall not write ill. Lawyers. Other disciplines. Computation. The art of Medicine.'

By providing local elementary schools, and by a slightly higher level of instruction dispensed by episcopal sees and monasteries, it was hoped to give Christian folk a minimum of religious knowledge, to recruit and educate a presentable parish clergy, and to give proper training for men destined to form the upper levels of society in the temporal and ecclesiastical orders. Though this may seem a fairly modest programme, taking into account the setting which gave rise to it, it was vast and ambitious. At all events, Charlemagne could never have embarked on it if he had not had the whole of Europe to draw on to provide a small 'general staff' of cultivated men. Moreover, its achievement was nowhere near completed in his own reign, and his work would never have survived him had it not matched the aspirations of a growing number of men within the clergy itself.

THE MEN WHO MADE THE 'RENAISSANCE'

We can learn a good deal about most of the men who surrounded Charlemagne and were instrumental in carrying out his plan for a revival of learning. A general picture can be gleaned from their actual works, in which they reveal their ideas, tastes and intellectual capacities. The letters they exchanged, and a few poems by Theodulf describing Charlemagne surrounded by his learned circle of friends, complete this picture: they show all their faults and absurdities, but also the touching greatness of their pioneer spirit. The composition of this group reflects inevitably the cultural map of Carolingian Europe. It includes no Franks, since the most the Franks could aspire to at this stage was to be good pupils. On the one hand there is the contribution of the old Romanized lands, Lombard Italy and Visigothic Spain, and, on the other, that of the British Isles: the Irish and Anglo-Saxons who were behind the revival which is evident from the end of the sixth century onwards.

It was the conquest of the Lombard kingdom that brought Charlemagne into contact with his earliest teachers. In June 774 the Lombard king Didier surrendered at Pavia and a month later Charlemagne placed on his own head the iron crown of the Lombards. Immediately afterwards we find the aged deacon, Peter of Pisa, who was an inferior poet but a competent grammarian, giving the king his first lessons and writing a very elementary grammar for his use. His chief merit lay in being the first, and he did not even enjoy any great influence at court. Two or three years later he was joined by Paulinus of Friuli. Paulinus too was a grammarian and a poet, but in him there was also the stuff of a theologian which revealed itself when Charlemagne later appointed him to the See of Aquileia.

A much more valuable acquisition a few years later was Paul Warnefrid, better known as Paul the Deacon. A member of a noble Lombard family and also a native of Friuli, he was brought up at the court of Pavia, but at an early age he entered a monastery on near-by Lake Como, and later, in about 779, was transferred to Monte Cassino. When his brother was implicated in a rebellion at Friuli and thrown into prison by Frankish soldiers, Paul through the mediation of Peter of Pisa addressed to Charlemagne an eulogy in verse pleading for release of the rebel. He was obliged to pay for this boon with a stay at court and at the Abbey of St Martin at Metz, although he never ceased to mourn for his Monte Cassino, until at last in about 787 he was given permission to return and end his days there. All the same, his contribution should not be measured by the few years he spent with the king. He too was a grammarian; but more, he was a poet who restored the traditions of Latin poetry at the court. Still more important for us, he was a historian, and his history of his own people, the Lombards, is probably the most valuable of all his works. But at the time he performed an even greater service with a Roman history written before Charlemagne's accession, which familiarized the court with the memory of classical times that was to play such an important part in the restoration of the Empire in 800; and with his *History of the Bishops of Metz*, which provided an excellent model for what in the following centuries was to become an extremely fashionable genre. Finally, even after his return to Monte Cassino, he kept in close touch with the court and, as we shall see, continued to take a considerable part in Charlemagne's work.

In about 600, Visigothic Spain was the most highly cultivated kingdom in the West. A hundred years later the Arab conquest had overwhelmed it and cut it off from the West for several centuries. But it also led to a first wave of emigrations which scattered many fine illuminated manuscripts and sacred relics throughout Italy and southern France.

In about 782 the repressive measures resulting from Charlemagne's intervention produced a second wave of Spanish refugees, the most brilliant of whom was Theodulf. The exact part of Spain he came from is not known, but he is very much what might be expected from a country where an intimate knowledge of classical authors and interest in works of art seem to have been traditional for several centuries. As a poet Theodulf had assimilated the classical forms and used them with great ability to describe the antiquities and coins he liked to collect, the countries which had impressed him, and the court circles in which his witty, observant mind delighted. His reputation there was certainly great and, some time before 798, earned him a bishopric. As bishop of Orleans he was extremely energetic, and he also played a part in Charlemagne's religious work, writing a number of theological works at his request.

Another Spaniard, on the other hand, Felix, bishop of Urgel, was influential in a rather more negative way, by producing a brilliant defence of the opinions maintained at Toledo on Christ's 'adoption' by God the Father, and giving rise in the Frankish kingdom to one of those intense theological debates which enlivened the intellectual life of the times.

The full effect of some other Spaniards was felt only after the death of Charlemagne. Agobard, later bishop of Lyons, was an ardent polemicist, and Claude, later bishop of Turin, wrote commentaries on the Scriptures of an originality occasionally bordering on heresy.

Naturally the Irish were to be found at the Court of Charlemagne as they had been in so many monasteries for nearly two centuries. Their intransigence seems to have earned them some enemies. Very little is known about even the most outstanding of them: the grammarian Clemens Scotus, Dungal the monk of St Denis from whom Charlemagne learned the 'nature of darkness' and the eclipses observed in 810, and a little later, Dicuil, who has left behind a treatise on computation and a curious little manual of geography. What these men had to offer was not so much a wide cultural experience as a sound knowledge of grammar, the Bible and the Fathers, and an interest in matters of computation, geography and astronomy. The death of Alcuin lent an increased importance to their role.

This brings us back to the man who, it is generally agreed, emerges as the central figure of the group which formed around Charlemagne. In Etienne Gilson's words, the Italians used by Charlemagne were like visiting professors willing to be seduced by attractive offers but clearly suffering from the disruption of their own work and habits. They did their jobs but they did not really contribute. Theodulf and Agobard were refugees. Alcuin, on the other hand, devoted himself heart and soul to carrying out the aims of a ruler whose beneficence he fully appreciated.

He was however already nearing the end of his life when he entered Charlemagne's service, a fact which contributed to his reception at court as a teacher already famous and worthy of every respect. He came from a noble Northumbrian family and more than one among his forebears had been called a saint. His birth must have coincided more or less with the death of Bede in 735. At an early age he attended at the archiepiscopal school at York, which was then at its most brilliant. Alcuin himself, in one of his poems, has left a valuable description of the teaching of his beloved master, Aelbert, and of the school library which contained works by Cicero, Virgil and Lucan, indicating that while still based chiefly on the Irish and Anglo-Saxon tradition of grammar, computation and astronomy, the teaching of the school also had a broader tendency to revive its links with the dying culture of Rome.

From the time when Aelbert ascended the archiepiscopal throne of York until his retirement in 778 Alcuin first assisted him and later carried on his work. His pupils included Anglo-Saxons, Irish and Frisians, and it gave him, in his own words, 'a great joy to see [his] sons flourishing in the purity of their lives and their love of learning'. By about 780, at the time of his meeting with Charlemagne, he was nearing fifty and still only a deacon and abbot of a small monastery near the Humber; but his fame as a scholar was immense.

For eight years, from 782 to 790, Alcuin devoted himself to the education of Charlemagne and his court. At first he worked alongside Italian teachers; when they left, he remained in sole charge of all instruction, assisted by some former pupils of his own from York. It was a unique gathering before which he then enjoyed the satisfaction of 'being alone listened to, while all the rest were silent'. In 790 he obtained permission to go back to Northumbria, with which he remained in constant touch. By 793, however, Charlemagne was begging him to return and lead the fight against the adoptionist heresy maintained by the Spanish clergy which was threatening to spread through southern Gaul. Alcuin fully justified the king's confidence, and it is his fine figure which dominates the ecclesiastical synod of Frankfort, where major decisions were taken. His authority was then at its height and he used it to the full – with no small courage – recalling the lords and prelates to their duties, exhorting them to maintain peace, and even venturing to criticize Charlemagne himself for the mass baptisms he had enforced in Saxony. 'It is inadmissible for the body to receive the sacrament of baptism, unless the soul has first welcomed the truth of the Faith.'

Charlemagne had already rewarded him with the gift of a number of abbeys: St Loup at Troyes, Ferrières in the Gatinais, Flavigny in Burgundy and the small monastery (*cella*) of St Josse-sur-mer, near Boulogne, which was a halt for Anglo-Saxon pilgrims. By 796 Alcuin was complaining of old age and bad health. The troubles ravaging England discouraged him from returning there and it was then that the king offered him the abbacy of one of the most venerable monasteries in the Frankish kingdom. St Martin of Tours, overlooking the sleepy old town with its 'smoky roofs', was a huge and extremely wealthy seminary with over two hundred monks, and even its administration represented a considerable task. Alcuin also tried, without much success, to give its life a more ascetic and edifying tone. He enlarged the monastery school and attracted such distinguished students as Hrabanus Maurus, but he complained of 'not finding here those excellent works of erudition and scholarship which he had in his own country', and begged Charlemagne's permission to have a number of manuscripts sent over from York. He also set the monks to work copying manuscripts. None of this was easy, and Alcuin encountered a good deal of opposition from the monks, who resented this influx of foreigners. 'Oh Lord,' four of them complained one day, 'deliver our monastery from these British who flock here to find him like bees swarming to their queen.'

In spite of these setbacks, added to the trials of old age and the heavy duties of an abbot, Alcuin wrote some of his most important works at Tours. At Charlemagne's request he edited a definitive text of the Scriptures to be used throughout the kingdom. He kept up a constant correspondence with the king and those close to him, and everything points to the fact that by his letters and by a talk he had with Charlemagne when the latter paid a visit to Tours, Alcuin played a major part in the events of December 800 and the restoration of the Empire. He lived a few years more; then, old and blind, he died on Whit Sunday in the year 804 aged about seventy-five.

His character may strike us today as lacking in individuality. Alcuin was not an original thinker, but his influence over Charlemagne and his court, his infectious enthusiasm and his capacity for work made him the real moving spirit behind the 'renaissance' so dear to his sovereign's heart. All tributes to him acknowledge that he was an outstanding teacher, and his influence in this respect went far beyond his own time. It is interesting to note what might be called the family trees of his pupils. One takes us by way of Hrabanus Maurus and the abbey of Fulda, right down to the Ottonian renaissance of the tenth century. In France itself we find Aldric, abbot of Ferrières, handing on the teaching of Alcuin to his successor, Loup, who in turn transmitted it to Heric, a monk of St Germain d'Auxerre; and via Hucbald and Remi of Auxerre it came at last to Odo, abbot of Cluny. Remi of Auxerre also restored the schools of Rheims, where Gerbert later shone.

Before leaving Charlemagne and his followers, let us take another look at them in the setting of two institutions the nature of which might easily be misinterpreted. The first of these was the Palatine Academy, an imposing name (actually invented later) for the highly 'informal' meetings at which the king and his friends forgot the cares of state for a while and gave themselves up to learned argument. They had the absurd and rather touching custom of giving one another nicknames drawn either from Holy Scripture (Charlemagne himself was David), or from classical authors. Alcuin was known as Flaccus, Angilbert as Homer, Maganfred, lord of the bed-chamber, and the seneschal Audulf became the Virgilian characters, Thyrsis and Menalcas. Our knowledge of these conversational get-togethers comes chiefly from the poems of Theodulf and from Alcuin's own letters.

Theodulf describes the group feasting with Charlemagne: 'In the midst David presides with sceptre, dealing out mighty portions in order unperturbed.' A place of honour was clearly reserved for Alcuin: 'And father Albinus would sit, ever on the point of uttering pious words and freely partaking of food with lips and hand. And when the cups of beer or wine were handed round perchance he would accept of either. For he taught better and his pipe was better tuned when he wetted his learned whistle.' Theodulf exercised his wit on the busy diminutive figure of Einhard, who was then making his debut at court: 'Nardulus, scurrying hither and thither, never still, your busy feet pattering to and fro like the ant. A great guest dwells in that small house, and great thoughts fill the hollow of his tiny heart.' There is even a sting in his words about one of the Irishmen who frequented the court: 'Before I, the Goth, make friends with the Scot, the dog shall nurse the hares and the cat run away from the mouse. . . . Moreover take away his second letter and you will have his real name.'

Several of Alcuin's letters were written in reply to questions asked in this small group. Often these are grammatical queries. To a question from Angilbert-Homer as to the meaning of the word *rubus* (bramble or raspberry bush), Alcuin-Flaccus replies with a series of quotations from authors and grammarians concluding that 'the masculine seems more likely than the feminine'. On another occasion he tries to explain to Charlemagne the distinction between the words

aeternum and *sempiternum*, *perpetuum* and *immortale*, undoubtedly
a valuable exercise in differentiating between almost synonymous terms. He also turned his attention to matters of
astronomy, such as why the planet Mars should have vanished
from sight for a year, and why the moon seemed shrunk on
18 March 799. Exegesis was a subject of no less interest. We
find Alcuin reassuring Charlemagne as to an apparent contradiction in the Gospels: how Jesus could counsel his disciples
in one place: 'and he that hath no sword let him sell his
garment and buy one' (Luke xxii 36), and elsewhere command
Peter to put up his sword: 'for all they that take the sword
shall perish with the sword' (Matthew xxvi 52). The question
indicates both great seriousness in the study of Holy Scripture
and also a certain inability to see beyond its literal meaning.

The 'Palace School' should not however be regarded as a
fixed, well-organized institution. It was more a collection
of courses and study groups which varied from year to year
and from season to season, attended by Charlemagne and his
family, the lords of the court and youths who were sent to the
palace to serve their ruler and get an education at the same
time. In such good company they all learned 'the prior way of
life'. A later monk of St Gall who depicted this 'school' as being like that in his own monastery, and showed Charlemagne,
looking rather like God on the Day of Judgement, conducting
an examination, with the studious pupils of humble origin,
on his right, and the lazy ones, of noble birth, on his left, was
very much mistaken. Like many edifying tales this one is
totally unfounded.

AFTER CHARLEMAGNE

At the death of Charlemagne there was a shift of emphasis,
fresh moving spirits appeared, but the work went on.

Charlemagne's successors neither expanded nor even re-
iterated his instructions as to the spread of learning, probably
because they regarded the great emperor's legislation as still
valid. In future it was largely the Church itself, more conscious

of the responsibilities it had to discharge and better equipped to fulfil them, which carried on the work of the Palace. We must therefore turn to the Conciliar records in order to follow up these attempts. As early as 798 a Bavarian synod had laid down that all bishops were to establish schools in their own cities. The Council of Chalons in 813 decreed that the emperor's precepts must be enforced and schools opened for the teaching of letters and the Holy Scriptures. Even more important was the Council of Aix which, following the example set by Chrodegang, organized the cathedral clergy into chapters and laid down firm measures to guarantee the existence of a functioning school in each (816). It would be naïve to imagine that these measures were carried out fully everywhere. The fact that other councils in 822, 829, 855 and finally in 859, also dealt with the same question is proof that the results had not been wholly satisfactory.

One might expect the monastic schools to have been the most numerous and influential; the fact that alongside the oblates destined for the monastic life they were also attended by children who simply wanted an elementary education, may have been felt as an irritant. At all events, the monastic reforms put forward in 817 at the instigation of Benedict of Aniane specified that in future monastic schools should be open only to oblates. Fortunately this measure, which represents a retrograde step in the progress of culture, does not seem to have been enforced everywhere either.

All the same, that it may have made men more strongly aware of the need for public schools open to all, seems to be indicated by some of the petitions the bishops addressed to their rulers. In 829 they petitioned Louis the Pious, advocating the creation of public schools in three carefully selected places in the Empire. It can be assumed that the bishops envisaged these as colleges for instructing the most gifted students in the liberal arts, but their modest plea seems to have had no effect whatsoever. Louis the Pious, who was at the time torn between his sons, had other worries on his mind. Indeed, not very long afterwards he escaped deposition only by doing a humiliating public penance. Thirty years later, however, at a meeting at Savonnières, the bishops reviewed the progress of religious life and education within the Empire and asked Charles the Bald to set up public schools to teach the divine and human sciences wherever the existence of competent teachers allowed. Unfortunately, in the meantime, the clouds had gathered yet more thickly, and this noble ambition was never fulfilled. Many decades were to pass before any Councils would again be in a position to turn their attention to the problem of education.

We have touched briefly on what may be regarded as one of the tragedies of the ninth century. The seeds sown by Charlemagne and Alcuin had borne fruit and the need for education was felt ever more strongly. But the tares – the many troubles with which the period was beset – had thrived among the good corn and threatened to strangle it. This is the distressing but unavoidable conclusion forced on us by a glance at the successors of Alcuin and his circle. Even before the death of Charlemagne the team he had brought together was already largely dispersed. The Italians had gone and Alcuin had been in his grave for ten years. Theodulf was still living, but in 817 he was dismissed and sent into exile on suspicion of having dabbled in conspiracy. He survived this disgrace only by some four years. The Irish were still very much in evidence and the most notable of them actually belong to this period after Charlemagne. They include the poet Sedulius Scottus, who appeared mysteriously at Liège in about 848 and vanished ten years later; and, most important of all, the one philosopher of the period, John Scotus, better known as Erigen, who turns up at the court of Charles the Bald in 845, although nothing is known about him before this date. His subsequent career can be followed right up to 870 or thereabouts. It is possible that both he and Sedulius were driven out of Ireland by the Danish invasions.

But the really important fact is the rise of gifted and educated men among the Franks themselves, able to take over from the foreigners. It is not possible to mention more than a few of them here. Einhard, born in the valley of the Main *c.* 775 and educated at Fulda, was presented at court shortly after 790, although his position was still fairly obscure. His hour of triumph came with the accession of his erstwhile fellow student Louis the Pious. Einhard became the emperor's secretary, was endowed with rich abbeys and continued to play a major part in politics until 828, when the growing political strife inspired him with the prudent notion of retiring to his abbey at Seligenstadt. There he lived for another twelve years, writing his *Life of Charlemagne* and consoling his declining years with this edifying account of better times, which remains for us a historical work of the greatest importance.

Another student of Fulda but nearly ten years younger than Einhard was Hrabanus, a native of Mayence. Hrabanus was Alcuin's disciple at Tours, and it was Alcuin who gave him his surname, Maurus, after the chief helper of St Benedict. In about 804, Hrabanus left Tours and returned to Fulda. As head of the school and afterwards abbot (822–42), he raised the monastery to great renown. He devoted himself especially to the education of the German clergy. The textbooks he wrote were admittedly quite unoriginal and even lacking in that personal touch which marked the hand of Alcuin, but they and the rest of his earnest endeavours earned him the title conferred on him by later ages of 'preceptor of Germany'. He spent the last nine years of his life (847–56) as bishop of Mayence.

Appreciably younger still was Hincmar, the son of an aristocratic family; he was born in about 806 and brought up at the monastery of St Denis. When Hilduin, the abbot of St Denis, was appointed arch-chaplain and religious adviser to the emperor, Hincmar went with him to the Court. Once there he was well placed to insinuate himself into political life. Throughout the upheavals which shook this troubled period, Hincmar remained faithful to Louis the Pious, but it was

Charles the Bald to whom he owed his ultimate advancement. Charles conferred a number of abbeys on him and it was through his influence that in 845 Hincmar was made arch-bishop of Rheims, where he remained until his death in 882. Rheims was an extremely important see since St Remi, from whom it took its name, had brought about the conversion of Clovis. It was also a see very conveniently placed in relation to the kingdoms of Charles and Lothair. There Hincmar was able to lead an active political life and fully justified his patron's confidence in him. Although his written works cover a much wider field he is remembered chiefly as a canonist and historian, since he was apparently responsible, over a period of twenty years, for the writing of a unique source – the *Annals*, which were later discovered in the abbey of Saint-Bertin. Walafrid Strabo (squint-eyed) was a Swabian of much humbler origin, and had a much less distinguished public career. Born about 808 and educated at Reichenau and later at Fulda, where he was a pupil of Hrabanus, Walafrid was tutor to Charles the Bald, who made him abbot of Reichenau in 838. He died young in 849, drowned crossing the Loire on a mission to the same ruler. Walafrid was above all a poet with a very personal voice. At an early age he wrote a poem on gardening (*De cultura hortorum*) which contains meticulous accounts of twenty-three different plants, with detailed descriptions of their medical virtues, and concludes with a charming dedication to his friend the Abbot of St Gall.

Servat Loup was the same age as Strabo and must have been at Fulda at about the same time, although he outlived Strabo by thirteen years. He came of a Frankish family of good standing at court and he was a pupil of Aldric at Ferrières before being sent by him to study under Hrabanus at Fulda. There he attracted notice; he was already famous by the time he returned as a monk to Ferrières, where he later, in 840, became abbot. Charles the Bald was responsible for his appointment to this office and later made frequent use of him as secretary to a number of assemblies, administrative inspector and envoy to Rome. His work was highly varied, but he is known chiefly for 127 letters collected in the tenth century, which fortunately are still in existence. There is no document which gives a better picture of the life of a learned abbot of the period, his time divided between administration and his monastery, the enthusiastic search for manuscripts and official missions – all in the end overshadowed by the terrible threat of Norman invasion.

There are many others who could be mentioned. Most of them would carry us farther from the Carolingian courts with which these authors were in more or less close and continuous contact. Certainly the Palace was no longer, as it had been under Charlemagne, a kind of inevitable centre of cultural studies. True, a man like Charles the Bald could and did play a considerable part by encouraging and subsidizing the best scholars of his time, men such as John Scotus, Loup de Ferrières and Hincmar, and countless works were dedicated to him. But in future it was in the great monasteries such as Fulda, Corbie, Ferrières that writers were educated, lived and worked. These abbeys, most of which followed the Benedictine Rule, carried on the interrupted and much-enfeebled labours of the Carolingian rulers. Acting on the instructions of Charlemagne himself they had trained copyists and created libraries and schools. This first cultural equipment of Europe was both a cause and an effect of the Carolingian renaissance and as such deserves some attention.

Chapter 4

THE CULTURAL FOUNDATIONS
OF EUROPE

No intellectual work can proceed without libraries. One of the prime virtues of the Carolingian renaissance is that it began to endow these lands with collections of books which were both numerous and extensive for the period. It has been estimated that the Benedictine Rule laid down for the monks some 1,500 hours of reading per year which, at say ten pages an hour, means approximately 15,000 pages. To supply the needs of a single year this represents an average of fifty volumes of 300 pages. Apart from all purely intellectual aspirations, the mere regular exercise of monastic life demanded the provision of that much material. Moreover the number of seminaries was increasing rapidly and the Rule of St Benedict becoming increasingly widespread.

Accustomed as we are to living in a civilization based on the written word, it requires some effort of the imagination to picture the problems facing those who had to find this reading matter, and the difficulties they had to overcome.

Firstly, they had to start very nearly from scratch. This is a complaint that recurs continually in the writings of the period. One bishop of Lisieux complained that his see did not even possess a complete text of the Bible. When Alcuin arrived at Tours in 796 he wrote to Charlemagne: 'Your humble servant has not found here those excellent works of learning which he had in his own country, and which he owed to the dedication of his master and to his own researches.' He therefore asked permission to have a number of manuscripts sent from York and copies made of them in his monastery. He is also known to have borrowed from Rome a collection of letters by Pope Gregory the Great and begged the loan of Jordanes'

History of the Goths from his friend Angilbert, abbot of St Riquier, together with a number of treatises by his pupil Ricbod, archbishop of Trèves. Alcuin however enjoyed exceptionally wide contacts and by 796 a number of monasteries and bishoprics were beginning to acquire considerable collections of books. Half a century earlier there was a much greater shortage, and in the general neglect which prevailed – with monasteries failing to observe their rule and the episcopal throne left sometimes for years on end without an occupant – the rarest manuscripts which had been handed down from earlier times ran the risk of being lost. A bishop or abbot who wanted to present his house with much-needed books had the greatest difficulty in finding them anywhere within the Frankish kingdom, and was obliged to have them sent from distant but better-provided countries such as England, Ireland and Italy.

Borrowing books was no easy matter. The danger and difficulty of communication increased the risk of loss. More than one manuscript of the time winds up with terrible curses directed at any potential thief which, it was hoped, would make him restore his plunder out of sheer terror. Even if the worst did not happen, the slow speed of travel still meant that the loan would deprive the owner for a long time of a volume which might well be precious to him. The reluctance of some churches to lend books is quite understandable. Alcuin, requesting the loan of two books from his pupil Ricbod, admonishes him kindly: 'I beg you to lend them to me for a while although I have to admit that, while you are very willing to hold out your hand to receive, you draw it back when it comes to giving.' Moreover it was necessary to know just where to ask for the desired volume. Needless to say there were no catalogues to inform booklovers which churches owned copies of a particular book. Travellers would make inquiries into the resources of monasteries at which they stayed. Correspondence and the talk at ecclesiastical or administrative gatherings also helped in these always tricky investigations. With what joy the manuscripts brought by zealous Irish missionaries and the Spanish refugees must have been received, it is not hard to imagine.

In spite of everything the first libraries can only have grown up very slowly at the cost of a great deal of groping in the dark.

THE PROBLEM OF WRITING

Even writing itself posed a whole new set of problems. In a period with a huge demand for more reading matter for an increasing number of readers, writing had to be clear and neat and yet at the same time capable of fairly speedy execution. Towards the middle of the eighth century no such writing yet existed. The slow, laborious but highly artistic characters were in any case falling increasingly into disuse in the barbarian kingdoms. These were the 'capital', made up of carefully drawn capital letters, with exaggerated up and down strokes, and the 'uncial', which was also large but with characteristic stems and tails lying above and below lines drawn about the body of the letter. Scribes generally preferred to employ a small cursive script, with a great many ligatures which made it unnecessary to raise the hand from the page in between letters. The coarseness of life and the lack of any commonly accepted rules explain why such writing sometimes looks primitive and varies to such an extent that some experts wrongly credit it with national characteristics and label it Visigothic or Lombard.

By the eighth century at least, and perhaps as early as the seventh, we do find some effort being made to improve hand-writing. It is not always easy to describe these with any accuracy, since this would imply a knowledge of the origin of such manuscripts of the period as have survived – and to attri-bute them with any certainty is a delicate problem. But what is certain is that these attempts were made simultaneously in a number of widely separated places: proof that they answered to a general need, born of the increased demand for texts. In Ireland and England a small spiky script was developed, with characteristic abbreviations. This is the 'Scottish' script which was carried to a great many continental monasteries by scribes from these countries, or imitated by their pupils. Some Italian copyists remained faithful to the uncial script. Rhaetia, with Chur and later St Gall, had its own regular, large, round hand. But the decisive experiments were conducted in Gaul, where at the end of the seventh century an 'elongated, undulating and pointed hand', rather heavy and of medium size with a highly characteristic 'a', was in use. This script of Luxeuil, St Columban's foundation, spread to a number of other monasteries, in particular to Corbie, whose first abbot had come from Luxeuil. But while some scribes at Corbie stuck faithfully to the Luxovian script, others continued to experiment and finally produced some more regular styles, which continued to exist side by side until the beginning of the ninth century. One of these, used in a Bible copied in the early years of Charlemagne's reign, already shows most of the characteristics of 'Carolingian' writing.

This Carolingian script was, however, finalized not at Corbie but at St Martin of Tours, possibly under the influence of Alcuin and certainly of his pupil and successor the abbot Fredegise. From Tours it spread gradually until in a few decades it had come into general use throughout the Carolingian Empire, thus meriting the name by which it is now known.

It was deservedly a success. Carolingian script is a minuscule incorporating certain characteristics borrowed from the uncial. It was still based on the Latin alphabet and solved the problem of providing a happy compromise between speed and regularity. There are few ligatures, but words are carefully spaced with somewhat larger gaps between connecting phrases. The result was so successful that even today modern printing retains the basic forms of the Carolingian minuscule. It would be no exaggeration to link this development with that of printing itself as the two decisive steps in the growth of a civilization based on the written word.

The labour involved in actually practising this new writing cannot be too highly stressed. Ninth- and tenth-century documents contain frequent references to it. 'The man who cannot write, thinks little of the writer's toil, but those who have tried it know what hard work it is.' 'Although the pen is held only in three fingers,' asserts another, 'it is the whole body that labours.' 'And so', concludes a third, 'the sailor is not more glad to reach harbour than the weary scribe to arrive at the last line of his manuscript.'

This pain and labour must have been familiar to many who embarked, often at an advanced age, on an apprenticeship in the unfamiliar task of writing. Charlemagne never succeeded in mastering the art, but admittedly he was unable to devote a great deal of time to it. Undoubtedly reading and writing were not connected as they are nowadays. Quite a number of people, including in theory all the clergy, needed to be able to read, but writing remained a specialized skill, the province of a tiny minority. It certainly formed a part of elementary education, but the majority of pupils probably forgot the difficult art later for want of any occasion to practise it. However, the growing demand for books necessitated the training of more scribes. At St Martin of Tours all the monks, of whom there were more than two hundred, were probably called in to help in the *scriptorium*, and not all of them can have possessed a particular talent for it.

Writing was moreover something rather different from what it is today. Nowadays everyone who has to do much writing – and their number is legion – has learned the art so thoroughly at such an early age that it has become second nature to them, sometimes considerably to the discomfort of their readers. To the informed psychologist a person's normal handwriting, with its own individual rhythm and its own pattern in the size and shape of the letters, can be extremely revealing of character. No such relaxed, personal handwriting then existed. It is a fact that expert palaeographers can recognize from various details the different 'hands' which contributed to the copying of a manuscript, but these variations are minute compared to what was generally a uniform style.

Indeed, even before the middle of the ninth century this uniformity was quite the most striking thing about the use of the Carolingian minuscule. Writing was rather like copying an illustration today and carrying it out as quickly as possible.

The sheer length of the task also constituted a formidable obstacle. Of course the speeds at which these scribes could write must have varied enormously. One copy of St Augustine's commentary, of 109 sheets – say 218 pages – of twenty lines to the page, has a note attached to it with the information that in 823 it was copied in seven days and corrected on the eighth by the same scribe. This represents the amazing speed of thirty pages a day. On the other hand another manuscript of 304 sheets (608 pages), begun on 2 June 819, was not completed until 12 September which, taking holidays into account, represents an average of six or seven pages a day. But for a really accurate estimate we should have to know the number of hours a day devoted to the exercise. In any case speed was not yet a prime consideration, and the system of abbreviations designed to save the scribe's time (and incidentally causing the inexperienced palaeographer to waste a good deal of it) was not really developed until much later.

Finally, the work was carried out in conditions of absolute quiet which were clearly necessary to the efficient working of a copying studio, but must have been a torment to the scribes. The identical fact has been noted in our own day by teachers dealing with belated intellectual or religious 'vocations' among manual workers. As we have said, the periods of silent study obligatory in a great many religious institutions were regarded as a new and painful exercise, to such an extent that this actually came to form a part of monastic asceticism. Moreover, in the Carolingian age an active life must have been far more natural to these country-bred monks. Some scribes found relief from this imposed silence in brief notes scribbled in the margins of manuscripts. An Irishman comments in his own language (which cannot have been understood by the object of his remarks) on the severity of the monk in charge,

adding, probably in response to some criticism: 'This page
was not copied slowly.' From Laon come more of these little
jottings: 'The lamp is not very bright.' 'It is time to start work.'
'This parchment is very rough.' 'I don't feel well today.'

We can picture the studio, a biggish room, its size depending
on the number of copyists, although not all of these would be
working at the same time. The monk in charge, who was the
librarian as well, dealt out the work. It was rare for a whole
manuscript to be entrusted to a single scribe, and often several
would be working in relays on the same text. Generally the
sheets of the text to be copied would be distributed among
the scribes, who had to take great care with their spacing in
order to finish the page on the same word. The instructor kept
a close eye on the apprentices, often tracing a few lines or
pages himself as an example for them to copy. He also had to
go over the work done in the studio and correct it. Finally,
he had a free hand as to the materials used.

BOOKS AND LIBRARIES

The fragile papyrus which was imported from Egypt and
consequently became increasingly rare and expensive as
navigation in the Mediterranean declined, was more or less
abandoned by the copyists by the middle of the eighth
century and replaced by the more substantial parchment,
although a few chancelleries occasionally used it until the
eleventh. Even so, for a time when animal husbandry was not
particularly advanced, parchment was not very easily ob-
tainable, while thicker skins were also required to make
covers. In 774 Charlemagne gave the monastery of St Denis a
complete forest, with all the wild beasts it contained, as a
source of skins for binding its volumes. In the sixth and seventh
centuries monasteries were so poor that some were compelled
to wash and scrape the pages of old manuscripts – copies of
religious as well as secular works – and re-use them, but as
time went on, despite increased needs, they were better pro-

vided. There is a ninth-century manuscript describing how the parchments were prepared: the skins were soaked in lime for three days before being stretched and dressed; after that they were ready to be cut into the required sizes.

Great strides forward were made during the first half of the ninth century. Not only was the number of churches copying manuscripts greatly increased, but some of the *scriptoria* began to undertake outside work, becoming in fact genuine publishing houses of the period. The most outstanding example is the monastery of St Martin of Tours, which also worked in conjunction with neighbouring monasteries. One expert, Monsignor Lesne, has stated that 'there was no other *scriptorium* whose products were so widely disseminated. The present distribution of these manuscripts throughout Europe and even America is merely an extension of the movement which in the ninth and tenth centuries had already carried them to every corner of western christendom.' The manuscripts copied at Tours included Bibles, Gospels, liturgies, works of dogma and even profane literature, sometimes in sequences destined for kings, great lords, episcopal schools and monasteries.

Some of these manuscripts, especially those of the Bible and Gospels, were most beautifully executed. The writing was skilfully varied, with capitals and uncials for the titles, semi-uncial for the first lines of chapters and minuscule for the remainder. Sometimes the parchment was dyed purple and the text written in gold or silver ink. Decorative illumination became increasingly elaborate. Simple at first, and confined to a few initial letters, this was gradually extended to cover whole pages. Foliage, strap work and stylized animals gave way to the rediscovered human form. Pictures were added, cunningly arranged in horizontal layers on the page. The famous Bible presented to Charles the Bald remains one of the finest examples of the art of book production as practised at Tours during the ninth century, but we know of a further thirty or so Bibles produced by the same studio.

This lavish profusion of detailed ornament shows a love

of books borne out by many direct statements and which has persisted into our present-day civilization. It is, however, true that this reverence was directed primarily towards the Word of God enshrined in these manuscripts. For this the monks reserved their most magnificent work, the sumptuous bindings with boards of carved ivory and plaques of gold studded with pearls and precious stones. In these books is already manifest that fervour for the Godhead revealed which was to inspire the later builders of churches, while their miniatures provided a kind of anthology for the sculptors of capitals and tympana to draw on. But gradually this love extended to all the volumes which normally formed part of the 'treasure' of a church. 'A monastery without books', ran the adage, 'is a fortress without victuals.'

But there was also an awakening urge to possess more accurate texts. Copyists who were inattentive and whose knowledge of Latin was inadequate, together with the difficulties of deciphering original manuscripts which were themselves frequently corrupt (sixth- and seventh-century copyists had been careless in the extreme), combined to produce a great many mistakes which sometimes made nonsense of whole passages. Emendations had to be made, and this was always a delicate operation, especially where there was no better copy available for comparison. In such cases it was a matter of working by judgement, guess-work and common sense, and even the most intelligent could make mistakes. One example of this is in a letter of Pope Gregory the Great in which the scribe, misunderstanding the abbreviation *mag. mil.* (for *magister militum*, the Roman military rank) copied it as *magni l*, which was meaningless, and this in turn was later amended by Paul the Deacon to *magnificus*. Loup de Ferrières, in particular, took great pains to bring together several copies of the same text and collate them. In about 830 he was writing to Einhard:

Having once broken the bounds of all restraint, I ask you again to lend me some of your books during my stay here: to beg the loan of a book is infinitely less presumptuous than to demand the gift of friendship. The book is Cicero's treatise on Rhetoric: it is true that I have it, but it is full of errors in many places, which is why I have collated my copy against a manuscript I discovered here. I thought this was better than mine, but it is even worse . . .

Another source of error apart from the misinterpretation of abbreviations was deficiencies in punctuation. Alcuin insisted particularly that his scribes must put in the punctuation and even completed it himself.

Thanks to all these endeavours Europe in the ninth century was beginning to accumulate its first significant collection of libraries. Nearly all of them belonged to religious institutions, chiefly to monasteries. A few laymen did possess books, but these collections were either bequeathed to churches or dispersed when their owners died. Even Charlemagne in his will left instructions for his books to be sold – they represented a considerable fortune – and the money distributed among the poor. The idea of creating a permanent palatine library did not occur to any ruler.

Churches which, like the monastery of St Gall, have preserved up to the present day a library begun in the Carolingian age, are few and far between. Normally, to obtain a reasonably accurate picture of what resources were available in these libraries, all we have to go by is a handful of old catalogues and the indirect evidence to be gathered from certain documentary accounts or from the sources used by a particular author whom we know to have worked in a specific place.

Fulda seems to have possessed the richest of these libraries, possibly almost a thousand volumes. The monastery of Murbach in Alsace had 400 in about 870, and Bobbio in Italy, more than six hundred in the tenth century. A reasonably important church generally owned between two and three hundred books.

Naturally the contents of these libraries were not entirely uniform, but reflected the interests which predominated in a particular place. On the whole, however, the collections fulfilled much the same needs everywhere. They fell into several categories which were always the same and varied only proportionally from one place to another. First of all came the liturgical works, which were adapted to the needs of each individual church with its particular saints and feast days. These were often kept separately near the sanctuary. In the library itself pride of place was reserved for religious works; the Scriptures, the works of the Fathers, and various commentaries. Historical and legal works constituted an intermediate category including, alongside the volumes of Church history and collections of canon law, the works of secular historians and texts of Roman or barbarian law. Lastly there was the section devoted to the 'arts', the products of human wisdom rather than of divine inspiration: treatises on grammar and prosody, the masterpieces of classical poets and prose writers, a smattering of textbooks of logic and rhetoric and, more rarely, of works on computation, geography and medicine.

EDUCATION AND TEACHING

The books last mentioned were intended specifically for educational purposes, but unfortunately we have very little information about the way in which education was imparted. We do not even know exactly how far Charlemagne's orders were implemented by the actual opening of schools. The most direct evidence comes from Lyons and Orleans. A letter written to Charlemagne by Leidrade, archbishop of Lyons, shows what had been done in the former:

I now have singing schools and of these pupils several are grown so learned that they are able to become teachers. I also have schools of reading, in which is practised not only the proper reading of the 'lessons' for the office, but also the endeavour by a study of Holy Writ to reach an understanding of the spiritual meaning. Many of my pupils are already capable of making out the precise meaning of the Gospel. . . . What was needful to provide for the transcription of the books has also been done.

This was obviously a specifically religious programme, but it does imply the existence of some basic general education, without which it could never have been carried out.

Theodulf in particular is remarkable for the pains he took to establish the elements of education in the region of his diocese of Orleans. He encouraged village priests to keep schools and to teach their letters to all pupils entrusted to them, 'in all charity' and without asking for payment. The most promising children were to be sent to the cathedral church in Orleans or to the monasteries of the diocese.

These endeavours undoubtedly continued and were even amplified after Charlemagne, but we should beware of too many illusions as to results. A synod held at Rome in 826 deplored the shortage of teachers and the general lack of interest in the study of letters. A few years later Loup de Ferrières expressed the same regret: 'If the want of teachers had not prevented it and if the study of the classics had not been on the point of perishing from long disuse, I might perhaps, with God's help, have been able to satisfy my hunger ...'

The decree of 817 ordering monasteries to confine themselves to the teaching of oblates is at the same time an indication of the active work of certain monastic schools and of the obstacles placed in the way of their development. Fortunately it seems likely that more than one monastery ignored this prohibition. Plans for the projected rebuilding of the monastery of St Gall seem to have included both a *schola claustri* within the monastery itself, and also a *schola exterior*, situated in an adjacent building to the north of it. This duplication, which safeguarded the peace of the cloister, must have been the rule in other seminaries, such as Corbie.

Elementary education amounted to very little and even this was only acquired with great pains and enforced by strict discipline which did not exclude corporal punishment. Some masters were inclined to overdo it. 'Knowledge is not imparted by blows', one of these had to be reminded a century later, 'but by the inner working of the spirit; you may break an entire forest on the backs of your wretched pupils but you will achieve nothing without the cooperation of their minds!' But some pupils grew up to look back with gratitude on the correction administered by more moderate teachers. Reading and writing were taught from the Psalter which the pupils learned by heart and which for many clerics remained the thing they knew best. In the absence of alphabet books the letters had to be picked out separately from words – a far cry from the methods in use anywhere today. Some elements of arithmetic and a few singing exercises completed a programme which was to be the whole sum of education for many monks and clerics.

Any advance on this meant chiefly a detailed study of Latin grammar. This was particularly true for pupils of Germanic origin but also applied to the descendants of Italian, Spanish or Gallo-Roman families for whom the spoken language was growing farther and farther removed from the reinstated classical Latin. Of all the liberal arts, grammar was the only one studied in any depth, but it should be defined in a fairly broad sense such as that used by Alcuin himself: 'Grammar is the science of letters and the guardian of right speech and writing; it depends on nature, reason, authority and custom.' It was studied initially from the *Ars Minor* of Donatus, and in the compilations of Bede and Alcuin. More advanced pupils reached the *Ars Maior* of Donatus and the treatise of Priscian. Apart from the study of letters, syllables, words and parts of speech, they also worked at figures of speech and prosody. Examples chosen from Latin literature also ensured a greater or lesser degree of familiarity with this.

The teaching of rhetoric and dialectic (lumped together with logic) remained much more rudimentary and was usually based on Alcuin's extremely perfunctory textbooks. The study of *quadrivium* was even more neglected and, except for computation, scarcely went beyond the elementary information to be found in the *Etymologies* of Isidore of Seville.

Both from a psychological and an educational standpoint there is something to be gained from a closer look at the textbooks in use in the ninth century. It is worth studying how a man like Alcuin set himself to simplify earlier treatises. One obvious aim was to ease the effort of memory by short mnemonic poems, the use of which went back to the ancient world. Some of these have strophes, or verses, beginning with the letters of the alphabet in order. Others were like this piece – a fine specimen of the second declension – with which Sedulius Scottus thanks a friend named Robert for a gift of wine:

> Bonus vir est Robertus,
> Laudes gliscunt Roberti,
> Christe, fave Roberto,
> Longaevum fac Robertum,

> Amen salve, Roberte,
> Christus sit cum Roberto –
> Sex casibus percurrit
> Vestri praeclarum nomen.*

The deliberate use of dialogue was also retained to introduce an element of life into what was often very dry material. By way of distraction such dialogue might be frankly amusing, based on riddles or word play. One example of this can be seen in Alcuin's *Discussion between the royal and most noble young Pepin and his master Albinus*. Pepin (who may have been a son of Charlemagne) asks the questions and Albinus (or Alcuin) replies:

P. What is life?
A. The joy of the blessed, the sorrow of sinners, the expectation of death.
P. What is death?
A. An unavoidable occurrence, an uncertain journey, the tears of the living, the confirmation of the testament, the thief of man.
P. What is man?

> *A right good man is Robert,
> High swells the praise of Robert,
> Be gracious, Christ, to Robert,
> Long-lived render Robert.

> So be it, prosper, Robert,
> May Christ abide with Robert;
> Thy glorious name's declension
> Its course runs through six cases.

*Translation M. L. W. Laistner, *Thought and Letters* . . . pp. 199–200.

A. The slave of death, a passing wayfarer, the guest of a place.
P. To what is man [*homo*] like?
A. A fruit [*pomo*] . . .

Next it is the turn of Albinus to question the young man, who emerges more or less creditably from the test:

A. I lately saw a man standing, a dead man walking, even one who never was.
P. How can that be? Unfold to me.
A. A likeness reflected in the water.
P. Why did not I myself understand this, seeing that I have seen it so many times? . . .
A. I have seen the dead create the living and the dead consumed by the breath of the living.
P. From the rubbing together of sticks fire is born which consumes them.*

In the very limited extent to which we are able to identify them, these schools, libraries and centres for the copying of manuscripts can be related to a distinct and characteristic 'map of the Carolingian Renaissance'. Especially fruitful are the regions of communication, such as northern Gaul, which was a stopping place for Irish and Anglo-Saxon missionaries; the Rhine district between Gaul and Germany, the heart of the Carolingian State; Rhaetia (with St Gall and Reichenau), where there was the most intensive contact between Germany and Italy. The importance of England has been stressed. In Gaul, apart from the north-eastern corner already mentioned, the valleys of the Loire and the Rhone had long been major arteries of cultural life. In Italy, Bobbio was still, with Rome (although for different reasons), the only really important centre. Monte Cassino did not play a cultural role until later on. The greatest achievements in Germany are to be found in the growth of model monasteries, of which Fulda was the most complete example. By contrast southern Gaul generally, formerly heavily romanized but ruined by the long struggle against Arab aggression, is a noticeably backward area.

* ibid., p. 390.

Chapter 5

THE LEGACY OF THE
CAROLINGIAN RENAISSANCE

IT is out of the question here to draw up a complete reckoning of the Carolingian renaissance. All that can be done is to underline its importance in the development of European culture and to point to at least a few of its gaps and weaknesses.

PROGRESS IN RELIGIOUS KNOWLEDGE

First of all, this renaissance must be viewed in its proper perspective, which is that of the writers of the period, even if for some (or even a great many) people today this is not what constitutes its chief value. Now there can be no doubt that the ultimate goal of Charlemagne, Alcuin and their colleagues was to arrive at a real understanding of the Holy Writ and to disseminate this knowledge among the clergy as a whole. The key phrase in the Capitulary *Of Art and Letters*, already quoted, is certainly that in which Charlemagne expressed his fears 'lest . . . wisdom to understand the Sacred Scriptures be far less than it ought rightly to be'.

In the first place it was necessary to possess an accurate, complete and uniform text of these Scriptures. At the time of Charlemagne's accession this was far from being the case. A great many churches possessed only incomplete versions of the Bible. Elsewhere this might be complete but with the books of the Old Testament appearing in variable order. Finally, a great many discrepancies of detail were to be found in the text itself. How this came about is something which must be briefly explained if we are to understand the full extent of the work accomplished under the aegis of Charlemagne.

The responsibility for the muddle lay first and foremost with the conditions under which the Latin text of the Scriptures had been originally assembled. To begin with, the Old Testament was translated from Hebrew into Greek by the Septuagint. Legend has it that this was a group of seventy (or seventy-two) translators despatched from Jerusalem to Alexandria by the High Priest Eleazar at the request of king Ptolemy Philadelphus about the middle of the third century B.C. The legend is probably not without some factual basis. Ptolemy may have fostered an attempt at translation carried out by the Jewish community in Alexandria during the third and second centuries B.C. The Septuagint took a good many liberties with the original text, as well as changing the order of the books, which had hitherto been grouped in three sections: the Pentateuch, the Prophets and the Writ. This Greek text by the Septuagint remained in use among Roman Christians until the fourth century. It was held in extraordinary reverence because it was believed that the seventy or seventy-two translators (the figures have a particular symbolic significance) had worked directly under the inspiration of the Holy Ghost. At the very most, a few hasty translations into vulgar Latin, full of inaccuracies, were got together for the benefit of the many ordinary folk among the early Christians who did not understand Greek.

As for the New Testament – although there may have been primitive Aramaic versions in existence, and this is an extremely vexed question – Latin translations of the Greek text were made at a very early date. St Augustine was to observe later that every Christian with a smattering of Greek thought himself entitled to produce his own version. Modern scholars have succeeded in dividing these numerous pre-hieronymian versions into three main categories: the 'African', 'European' and 'Italian', although all of them differ immensely in detail.

Then came Jerome. His figure dominates the history of the Scriptures as they have been handed down to us, although in fact not all his work is of equal importance. Working from the Greek text, Jerome began at the request of Pope Damasius by carrying out a revision – reduced to the bare essentials – of the Latin translation of the Gospels in use in Rome (382–3). He may have done the same for the remainder of the New Testament, although this is uncertain. He then revised the Latin words of the Psalms, according to the Greek text of the Septuagint. But for the rest of the Old Testament he went back to the original Hebrew and translated directly into Latin. He carried out the work in Bethlehem, between approximately 390 and 405, and it is this which naturally bears the strongest imprint of his own personality. It was also, however, the part of his work which was given the coolest reception, since the text of the Septuagint was still held in immense veneration. At all events, in competition with earlier texts Jerome's version of the Scriptures – which came to be known as the Vulgate – was only slowly and sporadically accepted in the West.

The catastrophe of the great invasions, the break in continuity of Roman influence in the West, accentuated the chaos which developed quite naturally from an already confused situation. This chaos was partly due to dogmatic causes. People wanted to reduce what they regarded as contradictions in the Sacred Books, correcting one Gospel with the help of others, and inevitably these corrections were carried out haphazardly according to the whim of the individual. Alterations were also made in the Scriptural text in order to make it express certain truths of the Faith more clearly. Thus the passage in the second book of Maccabees (XII, 44–5) in which the prayer for the dead is recommended as 'a holy and pious thought' was frequently altered so as to make it appear as a firm command, and the page containing a text of Esdras which seemed to contradict this injunction was omitted. In the same way the First Epistle of Saint John (v, 7–8) was interpolated in Spain as follows, the better to demonstrate the mystery of the Holy Trinity:

For there are three that bear record (in heaven, the Father, the Word and the Holy Ghost, and these three are one in Christ Jesus; and there are three that bear witness in earth): the Spirit, the water and the blood, and these three are one.

In the midst of this extreme confusion two distinct traditions grew up in two comparatively isolated places. Spain possessed the complete Bible, but the order of the books varied a great deal, at least as regards the Old Testament, and, even more important, the text was very mixed, being full of interpolations by authors such as Priscillian. In Ireland few Bibles were complete, and very often manuscripts contained only the Gospels, plus the Psalms and a few books of Wisdom. The interpolations, although numerous, were perhaps less systematic and far-reaching than in Spain. A reference to what has been said about the Irish influence on the continent and of the spread of Visigothic manuscripts brought about by the Arab conquest will give some idea of the confusion which Charlemagne found in his domains.

A deplorable jumble of excellent and execrable texts, sometimes two translations of the same book set side by side, the older versions mixed up with the Vulgate in an inextricable confusion and the books of the Bible copied in a different order in each manuscript,

is how one scholar, Samuel Berger, has summed it up.

This confusion must have been shocking to minds convinced that there could be only one definitive text of the Scriptures. Here and there, some stirrings to word reform were evident, but the initiative was to come from Charlemagne and it is in the light of this situation that his often repeated wish to have 'Catholic books carefully corrected' must be understood.

Then came Alcuin. After Jerome, and on a much lower level, his activities were all-important in the communication of the Scriptures. To him was entrusted the task of establishing this single text which Charlemagne was determined to have. From constant references in his letters, although these are not always easy to date, it can be calculated that he began his work in about 797, shortly after settling at Tours, and completed it between Easter 800 and Easter 801. He may even have presented his manuscript to Charlemagne at Christmas 800 for the occasion of the latter's coronation as emperor of Rome. It would form a pretty coincidence between the two peaks of Charlemagne's achievement in different fields.

Although Alcuin's original manuscript has vanished we do possess several texts derived directly from it and can therefore form a fairly accurate assessment of his work. The general impression is rather dull at first glance, but a more detailed examination shows that Alcuin used very varied manuscripts and made substantial and occasionally daring emendations, some based on grammatical considerations and others influenced by the Commentaries of the Fathers of the Church. The quest for an uncorrupt text is obvious. Many major interpolations have been eliminated; on the whole the problems are resolved according to the same principles, and there are many excellent readings. More often than not the text is reconstructed from that of St Jerome.

Acting very much on his own initiative, Theodulf also carried out a similar work. It betrays a mind more flexible and more open to doubt than Alcuin's. In the final result, Theodulf's text may have been closer to the spirit of the original Hebrew. Unlike Alcuin he did not eliminate unusual variants but noted them carefully and to some extent collected them. This is useful from the point of view of modern scholars, but was much farther from what Charlemagne wanted and from what were certainly the needs of the times. Consequently Theodulf's work achieved little fame.

Alcuin's, on the other hand, was to exercise a considerable influence. His was the text largely accepted throughout the Middle Ages, though not without a multitude of variations in detail, which can be put down to hasty copying and careless correcting, and which appear even in Bibles copied at Tours itself less than half a century after Alcuin's death. Alcuin's text was re-integrated in the thirteenth century, and in this form it has persisted as the basis of the Vulgate, retained until the present day in the Roman Catholic Church. This reveals the full historical significance of Alcuin's work in what, to him, was the vital field of study.

The correction and unification of other 'catholic books' was also undertaken at Charlemagne's instigation. A brief mention may be made of Alcuin's work on liturgical matters. Although identical in broad outline, the sum total of Christian ritual – the order and continuity of the different parts of the Mass, the celebration of the various sacraments, the prayers laid down for special offices, the list of feast days celebrated throughout the year – had acquired an immense diversity of detail in the countries of Western Europe. In Rome itself, successive revisions had combined to produce a tradition remarkable for its restraint. These revisions spread outwards, to Gaul in particular, where they were incorporated in the 'Gallican' liturgy which was on the whole more formalized and expressive, and hence better adapted to the Frankish character. The sumptuous 'Visigothic' liturgy of Spain, with its amazing proliferation of offices and rituals, also took root in some regions conquered by Charlemagne. Impressed by the ceremonies he attended in Rome in 781, Charlemagne begged the Pope to send him the official Roman Sacramentary and entrusted Alcuin with the job of adapting it. Alcuin had to correct the rather faulty copy sent to him and he supplemented it with the addition of prayers and rites in common use among the Franks and Spaniards, to be employed here and there as required. Shortly after 800 Charlemagne gave orders for the exclusive use of this revised Sacramentary in his domains, a use which later spread to Rome itself. The Missal of the Roman Church as we know it today owes a great deal to it. In the same way Charlemagne wanted one book which should contain the basic outlines of sermons for the Christian clergy to deliver to their congregations. This 'homiliary', derived from numerous different sources, was the work of Paul the

Deacon and it too was an immense success throughout the Middle Ages.

CAROLINGIAN HUMANISM

The same movement which led Alcuin and his imitators to correct the 'catholic books' also brought them into contact with the best Latin writers, belonging to the classical Roman age of the Latin language, as defined by Isidore of Seville. In other words they read profane authors since without them there was no means of acquiring the intimate knowledge of the Latin tongue which was a necessity for their work. But the effects of this acquaintance went far beyond the Carolingian era. How much would we know about the Latin classics today but for the texts bequeathed us by librarians and copyists of this first renaissance?

To take only a few examples: the two oldest manuscripts of Caesar's *Gallic Wars* date from the ninth century, and one of these is from Corbie. The only text of the first five books of the fifth decade of Livy's *History of Rome* was copied in the fifth century but was preserved in the abbey of Lorsch on the Rhine where the humanist Symon Grynaeus found it in about 1527. St Denis and St Gall likewise kept the oldest texts of Virgil in fourth-century capitals. The two best manuscripts of Lucretius' *De rerum natura*, now in the library of the University of Leyden, date from the ninth century, and one of these almost certainly originated in the monastery of St Bertin. Of Tacitus we would know almost nothing if it were not for the ninth-century copyists; and the only manuscript to contain the first six books of his 'Annals', the *Mediceus prior* in the Laurentian Library in Florence, was probably copied at Fulda in the ninth century and sent to Corvey, where it was found towards the end of the fifteenth century. All our manuscripts of his 'minor' works, the *Dialogue on Orators*, the *Germania* and *Agricola*, are based on a ninth- or tenth-century text, now lost, which a monk of Hersfeld offered for sale to the humanist Il Poggio in 1425.

The comparative abundance of such manuscripts, no less than the frequency of borrowings from or imitations of classical authors, reveals the popularity – however unequal – which they enjoyed in the ninth century. It was then that Cicero entered the field of Latin studies and has remained its mainstay ever since. Loup de Ferrières took great pains to seek out manuscripts of his work. He praised 'that gravity which is found in Cicero and in all other classical authors and which the Fathers of the Church also copied', and loved to quote him alongside the Holy Scriptures. Einhard valued: 'his clear judgements . . . condensed into brief aphorisms' and concludes the preface to his *Life of Charlemagne* with a precept of Cicero's from the *Tusculans*. Alongside Cicero, Virgil became the basic author. True, he had never been forgotten but it was at this period that his *Eclogues* were rediscovered. Alcuin tells how in his youth he actually preferred reading them to the Psalms. In his old age he rebuked his pupil Ricbod, archbishop of Trèves, who had not written to him for some time, for the same weakness.

Perhaps the love of Virgil has erased my memory? Ah, if my name were only Virgil! Then I should be always before your eyes and you would spend your time studying my slightest word and, as the proverb says, then I should be happier than anyone could ever be again. But Alcuin is gone and Virgil has come, and Maro sits in your teacher's place. . . . I could wish your heart were filled with the four Gospels and not with the twelve books of the *Aeneid*.

But Einhard also took Suetonius for a model, and men were beginning to relish Horace and Ovid.

To Alcuin these treasures of classical wisdom were valuable chiefly because they led to a better understanding of the Scriptures. He speaks of them with a fervour that makes them to some extent sacred: 'the steps of grammatical and of philosophical disciplines lead to the summit of evangelical perfection'. Without denying the greatness they confer on the period of their origin, he claims that in future, in their new function, they will be of the most outstanding value. This explains the enthusiasm behind his famous exclamation to Charlemagne:

If many are infected by your aims, a new Athens will be created in France, nay, an Athens finer than the old, for ours, ennobled by the teachings of Christ, will surpass all the wisdom of the Academy. The old had only the disciplines of Plato for teacher and yet inspired by the seven liberal arts it still shone with splendour: but ours will be endowed besides with the sevenfold plenitude of the Holy Ghost and will outshine all the dignity of secular wisdom.

Besides, was not science also the unfolding of the order set by God in the universe? The liberal arts, Alcuin informed his master Egbert, are not the creation of man but of God, who placed them in nature.

All the same, as we have seen, Alcuin was careful not to enjoy profane authors too much for their own sake. Even in the ninth century more than one protest was raised against the excessive enthusiasm with which they were read. The very strength of these reactions is evidence in itself. What our ninth-century writers were discovering, and relishing almost in spite of themselves, was a knowledge which owed nothing to religion. No one had more praise for it than Loup de Ferrières, but even he makes his position quite clear: 'The love of letters was born in me almost from my tenderest youth, and I have never scorned what most of our contemporaries call their superfluous and superstitious leisure.' For him, then, it was a natural inclination, but one confirmed by reflection, for 'knowledge deserves to be coveted for its own sake' because it helps to develop in man that reason to whose control he ought to submit his feelings and emotions. Highly typical is a letter in which Loup endeavours to comfort Einhard on the death of his much-loved wife. In it reflections drawn from 'philosophy' are mingled inextricably with the dictates of religion. 'I would wish for you', he writes,

that which, in the opinion of the philosophers, may be the lot of the wise man, to know that the wisdom of your mind gradually softens the harshness of events which seem contrary to us at first and commonly crush the ignorant mass of humanity, and that it should bring your will into accord with the divine will.

He goes on to remind his friend of the example of David who, 'having tested the vanity of his urgent prayers, found comfort in his reason and submitting to God's justice, resigned himself in all humility.' This may well be regarded as a form of Christian humanism, but it also foreshadows the difficulties which later generations were to face in reconciling Christianity with profane wisdom.

THE BIRTH OF EUROPEAN LANGUAGES

A considered examination of the birth of European languages, which forms an essential part of the legacy of the period known as the Middle Ages, reveals something in the nature of a linguistic revolution. This is especially true of the Romance languages, although similarities may also be discerned in the origins of Germanic tongues. It marks the transition from inflected to analytical speech.

Classical Latin literature provided a model of an inflectional language in which the functions of the words within the sentence are indicated by terminal modifications. This is true not only of verbs but also of nouns and adjectives, which, as anyone who ever studied the language at school is unlikely to forget, decline in six cases. The wealth and complexity of this system of inflexions results in great economy in the use of such 'empty words' as the definite and indefinite article, personal pronouns, and prepositions with which our sentences are encumbered today. A Roman could write simply *eo rus* to express an intention which the modern Englishman or Frenchman could only convey at much greater length: 'I'm going to the country.' 'Je vais à la campagne.' This system also allows Latin a greater flexibility in the arrangement of a sentence and makes it possible, at least to a great extent, to invert the word order so as to produce the strongest effect. Latin authors made full use of this wonderful logic to carry a complex train of reasoning in a single sentence. Our present-day languages, as well as relying in varying degrees on an 'analytical' sentence structure involving the use of 'empty words', are also in general much more rigid in word order and simpler in their syntax. It may be that this kind of linguistic change reveals a change in the psychological attitudes of those using the languages as well.

We know, of course, that literary Latin was not exactly the spoken language of the Roman world. The discovery of some five thousand graffiti at Pompeii, to which a definite date can be assigned (A.D. 79), has shown that even in Italy at the height of the classical era the system of inflexions was less rigorously observed in the mouth of the man in the street than by the pens of grammarians and authors. The frequent omission of terminal vowels (such as m), and confusion between the various declensions makes clear the gulf which existed between literary and 'vulgar' Latin (the word is not used in any pejorative sense). And even a great writer such as Cicero could, in his private letters, relax and permit himself a word or two ordinarily banned from literary usage, or use a preposition (*aptus ad aliquam rem* – i.e., apt at something) where an inflexion would have served (*aptus alicui rei*).

We also know that in the first century A.D., Latin was spoken not only by Italians but also by countless provincials whose forbears, or even whose parents, had spoken a Celtic or Hispanic language. However complex the problem of these 'substrata', it seems very likely that, even in classical times, this would have given each province its own linguistic peculiarities, and that the way to the future divergence of Romance languages already lay open.

All the same, there was still a long way to go and most of this ground was covered between the third and the ninth century. For the present this crucial period is shrouded in mystery for lack of documentary evidence. However, writing and tradition generally go hand in hand, and such texts of these centuries as we possess, while certainly providing only a faint reflexion of the spoken languages, bear witness to a degeneration in the use of the Latin tongue. In order to trace this development, and date it more or less accurately, linguistic scholars have been obliged to evolve highly complicated methods. There is still argument as to whether these divergences were essentially complete by the sixth century or whether they occurred at a later date.

They were certainly related to the shattering upheavals which took place at this time in the Roman world and its environs, most notably the great invasions and the adoption by the newcomers of this richer, more flexible language, which, as a consequence of countless marriages between 'barbarian' soldiers and local women, was in many cases to become the mother tongue of their descendants. The Romans, on the other hand, never bothered to learn the Germanic dialects. Within a few centuries Latin had become the current language everywhere except in a very few places, such as Belgium, Alsace, the left bank of the Rhine, and England, where it failed to hold its ground. Roughly speaking, it is the boundaries of the old Roman Empire which mark the division between Romance and Germanic languages in Europe today. To a varying degree this triumph of Latin was accompanied everywhere by a certain transformation of the language under the influence of the 'barbarians'' own vocabulary, pronunciation and even syntactical habits. French, of all the Romance languages, was the one which moved farthest away from Latin, but in the Iberian peninsula the process was continued in another form by the Arab conquest.

These invasions also precipitated a whole political and social movement, which had its beginnings even earlier. This was the collapse of Roman administration, the decline of the schools of which such administrative careers constituted the normal outlet, the shrinking of cities, the ruin of the middle classes and the partial re-emergence of an elite. In this general disintegration only the Church stood firm, with its role immensely increased. The next question therefore concerns the expansion of Christianity and its effect on language.

This effect was not confined simply to the introduction of a whole new ecclesiastical vocabulary, although this was often destined for a wider future. The word 'parabolare' for instance, which originally meant the Word of the Lord, was gradually adapted to give the French *parler* and the Italian *parlare*, and so on. The Fathers of the Church laid great stress on the need to use the language of the common people for purposes of conversion and instruction, in writing as well as in preaching by word of mouth – for example in the lives of the saints, and in educational works. This new attitude ensured the survival of a great many everyday words hitherto frowned on by purists. It resulted in simple, lively syntax, relying on short, juxtaposed sentences. It meant, in fact, the promotion of vulgar Latin to the status of a written language. Lastly, it is not impossible that a number of new features, such as the appearance of the definite article, the spread of the personal pronoun and the emergence of the polite forms may have been related to the new, and specifically Christian concept of mankind and of human relations.

By about the end of the eighth century, at all events, the new languages were born. The same is also true of the Germanic languages, which underwent a similar process of divergence and stabilization. In the Carolingian age, people became consciously aware of this new development and at the same time the question of how these various languages were to be regarded emerged with new force. To understand this we must refer back to the Irish and Anglo-Saxon origins of Carolingian culture. These were lands where Latin had either never been spoken or was spoken no longer and no corruption was to be feared on that score. The language men learned – by dint of earnest grammatical study – and the language they wrote was a comparatively pure classical Latin. This was the Latin which Alcuin and his island colleagues reintroduced into the court of Charlemagne and which then spread to the Frankish clergy as a whole.

A great deal of study has been devoted to the decadent Latin of the sixth and seventh centuries. Very little, on the other hand, has been bestowed on the Latin written during the Carolingian era. It is as though scholars have taken more pleasure in castigating the bad pupils than in reading the good ones. And yet it is a fact that the Latin of Alcuin and those who emulated him was, if not exactly Ciceronian, at least correct and purged of the faults which had been widespread in the preceding centuries. In the case of men like Theodulf or Loup de Ferrières it actually achieved a certain elegance while even the Latin used in legal documents, capitularies, precepts and charters reaped some benefit from the new trend.

These results were achieved by careful study of Latin grammar. At a time when more or less everything had to be done by a few cultivated men it would be true to say that virtually all writers had first and foremost to be grammarians. Alcuin was not the only one who wrote a Latin grammar for his pupils. Sedulius Scotus, Clemens Scotus, Smaragdus, Peter of Pisa, Paulinus of Aquileia and Hrabanus Maurus all did so. The Irish were particularly indefatigable in this respect. These teachers also enriched the current Latin vocabulary by introducing extracts from classical authors and by the composition of glossaries to explain unfamiliar terms.

It has been said that this scholarly Latin, learned chiefly for purposes of writing, was a dead language. This is probably an overstatement: this Latin was also spoken. Einhard goes into raptures, not without a suspicion of flattery, at the ease with which Charlemagne could express himself in the language. More to the point, the better educated clergy were also learning to use it naturally again. But such men were few, and as time went on there was a huge gulf between this Latin and the language of common speech.

Thanks to Nithard, who recorded it, we possess the text of the oaths of alliance sworn by the kings Louis the German and Charles the Bald against their elder brother Lothair in the presence of their armies at Strasbourg in February 842. Louis the German spoke to be understood by his brother's soldiers, who hailed from western Francia, or what was to become modern France, and the text of this speech is regarded as the first monument of the French language. It has no longer any but the remotest connexion with Latin, a connexion perceptible only to scholars. There can be no doubt that the people who spoke this language no longer understood Latin without specifically learning it. To the question: at what time did people stop speaking Latin? a cautious historian like Ferdinand Lot would answer: 'in the Carolingian era'. Today we believe that orally the new language was born well before this period, but it was then that a clear division emerged between the various dialects and classical Latin as rediscovered. There was some awareness of this at the time, and the ninth-century documents make a rough distinction between three languages current in Charlemagne's domains: the *lingua romana* spoken in what had once been Roman territories, the *lingua theotisca*, used in the Germanic regions, and finally Latin, which was the language of administration and culture.

Naturally the truth was slightly more complicated. The reinstatement of classical Latin scarcely affected southern Gaul or the Spanish marches – the area later to become Catalonia – which lay to the south of it. On the other hand the term *lingua romana*, as we have seen, actually covered all emergent Romance languages. Over and above this diversity, however, there remained a conscious linguistic affinity which the phrase made quite clear.

It was the same with the Germanic regions. Here the dialects all belonged to the same linguistic family, and were differentiated only in detail. On the continent Frankish tended to predominate and was to form the basis of the Old High German. It seems an odd fate for the Franks! But even before the dissolution of Charlemagne's empire their linguistic unity had been disrupted. The Western Franks had abandoned Frankish. Loup de Ferrières, for example, though a Frank by birth, no longer understood it and gave up all idea of 'setting himself . . . the long, and arduous task of learning it'. In any case, the uncouth German names repelled him. But some slender thread of this ancient unity survived. The linguist Walter von Wartburg has observed that 'archaic French and the old high German are linked together by common evolutionary trends and have borrowed from one another constantly from the first'.

But it was Latin which remained the language of administration and culture. Latin alone possessed the strong structure, logical grammar and rich vocabulary which fitted it for this role. Moreover, the memory of the ancient Roman unity and its advantages was still too strong, and in addition Christian authors bestowed on the Roman Empire a providential vocation which was to make it as enduring as the world itself. Rome was the 'terrestrial city', gathering all men together in Christ for their salvation, foreshadowing the 'celestial city' of Paradise. It was this empire which persisted under Charlemagne and, inevitably, retained its own language, Latin.

However, Charlemagne had no intention of imposing Latin as the universal language, although the question might well have arisen. For a long time men had wondered about the strange fact that a great many different languages should exist on earth. The Scriptures offered one explanation which to the ninth century was clearly fundamental. All mankind, being descended from Adam, originally spoke the same language. Even after the Flood, when the descendants of Noah began to re-people the earth, 'the whole earth was of one language and one speech' (Genesis xi. 1).

It was men in their pride, by building the Tower of Babel 'whose top may reach unto heaven' (Genesis xi, 4) who unleashed the wrath of God. He decided to 'confound their language that they may not understand one another's speech. So the Lord scattered them abroad from thence upon the face of all the earth and they left off to build the city'. (Genesis xi, 7–8). Hence the diversity of languages. But just as the Passion redeemed man from original sin, so Pentecost enabled him to overcome the obstacle of this diversity. On that day the Holy

Ghost gave the Apostles the miraculous gift of speaking and understanding all the tongues of men (Acts ii, 5–12).

This still left many problems unexplained. It was generally accepted that the original common language had been Hebrew, but was it in actual fact possible to trace back all the languages commonly spoken in the ninth century, and consequently all the peoples who used them, to the miracle of Babel itself and to the descendants of Noah? On the other hand it was still possible to regard these languages in at least two different ways. The first and fundamentally pessimistic view was that the confusion of languages, the punishment of mankind's pride, was in itself an evil. Man must try and find his way back to the original unity. The three languages likely to achieve this were obviously Hebrew, Greek and Latin – that is to say the three languages of the inscription on the Cross: 'Jesus of Nazareth, the King of the Jews' (Gospel according to St John XIX, 19–20). There was an entire patristic tradition to proclaim their supremacy: St Hilary of Poitiers saw them as the 'principal languages' used by God. St Augustine proclaimed their excellence: had they not embodied divine law (Hebrew), human wisdom (Greek) and the State (Latin)? Isidore of Seville went so far as to designate them 'holy languages', the instruments of Redemption and Revelation. And of the three the only one available to the West was clearly Latin.

To other more optimistic and less exclusive ways of thinking, the diversity of tongues could not be absolutely evil since it had been decreed by God. These languages were not bad in themselves, because God had created them. Moreover, at the time people were extremely conscious of a symbolic value of numbers. The number seventy-two especially was thought to be perfect and was often believed to be the number of languages in existence. It was a sign of harmony, the manifestation of a providential order. In any case the miracle of Pentecost had lifted the curse which weighed on the diversity of languages. The miracle continued within the Church: what had been given to some at Pentecost was henceforth available to all Christians not as individuals but as members of a body which spoke all languages. There was no privileged tongue. God was the Father of all peoples and His praise should be sung in all idioms. St Augustine admirably expressed this meaning of Pentecost, and after him, even in the midst of the terrible invasions, there were still some Christians who accepted it as the source of a new Christian universalism.

Both these trends therefore existed in the Carolingian age and, in theory at least, it was in these terms that the problem of language presented itself to the small group of educated men. Charlemagne succeeded in maintaining a remarkably moderate attitude. He learned Latin and preserved it as the language of his administration. Einhard even states quite definitely that he attempted to learn a few words of Greek. But for all this he did not despise Frankish, which was his mother tongue. According to Einhard again:

He caused to be transcribed . . . the ancient barbarian poems in which were sung the stories and battles of the old kings, so that the memory of them should not be lost. He further undertook to provide a grammar of his native language and to all the months which had hitherto been known among the Franks, some by their Latin and others by their barbarian names, he gave names in his mother tongue. He did the same for each of the twelve winds, four of which, at most, had been named in his language before him. (Chapter 29.)

In the same spirit of balance and moderation Charlemagne tackled the linguistic problems posed by the religious life of his subjects. He had the Latin text of the Scriptures revised and disseminated. Here, too, Latin remained the liturgical language, though other languages also had their place in prayer and preaching. 'Let no one believe', announced the Synod of Frankfort in 794 (§ 52) – largely inspired by Alcuin, 'that God must be worshipped only in three languages. Let God be worshipped in every tongue and if a man's requests are just, he will be satisfied.' This was clearly a reaction against those clerics who, following Isidore of Seville, were demanding primacy for the three 'sacred languages' and seeking to impose the use of Latin in every aspect of religious life. In the same way, nearly twenty years later, the Council of Tours in 813 commanded clerics to expound the word of God in the vulgar tongue, whether German or Romance. It is perhaps an exaggeration to call this verdict, as Walter von Wartburg does, 'the birth certificate of European national languages'. All Charlemagne and his clergy were doing was to ratify the inevitable practice of all missionaries. Nevertheless, some such official sanction was important.

In fact, after Charlemagne opinions diverged. The supporters of Latin as a sacred tongue expressed their views energetically. One of these was Smaragdus, abbot of the monastery of St Mihiel in Lorraine around 820. He is a somewhat mysterious character, possibly an Irishman, author of a commentary dedicated to the grammarian Donatus which was much read for several centuries. For Smaragdus, Latin was a providential language and he used all possible arguments to demonstrate this. He pointed out that the number of parts of speech in Latin was eight (the figure symbolizing eternal life), because the study of Latin brought the elect to a knowledge of the Trinity and of Salvation. Smaragdus believed that the Latin text of the Bible had been written literally under the direct inspiration of the Holy Ghost and was consequently a higher authority than Donatus even in matters of grammar. For example, whereas Donatus asserted that the word *scalae* (ladder or staircase) should be used only in the plural, the Bible used *scala* in the singular, consequently 'we shall not follow Donatus, because we have a stronger authority in the Holy Scriptures'. This superstitious belief in Latin crops up alongside the unitarian tendencies of the ruling classes under Louis the Pious: Charlemagne's son spoke Latin as his mother tongue, and even a little Greek, and despised the 'national poems' collected by his father.

But this deliberate unitarianism clashed with much more powerful divergent forces which were to rend the Carolingian empire apart. At the opposite pole to Smaragdus, is Nithard, who was so interested in vulgar speech that he actually wrote down the text of the oaths of Strasbourg. This was the direction in which, in the immediate future at least, history was about to be made.

All the same, ninth-century literature in the vulgar tongue, or at least what remains of it today, naturally amounts to very little, since all of the barbarian poems collected byCharlemagne and the Frankish grammar begun by him have been lost. No contemporary work written in a Romance language has survived. We are slightly better off as regards Anglo-Saxon literature and that written in the Old High German. Of the first, the most remarkable monument is clearly the still half-pagan epic *Beowulf*. The second offers a few poems disseminating the truths of the Christian faith: the old Saxon *Heliand* (Saviour) and the 'Gospel Book' in old Franconian.

Even so, by the end of the century, at the opposite ends of Christendom and only a few years apart, we find two advances being made. In Wessex, under attack by the Danes, King Alfred the Great (871–99) supervised the translation of what were regarded as essential Latin works (by Gregory the Great, Bede and Boethius) into his native tongue. In the Slavonic regions, between 862 and 884, the Byzantine missionaries, Cyril and Methodius evolved a Slavonic alphabet, translated parts of the Bible into Slavonic and employed it as a liturgical language. Pope John VIII upheld them in this against the German clergy, who accused them of departing from the three prime languages, on the grounds that God might be worshipped in all tongues.

The linguistic face of Europe was now fixed for several centuries to come. On the one hand there was Latin, which had acquired a new purity and correctness and was the normal written language, the language of the Church, of culture and administration and a factor in European unity. But this was the language of a small, scholarly caste, chiefly attached to the Church, and consequently a language cut off from the roots of popular life, and from all new developments. On the other hand, there were the vulgar tongues, still hesitant, ungrammatical, almost entirely oral, and looked down on by scholars. In a Europe which was split up into so many small local units these could only crystallize in the form of dialects.

AN OUTLINE OF LITERARY PRODUCTION

The immediate effect of this familiarity with ancient writers was to encourage literary output and to raise its level. We only have to compare such work as Einhard's *Life of Charlemagne* with the shapeless chronicle attributed to Fredegar in the seventh century to measure what the Carolingian writer owed to the knowledge of Suetonius which he had acquired, no doubt, at Fulda. Admittedly we sometimes lose in spontaneity what is gained in literary merit. A close examination of the terms Einhard used to describe Charlemagne shows them to be quite literally borrowed from portraits of the various Roman emperors: The Frankish king has big eyes like Tiberius, a rather long nose like Augustus, a thick neck and a somewhat protruding stomach like Nero. ... How much of the real Charlemagne is left in all this we shall never know.

The first thing that strikes us when we try to make out the general characteristics of this Carolingian literature and its underlying psychological trends is its sheer abundance. Even if we confine ourselves to the century or so from 780 to 880, the writings which have come down to us take up nearly forty volumes of the *Patrologia Latina* collected and printed by the Abbé Migne in the nineteenth century. Each handsome octavo volume averages around 650 pages, and even then it must be remembered that a great many ninth-century works must have been lost. Of the works of Alcuin alone, we know only by repute of his treatise on music and of his commentaries on the Epistles of St Paul and the Proverbs of Solomon, while only a tiny fragment of his correspondence has been preserved. Even taking these losses into account the total may seem small in relation to our vast output today, but compared with the extreme poverty of the preceding century it represents enormous progress.

Comparison with our own times may also tend to conceal from us the variety of this literary output. The greater part of this literature was didactic, directed to the acquisition and communication of knowledge. On the whole and seen in relation to its time it was a scholarly literature. Its variety lay chiefly in subject matter and in the audience to which it was addressed.

First of all there were purely religious works: these included commentaries on the Scriptures and the Fathers of the Church, written to assist understanding and to direct it into orthodox paths; arguments composed in the heat of great theological debates on the relations of the Holy Ghost to the Father and to the Son or the real Presence in the Eucharist; and pastoral works, dealing with liturgy and containing model sermons. These last were aimed, through the clergy, at a larger public.

But it was hagiography that constituted the really popular genre of religious writing. Accounts of the lives of saints and the enumeration of their miracles transmitted to the people by their preachers must in their way have satisfied the need for self-identification and the appetite for the marvellous and amazing which in our own day find their outlet in sport and the cinema – and still more in the flood of *literature* about sport and the cinema.

Next there was properly academic writing aimed at communicating knowledge of the liberal arts. Enough has already been said of this, but in a neighbouring sphere some mention should be made of manuals intended for the instruction of kings and governments. These were extremely popular throughout the Middle Ages, a period in which the ideas of moral control exercised by the Church over the secular powers remained solidly entrenched. Alcuin's *Rhetoric*, written for Charlemagne, provides an early example of the

'Mirrors for Princes' which were later to appear in such profusion.

History was more than a single genre – it was a collection of different forms. The sequence of *Royal Annals* was simply an official history confined to a dry account of the facts, more or less angled, as was natural, but with no literary pretensions. The origin of works of this kind is to be found in the random notes written between the lines or in the margins of calendars used in monasteries to calculate the date of Easter and the moveable feasts. In time these notes were amplified and assembled into continuous year-by-year accounts. It seems to have been this example which was followed at the royal court.

Quite different again are those literary works devoted to a particular individual or sequence of events. The most notable examples here are Einhard's *Life of Charlemagne* and the four books of Nithard's *History*. The latter was in fact the great emperor's grandson, the offspring of an illicit union between Angilbert, the lay abbot of St Riquier, and Berthe, one of Charlemagne's daughters, whose father, according to Einhard, loved them so much that 'he would give none of them in marriage to any one whatsoever'. Nithard was deeply affected by the troubles which attended the end of the reign of Louis the Pious and the division of the Empire and had the idea of leaving an accurate account of them. Consequently both authors were actual eye-witnesses of the events they described. They do not conceal their sympathies, Einhard's for Charlemagne, and Nithard's for Charles the Bald, but at the same time they are sufficiently concerned with historical accuracy to include transcripts of actual documents in their works. Nithard's style is much simpler and less elegant than Einhard's, but even so both in their different ways have some literary pretensions. Both too try with a certain amount of psychological description of their subjects to explain the events which took place. For a long time to come psychological analysis of this kind was to remain a rarity in literature.

One step further, and we come to historical poems. One of

the most noteworthy of these is by Ermoldus Nigellus, a
cleric of Aquitaine, who extols the great deeds of the Emperor
Louis the Pious with the object of restoring himself in his
favour. It contains some happy touches of description but the
characters are distinguished at most by a few conventional
epithets, while its historical truth must be painstakingly un-
ravelled from the courtly and poetical exaggerations.

This brings us to the epic. The immense popularity which
this form was to enjoy in the eleventh and twelfth centuries
was already foreshadowed in the Latin *Waltharius*, harking
back to the struggles between Huns, Burgundians and Franks
at the time of the great invasions, and even more by the
Anglo-Saxon *Beowulf*, which is still deeply imbued with
pagan feeling.

It is important to stress the part played by poetry in all this
literature. It appears where we should expect to find it: in
occasional verse to express private emotion and in epic poems,
but it crops up too in places where its application is somewhat
surprising, such as in academic textbooks, collections of
proverbs, treatises on dogma and the lives of saints. It can
partly be explained by the academic nature of this poetry. The
study of Latin grammar was complemented by that of prosody, and Latin verse composition was a school exercise which
no serious scholar could escape. Quite understandably the
Carolingian poets went back to forms of classical Latin verse
based on combinations of long and short syllables, which had
been abandoned in previous centuries owing to the abandoning
of the rules of quantity. Some writers, of course, were better
at it than others. Alcuin attempted little beyond the hexameter
and the distich, whereas Theodulf was able to handle nearly
all the classical metres. Some versifiers even dabbled in
carmina figurata, in which the words could be read horizontally,
vertically or even diagonally, each time with a different
meaning – a piece of virtuosity more akin to a present-day
crossword than true poetry. But at least this familiarity with
Latin verse gave writers an intimate knowledge of the

language, a wealth of vocabulary and flexibility in construction similar to that which half a century ago our own grandfathers – or those of them who enjoyed the benefits of a classical education – derived from the same exercise.

More to the point, however, the distinction between prose and verse was at that time much more clear-cut than it is today. Now both can be read, whereas poetry then was not read but recited. The oldest surviving works on reading and verse-speaking date only from the eleventh century, but it is fairly certain that their advice was just as valid for earlier dates. Even so, they leave us in some doubt as to the methods of scansion used in reciting aloud, for instance, whether the voice was raised or lowered to mark the distinction between short and long. Later on (and this is discernible as early as the second half of the ninth century) rhythmic poetry reappeared, based on a combination of stressed and unstressed syllables, where the position of the stress was what mattered and there was frequently rhyme or assonance. It is highly probable that many of these poems, classical or rhythmic, were set to music. At all events, whether sung or recited, this poetry produced a very different effect from that felt by the private reader; moreover, it reached a large public which was unable to read. In this connexion it is possible to speak of a true 'auditory magic', and this makes it understandable that literature as such should at first have been largely poetic.

One last point. What was it beyond the fascination of the form itself and its recitation that attracted the public to this literature? Apart from religious feeling – and the pious excesses of later generations were largely unknown as yet – it contained little appeal to the emotions. There was also little or no psychological content (except in a very few historical works) and so it can hardly have been a matter of arousing or describing strong feelings. Its appeal was rather to the imagination, by conjuring up strange, fantastic and mysterious worlds. This was what lay behind the legends which very soon after his death began to gather around the person of Charle-

magne, the emperor 'of the flowery beard', or the epic tales
of the lives of the saints with the amazing virtues attributed
to them, their ecstasies and their miracles. The study of
classical mythology also revealed a strange new world, certainly very different from this one, and those astonishing
fables and stories of gods descending from Olympus must have
ravished even the most pious souls. At all events, they were
quite prepared to delve into Ovid's *Metamorphoses* in search
of them, and a man like Remi of Auxerre took the trouble to
make a painstaking catalogue of them. For several hundred
years more, Christian and pagan wonders continued to be
mixed up together.

The literature devoted to the marvels of this world provided
yet another source of astonishment and wonder. A great many
stories had grown up in ancient times around the conquests of
Alexander and the distant lands reached by him. One choice
example was a letter supposed to have been written by
Alexander to his tutor Aristotle about the marvels of India.
By the end of the eighth century the strange creatures,
monsters, and plants and stones with magical properties which
were mentioned in it had begun to filter through into western
literature. The result was a series of bestiaries, as well as an
inexhaustible supply of subjects for romanesque sculptors and
miniaturists.

In this way the products of the Carolingian age set the art
and literature of western Europe on to clearly defined paths
for several centuries to come.

Chapter 6

GAPS AND WEAKNESSES

BUT we must not let enthusiasm carry us away. The Carolingian era turned back to the heritage of Rome, but it was an impoverished heritage, cut off from the riches of Greek thought. And the Carolingians handled their inheritance with the clumsiness and, all too often, the unawareness of a child.

There was a time when some scholars were taken in by the claims made of Carolingian authors having a knowledge of Greek; closer examination has shown that any such illusions are naïve in the extreme. Alcuin occasionally quoted and construed a few words of Greek, but he was merely copying previous versions made by St Jerome or some other grammarian. Several monasteries did possess dictionaries from which the monks could learn the alphabet and dot their works with a sprinkling of Greek words to create a learned impression. Loup de Ferrières was more honest when he admitted to Einhard, in a reference to Boethius: 'I do not know if I rightly understand the meaning of these Greek words.'

Nevertheless there did exist in the West in the ninth century two sources of a more practical knowledge of Greek. Italy was a refuge for Greek monks and clerics fleeing from the Arab conquest and later on from the proscriptions let loose within the Byzantine Empire against the cult of images. Paul the Deacon succeeded in learning Greek in this way, although he subsequently forgot it almost completely. In the second half of the ninth century an ambitious and scheming cleric named Anastasius, whose abilities as a translator earned him a tempestuous career as the Pope's librarian and as a negotiator between Rome and Constantinople, also got his education in this way. The few other real hellenists then living in the West came from Ireland. How they came by their knowledge remains a greater mystery. These scholars had a few more or less gifted pupils in schools such as Laon, Liège and Rheims. The most eminent was John Scotus Erigen, of whom we shall have more to say farther on, but at all events their numbers can be counted on the fingers of one hand.

Besides, the attitude of western Europe generally – that is of the ruling classes – towards the Greek world was scarcely calculated to encourage disinterested study. Western claims to the imperial title, the assertion of the dogmatic supremacy of Rome and, later, the missionary rivalry for control of the Slavonic world, all conspired to turn the mutual ignorance which had grown up between the eastern and western Mediterranean in the course of the preceding centuries into an exasperated loathing. We have a clear instance of this in the Synod of Frankfort (794), in which Alcuin played a leading part. One of the subjects under discussion was the cult which had grown up around images of God, the Virgin and the saints, the question which was dividing the Byzantine empire. After sixty years of persecution the Council of Nicaea in 787 had just rehabilitated and re-defined the cult of images. A very inaccurate and misleading translation of the Acts of Nicaea was presented to the bishops assembled at Frankfort, who reacted violently. Alcuin wrote a *Capitulary of Images*, of which the following extract is typical:

A most arrogant wind of ambition and a most insolent appetite for vainglory have taken hold in the east not only of princes but of priests also. ... In their infamous and incompetent synods they transgress the teaching of their fathers and strive to win credence for beliefs never known to the Saviour or to the Apostles ...

In opposition to the wealthier and more cultivated Orient, the West reacted with the aggressive tantrums of a naughty child.

It is still true that even if there had been many more Greek scholars in Europe and if Western relations with the Greek world had been less bad, the West would have been in no state to profit by Eastern example to fill the gaps in the cultural heritage of Rome. It is impossible to overlook the generally superficial nature of European learning and its underlying weakness and inconsistency of thought. We have two striking examples of this among others.

Alcuin's only philosophical work – at least as regards subject matter – is a treatise 'on the nature of the soul' written at the request of Charlemagne's cousin, Gundrade. Alcuin confines himself to gathering together a number of ideas culled from St Augustine and set down with apparently no inkling of their philosophical implications. He quotes, for example, the Augustinian theory of sensation – that the senses are messengers informing the soul of what is going on in the body, but that it is the soul itself which forms its own sensations and images. Augustine regarded sensation as an act of the soul because, after Plato (interpreted by the Neoplatonist philosopher Plotinus), he defined man as a soul which makes use of a body. Alcuin repeats this statement without realizing that it commits him to a clear-cut philosophical course. Even if he had been aware of it, it would probably have been hopeless to try to convey any such idea to the mind of poor Gundrade.

Alcuin was likewise Charlemagne's adviser on matters of political philosophy, and here too his principal source was St Augustine. For several centuries the idea had grown of the religious obligations of a ruler, which was based on St Augustine, without preserving Augustine's clear distinction between Church and State. In this connexion a statement attributed to Pope Gelasius I (492–6) and often quoted subsequently asserted that:

There are . . . two [principles] by which this world is mainly ruled, the sacred authority of the popes and the royal power. Of these two, the weight of the priests is much more important, because it has to render account for the kings themselves at the divine tribunal.

A century later Isidore of Seville justified the power of 'secular princes' in this way: 'In the Church, these powers would not be necessary if they did not enforce through fear of discipline that which the priests are powerless to impose by words.'

Alcuin repeated these warnings to Charlemagne, in whom he found a willing pupil. In 802, he summed up his teaching as follows:

Charlemagne's imperial dignity, ordained by God, is destined for nothing else but to guide and help the people. Power and wisdom are given to those elected by God; power, so that the ruler may suppress the proud and defend the lowly against the unjust; wisdom, so that the ruler with pious care may rule and teach his subjects. Divine grace has exalted and honoured incomparable sublimity through those two gifts by sending the terror of his power over all the peoples everywhere, so that those people may come to Charlemagne in voluntary surrender whom war in earlier times could not subject to his rule, and so the people will live in peace.

Once temporal power was incorporated in this way into the ruler's religious duties the problem of his relations with the spiritual power inevitably became highly complex. But contemporary thinkers do not seem to have appreciated the gravity of the problem, which was to produce stormy consequences in later centuries, nor did they attempt to define any clear principles. The situation merely developed according to the balance of power, with Charlemagne taking it upon himself to defend the Church against its enemies within and without, and naïvely limiting the role of the Pope to 'raising his hands to heaven' and praying for the success of his efforts. By the middle of the ninth century, however, the Popes had emerged as the spiritual guides of Charlemagne's descendants. The problem had not yet passed wholly from the sphere of action to that of ideas.

Thus in the ninth century philosophical thought had not yet really awakened. The intellectuals of the time did not even have the proper tools in their hands, for their terminology was vague and their reasoning uncertain. It has been observed that nearly every writer of the period with the slightest initiative who attempted to elucidate any points of Christian dogma went astray at some point. Heresies such as adoptionism are largely explained by a misunderstanding of certain Scriptural passages. Argument was not on a very elevated plane, consisting principally of the two sides bombarding each other with a mass of quotations from the Scriptures and the Fathers of the Church. In this climate of intellectual uncertainty the strict doctrinal control exercised by the Councils is understandable, as are their verdicts and also the extreme caution displayed by the majority of exegetes.

This is the background to Alcuin's achievement in his commentary on the Gospels according to St John (a work not easy to grasp in all its richness). Alcuin had studied the gospel while still a young man, under the tutelage of Aelbert at York and probably on the basis of the commentary already given by St Augustine. Then Ghisla and Rotrude, Charlemagne's sister and daughter respectively, asked him for a commentary that would be less difficult than the bishop of Hippo's. Alcuin proceeded very much as though he was compiling an anthology, retaining some passages from St Augustine's commentary on the Passion (where the text was less difficult to follow), and for the entire first part of the Gospel, which is more complicated, substituting the simpler commentaries of Bede and Gregory the Great. Similarly, Hrabanus Maurus commenting on the Gospel according to St Matthew, confined himself more or less to plagiarizing a similar work by Claude, bishop of Turin, but without acknowledgement, since the bishop had been tried and condemned for his dogma! Plagiarism of this kind was considered quite normal at the time, and it was departure from tradition rather which seemed improper.

There are always exceptions. Among these may be counted the exegetical work of a monk of Corbie named Paschase Radbert. Radbert, too, produced a commentary on the Gospel of St Matthew, but underlining the disagreements between earlier commentators, and occasionally rejecting the opinions

of respected authors such as St Augustine himself and substituting his own views. Radbert lost no opportunity of formulating Christian dogma on points that were still ill-defined. His
definition of the Real Presence in the Eucharist was later
adopted by the Church of Rome as authoritative, a fairly
outstanding achievement for the representative of a period so
uncertain in its definitions. But Paschase in this field remains an
isolated case in between St Augustine and the eleventh-
century writers.

Even less is it possible to talk of any ninth-century scientific
thought. The whole field of what is now covered by the word
science was at that time something of a desert. On the one hand
there existed a fondness, inherited from classical times, for
seeking natural comparisons to illustrate certain dogmas: the
moon reflecting the light of the sun was like the Church
reflecting the divine light; the phoenix, reborn from its ashes,
was the image of Christ; the peacock whose flesh was supposed to be immune from corruption was the symbol of
eternity. These are constantly recurring images. Artists loved
to portray such themes as peacocks drinking at the Fountain
of Life (symbolizing the Christian imbibing the grace of
immortality) but these had nothing to do with any real
observation of nature. We may also be somewhat unsym-
pathetic to the speculations, highly fashionable at the time, on
the symbolic value of numbers: the figure 3 was a symbol of
God, the figure 7 of man (being made up of a body, 4,
because composed of the four elements, and a soul, 3, in the
image of God), the figure 8, of eternal life (beyond man), and
so forth.

On the other hand there were technical works of a more
practical nature. At about the time of Charlemagne a manual
of 'Dyeing Instructions' (*Compositiones ad tingenda*) was compiled. Many of these recipes must have been introduced into
the West some centuries earlier by 'Syrian' and Jewish
merchants: formulas for preparing pigments, gilding metals,
dyeing skins, producing gilded letters in manuscripts, colour-

ing glass, and so on. Their value is considerably reduced by their failure to mention any precise quantities. We might also cite collections of medicinal plants, such as the little poem by Walafrid Strabo, already mentioned, which were highly prized in monasteries. The use of 'simples' for their curative properties remains the most substantial achievement of a medicine still largely imbued with magic, as may be seen from the powder recommended by the fifth-century Bordeaux doctor Marcellus Empiricus, which crops up in many manuscripts. It is based on the dried blood of a virginal yearling ox which has been fed for three days on laurel before being killed on a Thursday or Sunday by a chaste person. A certain degree of astronomical observation was necessary to establish the date of Easter: Christ died on Friday the fourteenth of the Jewish month of Nisan, and the Jewish calendar was based on the phases of the moon. The Council of Nicaea had decreed that Easter was to be celebrated on the Sunday following the fourteenth day of the first full moon after 21 March. It remained to calculate the date of this full moon. For some time the Irish had a different computation from that of Rome, but finally the latter, which was based on the calculations of an obscure monk named Dionysius the Less (to whom we are also indebted for our habit of counting years from the birth of Christ), prevailed. By the ninth century the whole of western Christendom celebrated the great festival of Easter at the same time. The problem was solved, but it left behind an interest in the calendar and in the study of the heavens. This has already been seen in the correspondence between Charlemagne and Alcuin. Even so, the sum total is a fairly modest one.

To thi sad tally of ignorance of Greek works and a body of philosophical and scientific thought that was weak to the point of non-existence, the Carolingian West had one exception to offer – and that a fairly considerable one. It is time we said something about it.

In 827 the basileus Michael II sent an embassy 'to his dear

and honourable brother, Louis, glorious king of the Franks and Lombards and called by them Emperor' (neat evasion). It brought among other gifts a Greek manuscript of the works of a mysterious philosopher known by the name of Dionysius the Areopagite. 'Into this society of Latinized barbarians and grammarians with no metaphysical aspirations' as Étienne Gilson has put it, 'the *Corpus areopagiticum* fell like a meteor from another world.'

This work was prized chiefly on account of the author to whom it was attributed. Dionysius the Areopagite was one of the few who, after St Paul's preaching at Athens, 'clave unto him and believed' (Acts xvii. 34). With a lack of historical sense which need not surprise us, the monks of the monastery of St Denis, to whom Louis the Pious entrusted this work, persuaded themselves that this Dionysius was identical with the St Denis (or Dionysius), first bishop of Paris and martyr, whose remains reposed in their monastery. The abbot Hilduin undertook to prove this and to translate the work of his patron saint, an arduous task when we consider the ignorance of Greek then more or less general in the West. It was a task further complicated by the condition of the manuscript (now preserved in the Bibliothèque Nationale in Paris, Ms Grec 437). The scribe had made scarcely any division between the words and put in very few accents. It seems that one monk read the words out one at a time while a second produced the Latin equivalent and a third wrote it down. The result was a travesty and the text, already difficult enough in itself, became virtually incomprehensible.

Later on Charles the Bald commissioned a new translation from an Irishman who appeared at his court in 845 and distinguished himself by a knowledge of Greek which was quite exceptional for the period. This was John Scotus, known as Erigen. Though far from perfect – it contained a great many howlers, and occasional misrepresentations of the author's meaning – his translation was clearly superior to Hilduin's. It was now possible to read the Pseudo-Dionysius in Latin, and

John Scotus himself was influenced by him in his own work.

In actual fact, the author translated was a Syrian who probably lived in the fifth century. A Christian, though brought up on the Neoplatonic philosophy, he had set out to construct a system of philosophy to confute the pagan Neoplatonists, passing it off under the venerable name of St Paul's disciple in order to enhance its authority. The fraud succeeded only too well, with the paradoxical result that everything from such an august pen was bound to be accepted with reverence, even though there were many elements in the system extremely difficult to reconcile with Christianity.

It was to this task that John Scotus applied himself. This is no place for a detailed study of his somewhat elusive principal work, *On the Division of Nature*. It is enough to say that it is a study of the twofold movement of the being emerging from God and returning to God. In the beginning there was God, nature uncreated and creative; then there were Ideas, nature created in God and in its turn creative; then the world and mankind, which are the realization of these Ideas, a nature created and not creative. The second movement begins with the Christ's mediation of the Redemption which, by Love, restored created nature to its Creator, to be, in some way, swallowed up in Him, so that in the end there will be only God, nature uncreated and not creative. A system of this kind raises a multitude of difficulties, one of them being that if all creation is finally to be reabsorbed into God, what place can be assigned to a physical hell? And some of John Scotus' statements have a rationalist echo susceptible to misinterpretation. He believed that reason must be supported by Faith, but also that it is man's duty to develop the light given him by Faith by means of rational consideration of nature, since nature itself is a manifestation of God.

This is undoubtedly a work arising from intellectual progress, although as yet it is sometimes stumbling, its terminology insufficiently precise. John Scotus seems to have been dazzled by the revelation of Greek Christian thought. His work

towers above the society in which it was written, and by
contrast emphasizes the general mediocrity of its thought. It
was bound to be regarded with suspicion and to arouse at
least some moral condemnation. It exercised no direct influence.
However, to quote Étienne Gilson's evocative words again,
it 'lived underground' and remained for centuries a 'constant
temptation' to Christian philosophy.

Chapter 7

CONCLUSION

THE 'Carolingian renaissance' was only a beginning. As such it deserves a good deal of criticism. It has been called a movement lacking in breadth, almost entirely clerical and extending to no more than a few hundred clerks in the whole of Europe. An eminent historian like Henri Pirenne has actually described it as a decline, on the grounds that earlier centuries had possessed a greater number of educated laymen, although this was merely the tail-end of Roman society, and without issue. Western society was to be rebuilt on different foundations and the extraordinarily primitive conditions of its physical survival sufficiently explain that only a very few men should have had the leisure and inclination to devote themselves to intellectual pursuits.

It has also been called a movement lacking in originality, without any real philosophical and scientific thought, cut off by its ignorance of languages from all access to the superior cultural world of the Greeks, and, furthermore, incapable, even if it had possessed such access, of benefiting from it for lack of intellectual ambitions and techniques of thought.

This is true. These are the inherent weaknesses of a new beginning. But the great merit of the Carolingian renaissance was that it was a beginning at all. First and foremost it was a renaissance of learning, it provided a foundation of working copyists, libraries and schools, which was to form the infrastructure of our European cultural developments.

It is thanks to this that a great deal of our classical heritage has been saved. But for the copies made then, many texts would have been lost altogether, and at the same time a mental attitude was born which glorified classical learning and profane studies all the more because it incorporated them

into and used them for the development of religious knowledge. The work of ordering and unification which took
place at this period was to make its effects felt in this field for
centuries to come. The comment made by a late ninth-century
writer to the effect that 'so fruitful was Alcuin's teaching that
the modern Gauls or Frenchmen equal the ancients of Rome
and Athens' was more than simply a ridiculous exaggeration.
This theme of 'translated studies' became a tradition of
medieval writings presenting Paris as the heir of Athens and
of Rome.

This first 'renaissance', without which no others would have
been possible, was the result of the close collaboration between
natives and newcomers achieved in the Roman West after the
'barbarian' invasions. Such a collaboration could not come
about overnight. By the Carolingian age the West may be said
to have 'digested' its invaders, and found itself ready for more
positive tasks. Rome provided the entire basis of this culture
and some teachers came from heavily romanized lands such
as Italy and Spain. But the majority were from the isles of the
north-west, Ireland, the refuge of the Celts and Scots, or
England, a prey to the Angles and Saxons. These were
countries with little or no Roman influence, where classical
culture had followed in the wake of Christianity to which
the call had gone out from Lérins and from Rome. The Franks
provided the new political framework, the reunification of
Europe minus Spain, but extended as far as the Elbe, and soon
they too saw their harvest ripening.

However, the political situation was not long in deteriorat-
ing. Charlemagne's descendants were incapable of rising to the
concept of a Roman Empire, one and indivisible. Their
squabbles favoured the forces of disintegration and hastened
the decay of the Carolingian State. In addition a fresh wave
of invasions fell upon the West at this time. Alcuin had already
watched and wept from afar as the invading Danes landed in
Northumbria in 793, plundering the abbey of Lindisfarne and
pillaging the sanctuary where the holy remains of St Cuthbert

lay. 'What else can we do', he wrote to Ethelred, king of Northumbria, 'but weep with you before Christ's altar saying Spare, Lord, spare thy people, and deliver not thy heritage unto the Gentiles, for fear the pagans shall say: where is he, the God of the Christians?'

By the middle of the ninth century disasters of this kind had become common everywhere in the West. On 8 November 853 the Norman vessels made their way up the Loire and appeared unexpectedly before Tours. The city and the monastery of St Martin over which Alcuin had presided half a century earlier were burned, the archives, and probably also the library, which was one of the richest in Europe, destroyed. The abbot barely escaped with the body of St Martin. In 880 the monks of St Riquier were more fortunate in having time enough at the approach of the Normans to carry away with them some of their manuscripts, remnants of which came to light in a number of different monasteries. There were countless similar disasters. In Italy and in the south of France, the menace was from the Saracen pirates. And before long the marauding mounted Hungarians swept through the West, spreading terror and devastation.

Even so, the work begun by the Carolingian renaissance did not perish entirely. The troubled period of the mid-ninth century was, if anything, richer in talent than the reign of Charlemagne, and there has even been talk of a 'second Carolingian Renaissance' bearing the fruits of the first. The inroads of the new invaders subsequently destroyed some monasteries which were particularly remarkable as centres of learning, and ravaged certain regions which were especially rich in such centres, but the movement was under way, and they were already sufficiently numerous to avert any risk of total disaster.

The only explanation for this invaluable achievement is the enthusiastic reception given to Charlemagne's directives in enough cathedral churches where the clergy was beginning to organize itself into a community after the pattern set by

Chrodegang, and even more in the Benedictine monasteries, where the place set aside in the Rule for study was devoted to the highest intellectual tasks of the day. Thus the monasteries became, in a manner which not even St Benedict himself could have foreseen, the outstanding cultural centres of their time. The 'Carolingian renaissance' owed its scope and continuance to this 'Benedictine miracle'.

PART TWO

The Time of Gerbert

THE little town of Aurillac stands with its back to the volcanic hills, commanding a high plateau through which runs the River Jordanne. In spite of its situation among the bare uplands of the Cantal, it really seems to have been 'an outpost of the Midi in the heart of the mountains of Auvergne'. Its tough, cheerful people spoke a southern dialect and today it has more contact with Toulouse than with the much closer city of Clermont. In this small, isolated corner of Aquitaine, in the last years of the ninth century, the count Géraud – later canonized – founded a monastery of the Benedictine Rule which was in after years to bear his name. The abbey stood in the protective shadow of a castle and around it there soon sprang up a modest huddle of houses, forming the kernel of the future town.

The monastery of St Géraud (or Gerald) was therefore only some seventy years old, although already enjoying a considerable reputation, when Borrell, Count of Barcelona, halted there to pray to its sainted founder after his marriage, in Rodez, to the daughter of the Count of Rouergue, in 967. Borrell was making ready to depart after this brief stay and return to his distant domains on the borders of Islam when the abbot asked him 'if Spain possessed men well versed in the arts'. When the count replied in the affirmative, the abbot urged him to take with him a young brother of the monastery whom he praised for his exceptional intelligence.

Thus it came about that Gerbert embarked on the first of the journeys which were to fill his life, carrying him from Spain to Rheims and afterwards into Germany and Italy. He was never to re-visit the country of his youth. By sheer force of intellect alone he rose to be the counsellor of the greatest rulers of the age and end his days on the throne of St Peter in Rome. Deeply involved in the affairs of his time, Gerbert stands for all that was best in it. But he also dominated it from the height of his brilliance and was in many ways far ahead of it.

If we are to understand the opportunities he was offered and assess the use he made of them, we must first look at the man in his own setting. Gone was the comparative simplicity of Carolingian Europe, where everything centred on Charlemagne. Moreover, we must now begin to look beyond this dark, tormented Europe to a wider world, to the Empire of Byzantium and the Muslim world, then at the full height of their brilliance, some of which was to rub off on to the West. First, however, it is necessary to deal firmly with one quite illusory problem: the so-called 'terror of the millennium'.

Chapter 1

THE TERROR OF THE MILLENNIUM

IT was the universal belief in the Middle Ages that the world was to come to an end in the year one thousand A.D. .... This world beheld nothing but chaos within but it aspired to order and trusted to find it in death.... Trouble upon trouble, ruin upon ruin. There had to be something more to come, and the people waited for it. The captive waited in his black dungeon, in the sepulchral *in pace*; the serf waited in his furrow beneath the shadow of the hated keep; the monk waited, in the abstinence of the cloister, in the solitary tumults of the heart ...

Thus the eloquent prose of Jules Michelet describing the expiring tenth century, bowed in terror of the end of time, heaping offerings upon its altars, suspending its wars and its plans – until at last, when the fateful year had passed, humanity, 'hoping to endure a little longer', rose up 'from its agony'. If this view, which has been put forward by a number of historians from the eighteenth century onwards, is true, it is clear that there can have been little question of culture in such a desperate world, and that the movement born in the Carolingian age was doomed to failure.

Fortunately this was not the case. Nevertheless, Michelet and his less brilliant colleagues were basing themselves upon documents which are worthy of examination, especially since such a study enables us to isolate one element in the background to Gerbert's life and thought.

The beginnings of Christianity witnessed the growth of two attitudes of mind, bound together in many ways, which also aroused strong reactions. In the first place there was the belief in an imminent 'parousie', the conviction that the end of the world and the return of Christ in triumph as announced in the Gospels was to take place in the immediate future. St

Paul, without eliminating the possibility that his generation might behold these great events, disagreed with those Christians who asserted that 'the day of the Lord is already come', and recalled that before this there was to be the appearance of the man traditionally known as Anti-Christ.

In addition there grew up what has been called the cult of the millennium. This was based chiefly on an enigmatic passage in the Apocalypse: 'And I saw' says the writer,

an Angel come down from Heaven having the key of the bottomless pit and a great chain in his hand. And he laid hold on the Dragon, that old serpent, which is the Devil, and Satan, and bound him a thousand years ...

Then came the first resurrection, in which the saints, those who had suffered for Christ, came to life again around him, and reigned with him for a thousand years.

And when the thousand years are expired, Satan shall be loosed out of his prison, and shall go out to deceive the nations which are in the four quarters of the earth. . . . And fire came down from God out of Heaven and devoured them.

This was the final ordeal, followed by the second resurrection: 'and the dead were judged out of those things which were written in the books, according to their works'.

Were these visions to be taken literally? If so, when was the beginning of these thousand years supposed to be and to what known occurrence should they be connected? Or was it preferable to stick to an allegorical interpretation in which the figure 1000 stood simply for a long period? All this raised a great deal of argument among the early Christians. Moreover there was some doubt as to the canonical respectability of the Apocalypse which, though rejected by the majority of eastern churches, was accepted by the Church of Rome.

The disasters consequent on the great invasions led in the West to a revival of belief in the imminent end of the world: 'The earth succumbs beneath the weight of age,' wrote St Eucherius.

As old men are borne down with ills, so we see the world pullulating with misery: famine, pestilence, war, ruin and terror.... The last day, not only of our lives, but of the world, is upon us.

But the expression of such fears roused a protest from St Augustine and the eminent Doctor made a point of recalling Christ's own words, that 'none knows the date of this day, not the angels in heaven, nor the Son, none save the Father alone', and that it was therefore vain to plunge into calculations.

From the fifth century onwards these fears began to lose ground although they did not entirely disappear. They even can be found in deeds – especially donations – in the preambles made of pious sentiments which lawyers and scribes liked to include as an indication of the state of the donor's soul. 'The increase of ruins shows clearly the approach of the end of the world' was a common seventh-century saying. That the same sentiment was later reproduced in a number of documents should not surprise us, nor should much importance be attributed to what was often merely a mechanical repetition. All the same, by the second half of the eleventh century all this had completely disappeared.

The Apocalypse on the other hand acquired a new popularity in the latter half of the eighth century as a result of a commentary written by a Spanish monk from Asturias, Beatus, abbot of Liebana. This was an isolated region, on the borders of Christendom, but after Beatus had taken part in some fierce controversies, his commentary became widely known and was copied many times in the monasteries of France and most western countries. He even fired the imagination of miniaturists from whom romanesque sculptors later drew their inspiration. This was the source of the grandiose visions of Christ in Majesty adorning tympana in churches like the one at Moissac, or of these curious details – knights riding on lions, the Beast chained by the angel, and so on – fitted laboriously into the small spaces of the capitals. Their popularity shows how far the vision of St John was in tune

with the sensibility of a troubled age, quick to interpret its
sufferings as the signs of great Events to come.

This is very much the mental attitude expressed in the work
of a Burgundian monk who came somewhat after Gerbert.
Raoul Glaber – or Beardless – was born towards the end of the
tenth century and died in the middle of the eleventh. The stuff
of his *Histories* can be found in all modern authors who have
delved into the subject of the 'terrors of the millennium', and
especially in Michelet. To read Raoul Glaber is to be trans-
ported into a magical world filled with a host of miracles and
portents, where the ravages of ungodliness vie with natural
disasters and Satan gambols freely without even troubling to
disguise himself. More than once Raoul beheld him rise up at
the foot of his bed, 'a hideous little man . . . of puny stature,
with a skinny neck and wasted features . . . a goatee beard, his
ears pointed and hairy, his hair standing thickly on end, sharp
teeth, pointed head, pigeon chest, a hump on his back and
quivering flanks'. Raoul Glaber, who was writing somewhere
between 1026 and 1048, arranged his principal events about
the years 1000 and 1033, i.e. a thousand years after the
Nativity and Passion of Christ.

'Seven years before the year one thousand' a violent
eruption of Vesuvius occurred and 'at that time, nearly all
the cities of Gaul and Italy were devastated by fire'; 'at the
same time, in Italy and Gaul were seen to die all the most
eminent prelates, dukes and counts.' 'Three years before the
year one thousand' there appeared in the skies 'an enormous
dragon, coming out of the North and reaching the South,
throwing off sparks of lightning.' 'At the same time, a severe
famine which lasted for five years, covered all the Roman
world' . . . But 'by the coming of the third year after the year
1000, churches and buildings nearly everywhere were again
being rebuilt, especially in Italy and Gaul. . . . It was as if
the very world was shaking itself rid of its decrepitude and
everywhere put on a white mantle of churches.' The lines
have been so often quoted as to be almost too well known.

'At the approach of the millennium of Christ's Passion' we once again find heresies, deaths of famous men and a famine so terrible that 'it was feared almost the whole human race would be eliminated.' Then, 'in the year one thousand of the Passion of Our Lord, which came after this disastrous famine, the clouds ceased to pour down rain; obedient to the divine goodness and mercy, the smiling sky began to clear, to blow favourable winds and proclaim in its peace and serenity, the goodness of the Creator; all the earth was covered with pleasant verdure and began to produce an abundance of fruits which completely drove out want.' But the signs continued to appear, even after this year of 1033.

What are the conclusions to be drawn from this evidence? In the first place, we must take care not to regard Raoul Glaber as altogether typical of his time. This talkative, versatile, credulous monk who made such a nuisance of himself that he was expelled from one monastery after another, is something of a caricature in whom some characteristics of his time are exaggerated to the point of absurdity. He was entirely lacking in the balance and common sense which distinguished so many of his contemporaries.

Besides, what he foretold was not so much the end of the world as the signs which quite naturally marked the anniversaries of such important events as the Nativity and the Passion. Each time the stricken universe seemed to be 'shrugging off the old' before putting on the new.

Other things were told by those who believed in the 'terrors'. Abbon, abbot of the monastery of Fleury-sur-Loire, who was born about 940, tells how in his youth he heard a preacher in Paris announce the end of the world for the year 1000. He adds that a rumour was circulating in Lorraine in about 975 to the effect that the world would come to an end in the year in which the Annunciation coincided with Good Friday, that is in 992. Adson of Montierender, on the other hand, in a book about the Antichrist written for the Queen of France in 954, asserted that the end of the world and the

coming of the Antichrist need not be feared while the kingdoms were not divided from the Roman Empire. He acknowledged the fact that this Empire was partly destroyed,
but while there were kings among the Franks capable of
reviving it, all hope was not lost. ... Adson demonstrates
strongly the reaction of the Church to these alarms, which
Abbon, for his part, was opposing 'with all his strength', by
the Gospels, the Apocalypse and the Book of Daniel.

There was therefore no general belief that the end of the
world was destined to occur precisely in the year 1000.
Taking into account the chronological vagueness of the period
and the numerous undated documents which have come
down to us, this would seem to have been out of the question.
Far from universally employing our method of counting
from the beginning of the Christian era, people still relied on
a variety of aids, such as years of reigns, or pontificates, or
astronomical conjunctions. It is not surprising therefore that
the documents which have survived from the years 1000 to
1033 show men waging wars, governing, working and making
plans just as usual.

But what did exist was a vague sense of a twilight of the
world. Individuals, regions and years were all more or less
imbued with the same feeling. Here and there brief waves of
panic arose which the Church set itself to pacify. To borrow
Marc Bloch's evocative phrase: 'In spite of everything, life
fermented irresistibly in mankind. But whenever they paused
to think, there was no feeling more remote from them than of
a vast future open to the strength of youth.'

We cannot afford to overlook this attitude, since it was
probably that of the men we are going to look at next, and
even of Gerbert himself, who must certainly have been
influenced by their way of thought and their writings.

Chapter 2

THE HISTORICAL BACKGROUND:
THE EASTERN WORLD

THE TREASURES OF THE ANCIENT EAST

THE Roman culture with which the men of the Carolingian
Renaissance had renewed their ties had collected only scraps
of the wealth of observation, thought and knowledge which
had grown up in the countries of the eastern Mediterranean as
a result of religious beliefs and practical necessity.

In Mesopotamia, for example, which, as we should never
forget, was one of the cradles of our civilization, the belief that
the stars exercised a powerful influence over human destiny
had led men to increasingly accurate astronomical observations, allowing for the rudimentary methods at their disposal.
The Chaldeans learned to identify the planets, to mark the
irregularities of their apparent courses and note their positions
in relation to the ecliptic (that is, to the orbit which the sun
appears to describe around the earth in the course of a year),
and to plot this ecliptic by means of fixed stars and so divide
the 'zodiac' into twelve signs (libra, gemini and the rest).
From this basic material they even proceeded to calculations.
They measured time both by the phases of the moon and the
solar year, systems which roughly coincide at about 360 days.
This number acquired for them a mystical significance. They
divided the celestial globe and every circumference in the
same way, into 360 degrees – in which we still follow them
today.

Calculations of this kind clearly necessitated some practical
method of representing numerals. Accustomed as we are to
our own system, it requires a certain amount of thought for
us to understand the labour which must have gone into its
development. Suppose we take the number 16,861. Here the

first and last '1's, although they are both represented by the same sign, are clearly quite different in value. Their value varies according to their position from tens of thousands in the case of the first to single units in that of the last. It is the same with the two sixes, where the position of the one indicates thousands, of the other tens. Thus the figures indicate ones, tens or hundreds according to where they stand. By transposing a figure from one position to another we can multiply or divide by ten. Our system of representation is founded on the principle of 'notation by position', and on a basic unit of ten. If this system is to work properly it implies that if there is no figure to be put in one position in a given number, the space will be filled with a symbol, which is nought or zero. As it stands, it has proved right up until the twentieth century a highly workable system, able to support the complex mathematics necessary for the expansion of modern science.

In order fully to appreciate the benefits of this additional tool for the human mind we have only to compare it with Roman numerals, which we still use from time to time for purposes of classification, or pagination. The working out of even simple multiplication and division using Roman numerals alone – even supposing we could actually put back the clock and do so – would be an almost impossible task. We should have to resort to the kind of counting frame still used by children learning their first steps in arithmetic, just as the Romans did.

As early as the fourth century B.C. the Chaldeans had arrived at the principle of notation by position. But they used a basic unit of sixty, drawn from what was to them the mystical number of 360, which was much less convenient than our basic ten. Nevertheless it served their purpose for the calculations needed in their studies of astronomy. Much later, in about the third century B.C., they even invented a sign for zero.

Thus in the fields of astronomy and arithmetic vital progress had already been made in Mesopotamia, long before the

Christian era. Egypt, another cradle of a very ancient civilization, has a less impressive record of achievement. From about the third millennium before Christ, Egypt was developing, not so much an actual science as a systematic body of techniques whose importance has emerged only gradually with the discovery of documentary evidence. There is still the possibility of fresh information on the subject coming to light. In a country where the land fertilized by the Nile was immensely valuable and where its use was controlled by the state, problems of measurement and land-surveying demanded special consideration. The Egyptians arrived at the idea of a square being the sum of a number of other squares which led them ultimately to the famous theorem of Pythagoras. They made up tables (of multiplication, square roots, etc.) to avoid the necessity of repeating complex calculations. In medicine they were thought to have produced only a single pharmacopeia relying chiefly on magical formulas until the 'Smith papyrus', which was discovered in the mid-nineteenth century but not deciphered until much later, revealed the extent of their progress. It includes a detailed description of the entire human body which is, all things considered, quite remarkable in its accuracy, together with an analysis of possible treatments owing nothing to supernatural remedies, and a frank admission of the incurability of certain cases.

The Greeks reaped the benefit of this Eastern science, but they also added to it what constituted their own particular genius: the urge to find an explanation for natural phenomena, an attempt to synthesize the results obtained, and the desire to rise above the purely utilitarian motives which had previously predominated, into the sphere of pure, disinterested research. In this as in many other fields the 'Greek miracle' was one of those drastic transformations which occur now and then in the history of the human mind.

From its earliest beginnings in the colonies of Asia Minor, Greek thought concentrated on the incessant changes to be found in nature. How does the air around us turn into dew and rain? How does water evaporate and turn into air? How does wood become fire? Are all these simply different states in the existence of a unique matter, endowed with a life of its own and responsible for its own transformations? If so, what is this matter? But surely, others would object, it must be a contradiction to talk of matter which changes and yet remains the same? Perhaps, like Parmenides, we should deduce that these changes are only apparent, an illusion, and that the world as perceived by our senses is no more than appearance? This was the path followed by Plato in his famous metaphor of the cave, on the walls of which captive man can perceive only the shadows thrown by the brilliant light without. Like the shadows in the cave, physical objects were only reflexions of the eternal and immutable Ideas that alone were Real. The mathematicians alone among the scientists were able to uncover the enduring verities of geometry beneath these changing phenomena. In his ideal City, Plato gave place of honour to geometry. But, more than anything, he followed Socrates in turning to man and to the play of ideas in men's minds.

Another important trend in Greek thought, stemming from the school of Pythagoras, was the study of numbers. The Pythagoreans believed that everything in the world could be explained by numbers and the relation between them. An excellent illustration of this is to be found in the relation between the length of a vibrating cord and the musical note produced by it; it formed the basis of a musical theory which retained an important place in classical and medieval science. But by classifying numbers as odd, even, square, and so on, the Pythagoreans also laid the foundations of arithmetic. They invented the idea of the irrational quantity (such as π) which may be approached indefinitely but never reached. The problems of measurement raised by Pythagorean theory also culminated in Pythagoras' theorem. It must however be admitted that the mystical value attached to certain numbers contributed as much as these valuable acquisitions to the fashion for such speculations, which persisted throughout antiquity into the Middle Ages and even beyond.

No scientific advance was possible without some consideration of the art of reasoning and expression – without expanding the possibilities of grammar, the use of words and, lastly, of logic. Such consideration is apparent at a very early date and resulted ultimately in the excessive virtuosity of the sophists. But in the political sphere it was also at the root of Athenian democracy, which was based on the force of reason and eloquence. This is a point which deserves to be stressed, since the phenomenon repeated itself on a vastly more modest scale with Gerbert. Socrates and Plato, too, carried this attempt at mental analysis to a much higher level and learned the art of isolating complementary ideas from apparently contradictory opinions.

Aristotle – the man who, with Plato, was to exert over medieval thinkers a greater fascination than all others – stands at the crossroads of all these various currents, but also on the threshold of a new development in the eastern world. The son of the doctor Nicomachus, he studied at Athens under Plato and was himself the tutor of the young Alexander (343–340) whose fantastic conquests were to lay the foundations of the Hellenistic world in which the diverse trends of ancient thought were to meet to their mutual advantage.

At the risk of over-simplification, we may say that Aristotle's basic tenets look like a complete reaction against the system of Plato. He rejected any divorce between individual objects and the universal Ideas which were the only true reality. For him the universal existed only in the particular, and it was the job of the intellect to isolate it by abstraction. It was even possible to classify the sciences according to the degree of abstract thought involved. The physical sciences dealt with perishable things, joined to matter. The mathematical sciences studied things solely in their quantitative aspect, divorced from matter. Prime philosophy or metaphysics rose above all matter, all change, and all quantity, to the pure nature of the thing itself. But within this framework the observation of natural phenomena is reinstated in its place as a fundamental necessity.

If physical objects are real both in a permanent sense and in the transformations they undergo, then a distinction must be made between these two aspects of reality. This is at the root of the famous Aristotelian distinction between matter and the form or state in which it exists at a given moment. This distinction, for him, was basic and can be seen alike in his physics and in his theory of man.

No more than a brief summary can be given here of other, no less essential, aspects of Aristotle's genius. He was a first-class logician, a precise analyst of the various processes of thought, and in this way he helped to make mankind fully master of logic as a tool (*organon*). He was also a scientist, although he did not possess a mathematical turn of mind. His contribution lies particularly in his method, which gave a prime place to observation, and in his own application of it to zoology and botany. However primitive the techniques at his disposal, his zoology was not superseded in Europe until the eighteenth century. In botany he was less fortunate, being eclipsed by the work of his disciple Theophrastus, but even then by the use of his own methods.

Aristotle stood on the threshold of the Hellenistic world as the last wholly universal thinker. After him it was no longer possible for one man to conquer both philosophy and the newly developing sciences. In the new capital cities, such as Pergamum and to an even greater extent Alexandria, which was to remain the great intellectual metropolis of the Mediterranean world until the fifth century A.D., more specialist scholars in every scientific field were making discoveries that as a general rule would not be surpassed until the eighteenth century.

In mathematics, Euclid, working in Alexandria at the beginning of the third century B.C., collected and amplified the sum of existing knowledge in his *Elements*. But the subject did not rest on its laurels, and 600 years later Diophantus laid the first foundations of what was to be the study of algebra. In physics the discoveries of the Pythagoreans (in acoustics) and of Aristotle were only surpassed by Archimedes of Syracuse, a contemporary of Euclid whose brilliant work on levers and hydrostatics formed the basis of mathematical physics. In astronomy Hipparchus and Ptolemy carried the system based on the theories of Plato and Aristotle to their culmination: the first invented the astrolabe and was responsible for the development of trigonometry, while both worked out tables foretelling the movements of the stars for centuries ahead with astonishing accuracy. In medicine there was research based on the work of the Hippocratic school, and Galen of Pergamum collected the results of this in the second century A.D. in a volume which reigned supreme throughout the Middle Ages and even beyond.

The reader must forgive this brief and somewhat tedious summary on the grounds that the history of cultural and scientific developments can be little more than a meaningless list of names, titles and dates unless there is some attempt to bring to life the questions and ideas which concerned the men involved. Moreover we are limited here to the things which were the chief focus of attention in medieval Europe. How else than by trying to some extent to recreate them, can we understand the fascination which must have been exercised by this extraordinary collection of facts, principles and methods?

For all her avid exploitation of her eastern conquests, Rome had let slip the greatest prize they had to offer through inability to absorb and hand it on. More than one medieval author was to reproach her bitterly for the failure. But by the end of the tenth century a few flowers were beginning to bloom again on the old and apparently long-dead trunk, and there were breezes to waft their fragrance as far as the frontiers of Europe. This was the historical phenomenon which bestowed its real value on the time of Gerbert.

THE GLORY OF BYZANTIUM

The Roman Empire, which had been restored to Rome by Charlemagne at Christmas 800 and again, after a fresh lapse, by Otto the Great in 962, had suffered no such interruption in its eastern half. Theoretically a succession of emperors ruled from Constantinople over all the territory which at any given moment had come to make up the empire. One of these, Justinian, in the sixth century, decided to turn this polite fiction into a fact, and after a protracted struggle his armies succeeded in reconquering what is now Tunisia, Italy and a small part of Spain. In the end, however, all that remained for his successors was a few fragments of Italy.

Then, at a time when the Empire was exhausted by its hard-won victories over the Sassanid kingdom which occupied the area now covered by Iraq and Iran, came the Arab conquests. Even so, the defeats suffered by the imperial armies at the hands of the Bedouin tribes which had hitherto been lost in their desert fastnesses came as a rude shock. Within a few years the Empire had lost its richest eastern provinces, Syria and Palestine, as well as Egypt, the granary of Constantinople. Next the victorious enemy took to the seas, built up a fleet and sailed to lay siege to Constantinople. For four years (673-7) the capital of the world withstood the blockade, defending itself with the energy of despair. With the aid of Greek fire – a liquid with a naphtha base which would burn on the water – the Byzantines succeeded in destroying the enemy vessels, but the assault was renewed in 717. Meanwhile, at the other end of the old Roman world, the Arab armies had gained control of the Maghreb and now occupied Spain. But this second attack also failed and it became clear that the Empire would survive its terrible ordeal.

Survive it did, but so shrunken and impoverished that it was obliged to seek a new equilibrium. Morally the blow was no less crushing. It had become almost an article of faith, carried over from paganism to the Christian Empire, that the emperor, as the elect of God who aided him in his mission, was bound to triumph. The cross which surmounted his diadem was the symbol of his invincibility. More, the Roman Empire, incorporating in itself all the civilized races, seemed to be the ultimate and God-given framework for all mankind, a foretaste of the triumphant union within the celestial City. Such a view was not easily reconciled with the recent series of defeats, and it was the resultant demoralization that made the so-called Iconoclast controversy, which occurred in the eighth and ninth centuries, unusually serious.

In the second half of the ninth century the Byzantine Empire, as we shall call it in future to emphasize its specifically eastern character, was slowly emerging from the abyss into which it had so nearly fallen. Its territories, shrunk still further by the loss of nearly all the Balkan peninsula to invading Slavs and Bulgars, now covered an area scarcely greater than that of present-day France. It was still surrounded by hostile foes and partly cut off from the southern and western Mediterranean by Arab fleets. But the Iconoclast controversy was over and done with. A long line of brilliant and more or less related emperors – the Macedonian dynasty – succeeded one another with the minimum of bother, reorganizing the army and navy and overhauling the Empire's finances. Once again Constantinople became a rendezvous for merchants, Syrians, Slavs, Bulgars and Italians, all eager to trade their wares and acquire the luxury articles produced by her world-famous craftsmen. Guarded by impressive fortifications, set in the waters of the famous Golden Horn, adorned with churches and palaces and seething with the life of her 2–300,000 inhabitants – a fantastic number for the period – Constantinople was the city of marvels. Arab travellers never tired of describing it, while Slavs and Christians from the west gazed with greedy awe.

Above all, the Empire had discovered a new equilibrium and, as it were, a new mission in its influence over that very Slavonic world which had dealt it such crushing blows. From

864, when the Bulgarian king Boris had visited Constantinople to receive baptism, that country had come more or less strongly under Byzantine influence – intellectual, literary and artistic as well as religious. Closer relations had also been developing with the emergent Russian nation, and in 989 Vladimir, prince of Kiev, came to receive simultaneously the waters of Christian baptism and the hand of a Byzantine princess.

In due course, and exactly coinciding with the lifetime of Gerbert, this recovery found expression in a resumption of military expansion. The move against the Arabs began in about 960 with the reconquest of Crete and later of Cyprus, Cilicia and Antioch. This was followed up by the occupation of northern Syria as far as Tripoli (995–9) under the emperor Basil II who, while also annexing Armenia, reserved the brunt of his offensive for Bulgaria, which he finally brought into complete subjection after a long and bitter struggle (996–1018).

Particularly important in the present connexion are the Italian policies of these Byzantine emperors. By the end of the ninth century the whole of southern Italy, roughly as far as Naples, had been firmly reoccupied, although there could be no hope of dislodging the Arabs from Sicily, whence they continued to launch murderous expeditions. But all the way to the frontiers of Roman Italy was a land under Byzantine rule where Greek civilization flourished. It was a land of Basilean monks and hermits who implanted there an eastern form of monasticism, the most notable representative of which was Nilus of Rossano, a small town on the Gulf of Taranto. After a somewhat tempestuous youth, Nilus entered a monastery and was later forced on account of Saracen raids to take to a wandering life in the mountains. Sometimes alone, sometimes accompanied by a small group of cenobites, he practised a life of stringent asceticism and divided his time between prayer, working the land and copying manuscripts. He dressed in sackcloth which he never changed until it was crawling with vermin, fasted extravagantly, and enjoyed a reputation which brought those in trouble flocking to him in times of war and famine and which to some extent forced him into the role of a righter of wrongs. All over Calabria were small groups of cenobites living in cells hollowed out of the rock and decorated with primitive paintings in the style of Cappadocia. There was a certain amount of contact between these monks and their neighbours adhering to the Benedictine Rule.

Further consideration of the commercial ties which grew up between Constantinople and such Italian ports as Bari, Gaeta, Amalfi and, above all, Venice – where as early as 1008 we find Byzantine mosaicists at work on the cathedral of Torcello – gives some conception of how much Italy then had to offer the West in the way of contacts with the Byzantine Empire and its culture.

For – and this for us is the essential fact – Byzantium had also made a marked recovery in the field of culture. Even before the Arab conquests, Byzantine culture had lost much of its force. Various factors had, as it were, set the seal on this decline and brought about a collapse from which at any other period it might have been possible to recover. In the same way Alexandria had barely survived the slaughter of the scholar Hypatia by the Christian mob in 415, Athens the closing of the pagan school of philosophy on the orders of Justinian in 529, Antioch the sack by the Persians in 540, and Beirut the earthquake which destroyed its law schools in 551. Something, however, was salvaged from the gradual wreck. The university of Constantinople continued to provide teaching, and a few Syrian monasteries were responsible for translating many Greek manuscripts into Syriac. But a great many works were undoubtedly lost for ever.

In Constantinople, from the second quarter of the ninth century, there was a revival of interest in classical texts, although the precise factors which led to it are unknown. This first Byzantine renaissance, coming a little after the Carolingian, was similarly characterized by a reform of handwriting.

Prior to this, literary works had been copied in uncial characters (*cf.* p. 56). Then someone realized that by using the minuscule hand employed in administrative documents it was possible to get five or six times as many words into the same space and effect a valuable saving in time. Both these objectives suggest an increased demand for books and hence an expanding intellectual life. There were many copying schools, one of the best known the recently reformed monastery of Studios in Constantinople itself.

The movement towards a revival of classical studies was led by a few notable pioneers. Leo the Mathematician was born in Thessaly about 800 and partly self-educated from his own reading in various monastic libraries. He was modestly giving lessons to a few followers in the capital when a chance event led to his discovery by the emperor Theophilus. One of his pupils was taken prisoner by the Arabs and the emir who talked with him was so astonished at his learning that he sent him straight to the caliph al Mamun. The caliph promptly entreated the basileus to send the teacher of such a scholar to Baghdad. Theophilus did nothing of the kind, but he did appoint Leo to a chair at the university. The new professor was an encyclopedist and the author of works on mathematics, astrology and medicine. Tradition also credits him with a number of mechanical inventions, including an optical telegraph in use in the Empire.

As with Alcuin, an entire intellectual family tree can be traced from Leo. His best pupil, Photius, was especially remarkable for the wide variety of his knowledge, which ranged over theology, grammar, law, medicine, and natural sciences. Photius directed a copying school and himself possessed an extensive library. With his friends he formed a kind of club for reading and discussion on which he drew when compiling his *Myriobiblion*, a form of digest containing extracts and comments on 280 books, some of which would otherwise be unknown to us. Like Alcuin, Photius was a celebrated teacher, and such was the emperor's confidence in him that he was appointed, although a layman, to the office of Patriarch of Constantinople, in which role his activities were as outstanding as they were controversial. The breadth of his learning was so astounding that he was suspected of having sold his soul to the devil in return for magical powers, an experience in which he was by no means unique.

The movement reached its height with Arethas (c. 860–after 932), later archbishop of Caesarea in Cappadocia, who was probably a pupil of both Leo and Photius. He was keenly interested in the old uncial manuscripts, had them copied in minuscule, himself correcting the copies and adding a number of philological notes of the greatest interest. Today his manuscripts are divided among the European libraries: Venice has a Homer, the Bodleian at Oxford a Plato and a Euclid, while the British Museum, Rome and Vienna have to thank him for an Aristotle, a Marcus Aurelius and three copies of Lucan. And this is by no means a complete inventory of his work, which constituted a real salvage operation for Greek literature comparable to that achieved by the Carolingian renaissance on behalf of the heritage of Rome.

The work of Arethas brings us right into the tenth century. In Constantinople this was a century of inventories and encyclopedias. The work was fostered by several emperors, including Leo VI, a pupil of Photius, and Constantine VII, who occupied his enforced leisure while political authority was kept out of his hands by making compendious notes on imperial administration and court procedure. There was no original work in all this but it provided a collection of extracts from historians, medical, veterinary, zoological and agricultural encyclopedias, and major works of jurisprudence, all of which formed a sound basis for fresh educational progress and for more individual achievements.

Thus, at the very time when Gerbert was acquiring his own education, Constantinople had renewed its ties with the traditions of ancient Greece and had begun to function as a great intellectual centre once more. Nevertheless, of still more immediate importance to the West was the work being accomplished in the Muslim world.

THE MUSLIM WORLD

From the Iberian peninsula to the Indus plain – which was actually occupied by a Turkish Muslim chieftain around the year 1000 – and from the Caspian to the borders of the Sahara, the Arab conquest had created a huge world within which men, goods and ideas circulated freely. How best to describe this world? We may call it the Arab world, and it is true that the official language was Arabic, but the Arabs as such constituted only a tiny minority, and the indiscriminate appetites of the caliphs had resulted in the introduction of a good deal of foreign blood even into the ruling families. We may call it the Muslim world since religion was certainly a powerful unifying factor, but Islam was far from being the universal creed; considerable Christian, Jewish and Zoroastrian minorities persisted and were generally tolerated.

By the end of the tenth century this sprawling world had lost even its strict religious and political unity. The authority of the Abbasid caliph, resident in Baghdad, was no longer universally recognized. Other caliphs had emerged and equally demanded the obedience of all the Faithful. In Kairouan, for instance, a descendant of the Prophet's daughter Fatima had been acclaimed by his supporters as the successor of Mahomet in 909. Their persistent efforts carried his side as far as Egypt, where Cairo became its capital in 973. In 929 a caliph of the Ommayad family, Abd al Rahman III, was likewise recognized at Cordova, but apart from some small successes in the Maghreb his authority hardly extended beyond the Iberian peninsula.

All the same, these schisms did not prevent an abundant interplay of ideas moving throughout the Muslim world, fostering local initiative and contributing to the growth of populous cities with their own, highly civilized way of life.

The tenth and the first half of the eleventh centuries even marked a kind of climax in this respect.

It is not true that when the Arabs captured Alexandria in 641 they set fire to the famous library, but it is a fact that the mounted Bedouin tribesmen who now set out on a wave of conquest were almost entirely devoid of culture, while the men who ruled them, from Mecca and Medina, themselves possessed only the barest rudiments. However, the establishment of a definitive text of the Koran and the study of tradition which went with it, as well as the meditation on its teachings, did combine to produce an expansion of such specifically Arabic sciences as grammar, history, law and theology.

The Arab conquest also covered a great deal of the ground where Greek civilization had flourished hundreds of years earlier. A number of Syrian monasteries still preserved important manuscripts translated into Syriac, a language not far removed from Arabic. The school of Jundishapur in southern Persia extended a welcome to refugees from the Roman Empire, heretics condemned by the Councils and philosophers who had been expelled from Athens, and was also considerably indebted to Hindu science, especially medicine.

It was not until the caliphs had settled in Baghdad (in the middle of the eighth century) and had shed their Arab way of life in favour of the more luxurious and refined habits the traditions of which were still preserved in their new capital, that they came into contact with these survivals of Hellenistic culture. Men like Harun al Raschid and al Mamun, contemporaries of Charlemagne and Louis the Pious, were especially susceptible to the attractions of these precious remnants. They encouraged translations into Arabic and built up a magnificent library in Baghdad. Several decades of feverish activity ensued, and it was some time before the intellectuals who flocked to Baghdad – for the most part Iranian converts to Islam but including also a number of Christians and Jews – were able to absorb and master the formidable bulk of knowledge poured on them by this avalanche of translations.

For 200 years Baghdad remained the scientific capital of the Mediterranean world, as Alexandria had been before it. But here too the new caliphs were keen to dispute its supremacy. In Cordova, Abd al Rahman III, and even more his son al Hakam II after him, built up a library which is said to have contained 400,000 volumes. This figure is undoubtedly an exaggeration, but even so it is out of all proportion greater than anything we have been able to establish for Carolingian Europe. They attracted scholars. Jewish thinkers who were unpopular in the East at that time flocked eagerly to this welcoming city, which became the chief centre of Jewish scholarship. All this expansion was maintained by the prosperity then spreading throughout the Muslim West, the Maghreb and Spain. The time of Gerbert was one of a shift of balance within the Muslim world, and this was the beginning of the transference of Greek ideas and learning from East to West which the Romans had failed to achieve.

It is important to emphasize that this phenomenon was not confined to Cordova, nor to Muslim and Jewish circles. Cultivated courts began to appear from the end of the tenth century in smaller places such as Seville, Toledo and Saragossa which in the eleventh became the capitals of small Spanish Muslim principalities. Nor was the Christian population of Muslim Spain – the Mozarabs – immune from the attractions which this intellectual life had to offer its more educated elements. The mozarab clergy naturally continued to officiate in Latin but its real cultural language was Arabic. This astonishing fact is brought home to us today by the surprise we feel at the sight of Arabic manuscripts from the hands of mozarab bishops. In the peninsula, where religious hatred was still unknown, the effects of this enlightenment were felt by the Christian states of the north whose monasteries contained many mozarab monks and whose princes were sent to be educated among the Saracens.

At the end of the tenth century the finest fruits of this 'Arabic' learning were still in the future but already it had gone beyond the mere handing on of Hellenistic thought. It also took in a whole current of practical and theoretical knowledge from the Far East and India. In this way the game of chess; paper; porcelain and, before long, the compass penetrated to the Muslim world. But in addition to these and even more important, there was the spread of the Hindu system of numbers, the forerunner of our own. The basic theory was laid down in the ninth century by the Persian al Khwarizmi who also invented algebra*, using the work of Diophantus.

Moreover these 'Arabic' scholars also had their own original contribution to make. From the end of the ninth century they were developing trigonometry. In astronomy, al Battani accurately defined the important phenomenon known to experts as 'the precession of the equinoxes' and wrote a treatise which was long to remain a classic in its field. In physics, optics and the accurate measurement of the density of solids according to Archimedes' principle were studied in especial detail. Medicine was dominated by the towering figure of the Persian al Razi, whose observations even today are striking in their precision. His study of a perforated renal abscess is still exemplary. The eye diseases so common in the arid, glaring lands of Islam were also made the subject of original research.

Besides this brief summary, it is also worth stressing what was up to a point the most novel aspect of the general attitude to science in the Arab world. The search for a rational explanation of natural phenomena was no longer as fundamental as in Greek science and the desire to acquire power over nature by means of science played a much larger part. This admittedly utilitarian attitude helps to explain the passionate

* From the Arabic word *al djabr*, the method by which a figure is carried over from one side of an equation to the other by altering the sign from plus to minus.

enthusiasm for these studies both in the Muslim and later in the Christian worlds. It also highlights the practical nature of scientific research which we shall encounter again with Gerbert.

When Gerbert died in 1003, the young Persian ibn Sina – known to Christian authors as Avicenna – was just beginning a scientific work now recognized as one of the most remarkable of all time. Gerbert could not have known this work and would probably not have understood it if he had. Arabic science was still a long way ahead of all other. But the time had come for Western Christendom to rise above the tremendous ordeals which had driven it. The roots put down by the Carolingian renaissance proved deep enough and it was ready for more. Although unsuspected as yet, this, for the West, far from being the 'twilight of the world', was the dawn of a new day.

Chapter 3

THE HISTORICAL BACKGROUND: THE WEST

A FRESH WAVE OF INVASIONS

FROM about 800 until the early years of the eleventh century Europe suffered under a fresh wave of invasions: the last in her history to date, unless we count the Mongol tide of the thirteenth century which covered only eastern Europe – and even that only partially.

The earliest attacks go back as far as the time of Charlemagne when Alcuin was bewailing the first Danish assaults on his beloved Northumbria and the emperor was forced to attend to his northern seaboard defences. At about the same time Saracen ships were beginning to infest the western Mediterranean, and in 827 the Muslims landed in Sicily. For the next 150 years or more, western Europe was to be in the position of a besieged citadel, a citadel which, if the truth be told, the attackers sometimes succeeded in penetrating and where, when they did so, room had to be made for them.

The Muslim attacks in the south were, relatively speaking, the least serious because more localized. Sicily, which had been totally occupied by about 900, became a wealthy emirate and also a formidable base for further operations from which marauding bands moved up Italy, ravaging the countryside and threatening towns. One of these bands established itself in the Garigliano valley between Rome and Naples and wreaked havoc for twenty years before it could be wiped out (915). More troublesome still was one which came from Spain at about the same time and gained a foothold in the Massif des Maures, at La Garde-Freinet, near St Tropez, launching daring raids as far as the Alps and the valley of the upper Rhine. In the end it took the strong feelings roused by the capture of Maieul, abbot of Cluny, to produce a decisive attack on La Garde-Freinet (972). But maritime expeditions in search of booty continued along the coasts of Languedoc, Provence and Italy until the early years of the eleventh century.

In Spain, apart from a few inconclusive engagements, the influence of the caliphate of Cordova was initially quite pacific, with the Christian principalities of the north content on the whole to acknowledge some kind of suzerainty. After 980, however, an Arab chieftain known as al Mansur billah (the victorious by Allah) broke the truce and destroyed most of the Christian cities, among them Barcelona, Coimbra, Leon and Santiago de Compostela. Fortunately al Mansur was after booty and prestige rather than conquest. After his death in 1002 the situation was speedily reversed and before long Christian contingents were intervening in squabbles between the principalities which had grown up as a result of the decline of the caliphate. The sequence of events is instructive. These wars and raids were a sign of the political degeneration of the Muslim West and produced only negative results.

The Norman invasions appear to have been a very different matter. Western Europe was only one theatre of the remarkable adventures which, in the space of two centuries, carried the Scandinavian warriors and seamen across the Russian plains and out into the north Atlantic to Iceland, Greenland and America. To begin with, these expeditions seem to have been little more than raids. The slender ships loaded with fierce fighting men sailed along the coasts and up rivers, burning villages and monasteries as they went, and sometimes taking even fortified towns by storm. Their sphere of action extended to all the rivers of France and then took in Spain, and Normans even penetrated into the Mediterranean, where their ravages were frequently confused with those of the Saracens. As they ranged farther afield from their northern homes it became necessary for them to winter abroad and so to take wives and children with them. Sometimes the local peasants would overcome their fear and bring produce to trade with the strangers, turning the camp into a temporary market. This marks the transition to a permanent settlement.

A first small Norman principality appeared on the continent in Frisia, led by a Norman chief who had been converted to Christianity. It endured only a few years (882–5) but its example was soon followed. The Danes settled in the east of England, and in 911 came the famous treaty by which King Charles the Simple ceded to Rollo the province of France thereafter called Normandy. The rough adventurers were not transformed into peaceful neighbours overnight. Even when they were well settled in their new lands they continued to send out from them such vast expeditions as those which occupied southern Italy and Sicily, conquered England and took part in the Crusades. But they did become fully integrated into the western world which they had begun by ravaging so ferociously, bringing to it all their warlike instincts but also their talent for legislation and administration.

Thus, by the end of the tenth century, the whole northwest face of Europe from the North Cape to the Hebrides and Brittany was well on the way to stabilization. The conversion of the Norsemen to Christianity is a measure of this. It came about at first in a spontaneous and disorganized fashion as a particular chief, wintering on the continent, found it advisable to add the protection of Christ to that already accorded by his traditional gods, or as traders who had visited Christian lands brought home the occasional priest with the rest of their merchandise. It was an odd kind of Christianity, certainly, mingled with primitive beliefs, solar myths and the uncouth practices which the new converts did not abandon all at once. But they were also becoming part of the body of a Church which taught them and little by little brought their habits and customs into line. By the middle of the tenth century three Danish bishoprics were attached to the see of Hamburg. In Norway and Sweden progress was slower, although Olaf Trygvesson, the king later responsible for the conversion of

Norway, received baptism on English soil in 994 and the conversion of the Swedes to Christianity began in about the year 1000. Gerbert lived to witness this impressive spread of Christianity and to see it carried to still farther regions.

As early as the time of Charlemagne the conquest of Saxony as far as the frontier marked by the Elbe and the Saale had put the Frankish kingdom in constant touch with the Slavonic world. Border skirmishes alternated with trading expeditions and raids in search of the slaves for which there was a big demand in Muslim countries, and some enterprising missionaries also made attempts at conversion. In the early part of the tenth century Henry I, duke of Saxony, conducted a systematic programme of colonization in the Wend country, between the Elbe and the Oder.

But in the south-east a new enemy had appeared. Documents as early as 833 mention a yellow-skinned race from the region of the Azov Sea which crossed what is now south Russia to emerge a little before 900 on the plains of the Tisza and the middle Danube. From here the Hungarian horsemen set out on pillaging expeditions from which they returned laden with booty and dragging pathetic files of captives to their permanent camp. They scoured the plain of the Po for the first time in 899. The following year it was the turn of Bavaria, and from then on the raids became almost an annual event, pushing on occasion as far as Lorraine and Burgundy and once even into the region of Nîmes. They rarely attacked fortified towns but their sudden descents laid waste the countryside and drove all those able to flee in terror before them.

There were a few rulers who attempted to lead some resistance. Henry I of Saxony, by now king of eastern Francia, achieved considerable success, and his son Otto I inflicted a terrible defeat on one of their armies near the river Lech in August 955 which effectively put an end to their incursions. For some time the raids had been growing less frequent. The lands which had been ravaged so many times yielded less and less plunder. Gradually the marauding habits which harked back to the time when they had been a nomadic people in Asia gave way to agriculture and a changed pattern of society with their new, sedentary way of life in Hungary. The more or less loosely organized groups of tribes began to form themselves into a state, and a new era in the life of the Hungarians began.

In the same year as this victory Otto I won another against the Slavs on the Recknitz, inaugurating half a century of dazzling success for Christendom. In 986 Otto founded the see of Magdeburg which was to organize missionary expansion and the foundation of new dioceses. The Polish duke Mieszko was baptized about 966. In 973 the bishopric of Prague was created, and in the same year a Hungarian embassy arrived at Otto's court. Christianity had reached even the erstwhile robbers and it was possible to contemplate the creation of a Hungarian bishopric. The duke Vajk in turn was baptized in 985, taking the Christian name of Stephen, and from then on he encouraged missionaries to convert his people.

You behold the wrath of the Lord burst out before you. ... Nothing but depopulated cities, monasteries destroyed or burned, fields laid waste. ... Everywhere the powerful oppress the weak and men are like the fishes of the sea, devouring one another.

In these words the bishops of the province of Rheims, meeting in 909, deplored the evils of the time. By the end of the tenth century the new wave of invasions was over and the new peoples on the way to conversion entering for the most part into the vast community of Western Christendom. A new era was dawning but political and social life still bore the scars of this troubled period.

THE REMNANTS OF CAROLINGIAN EUROPE

The Carolingian Empire, 'this fragile masterpiece' in the words of the historian Henri Focillon, could not, however imposing the edifice constructed by Charlemagne, possess a great deal of stability in the face of the troubled mental and material conditions brought about by the new invasions. To administer and defend such an unwieldy whole was in the long run a task beyond human strength, and the Frankish sovereigns are not entirely to be blamed for their almost universal inability to rise to the concept of a state that was not to be divided up like a family estate. By the end of the ninth century or thereabouts the extinction of several branches of the line restored the realm as a whole once more into the hands of a single ruler, only to reveal his incapacity to hold it. Thus the partition effected by the Treaty of Verdun in 843 between Charlemagne's grandsons was ultimately to decide the fate of Europe for centuries to come.

Of these remnants of Carolingian Europe the most substantial was still, comparatively speaking, also the newest. By joining the previously unconquered region of Saxony to the existing peoples of Bavaria, Thuringia, Alemannia and Frankish Austrasia, Charlemagne had in fact made Germany into a political entity. At the partition the whole area was considered as the eastern part of the Frankish kingdom. The Carolingian rulers strove to endow it with its own traditions but it was by no means certain that this precarious unity would endure. But with the disappearance of the last of these rulers the chiefs of the *Stämme* or tribes assembled to elect one of their number as king. This was the real birth of Germany as a nation (911). Its contributory factors, in addition to the political wisdom of its leaders, were a certain community of language and customs and the pressing need for defence against the Slavs and Hungarians. Little by little the Frankish state became transformed into the Germanic kingdom (*regnum Teutonicorum*) and the Franks lost their dominant position there.

Even so, the young kingdom was still extremely fragile. Relations between the king and the heads of the great families who had proceeded to turn the old *Stämme* into duchies with themselves as overlords, were ill-defined. At the crucial moment it was the dukes of Saxony who saved the situation. Henry I was elected king in 919 and succeeded in establishing his overall authority and at the same time making himself liked and trusted to such effect that on his death in 936 his son, Otto I, was appointed to succeed him. To Otto must go the credit for rallying the dukes around him, making them the duly delegated representatives of the royal authority, and placing himself at their head against the Slavs and Hungarians as the victorious personification of the new power of Germany. Here, in Gerbert's time, lay the real strength of Europe.

The development of the western part of the Frankish kingdom followed a very different course. Here, resistance to the invasions was centred on the already long-established administrative units of the counties. The counties had tended to fall into groups, numbering some twenty or so in the kingdom as a whole, each of which was in the hands of some enterprising family which had come to regard it as its birthright. The Carolingian monarch himself, whose actual possessions were confined to a small principality, had gradually been reduced to the status of a mere figurehead. Furthermore, ever since in a moment of panic in 888 the nobility had elected as king that Count Eudes of Paris who, three years earlier, had distinguished himself by his heroic defence of the city against the Normans, the Carolingians had had to endure the often successful rivalry of this family. In this struggle for the throne it was in the long run the royal power which suffered most. The support of the German king, in fact, was the ultimate resort of the last Carolingians, and by breaking with Otto I they were preparing with their own hands for the accession of Eudes' descendant Hugh Capet. Hugh was elected king in 987 and thereafter the Capets would not release their grip on a power which, though puny at first, was to go from strength to strength.

Between western and eastern Francia lay the kingdom of Lothair the eldest. Although this included the Rhineland, the cradle of the dynasty, and the city of Rome, the capital of the Empire, it was perilously elongated from the Low Countries to southern Italy and, unlike the other kingdoms, had been unable to preserve itself intact. By the tenth century only a few fragments remained. Lorraine, in the north, was disputed among its neighbours for some time before being absorbed into the eastern kingdom. Further south the kingdom of Burgundy and Provence had grown up, not without a struggle, and led a precarious existence under some form of German protectorate. Finally, Italy had been divided up into secular and ecclesiastical principalities which no longer possessed even the theoretical ties of a proper monarchy. Even the imperial title, though there was some obscure bickering about it to begin with, lapsed after 924.

Lying on the fringe of this Carolingian Europe were the British Isles. Here the descendants of Alfred the Great, king of Wessex, had been carrying on his work. Athelstan (925–39) was able to style himself proudly 'king of all Britain', and to marry his sisters to the king of western Francia and to Otto the Great. But it was a fragile splendour. The Danelaw brought little more than a nominal truce, and from 980 onwards the resumption of the invasions from Norway and Denmark brought about the rapid disintegration of the Anglo-Saxon kingdom. In 1016 this was finally submerged in a Danish empire. Ireland, on the other hand, thanks to the stubborn and increasingly united resistance of her clan chiefs, managed to escape Scandinavian domination.

Such then was the map of Europe in the tenth century. But its appearance is deceptive. In all these kingdoms the decay of the Carolingian institutions was proceeding more or less rapidly. In those unsettled times the thing that mattered most to the still almost entirely agricultural population was the protection to be expected from their local lord and the shelter which they, their animals and such pathetic possessions as could be hastily flung together might find within his walls. The age of the castle had begun. From the ninth century their numbers had been growing, often without even the statutory request for royal permission. At first they were no more than crude, wooden buildings perched on top of a *motte* and

surrounded by a rudimentary palisade. Towards the end of
the tenth century the first stone keeps began to appear. Life
within walls pierced only by narrow *meurtrières* was a hard
business, but the power conferred by possessing a castle was
increasingly certain. For these peasants the real authority was
the lord whose castle they had helped to build with their own
hands and for whose protection they paid by submitting to
his frequently ferocious and overbearing temper.

In this way there grew up what may be called the seigneurial
system. The *seigneur* was the landowner or castellan who had
taken advantage of the decline of civil authority to assume
powers of command over his fellow men – what was called at
the time the *droit de ban*. In practice it allowed him to exploit
them to his own advantage, press them into his service,
impose a monopoly of such communal institutions as the
mill, the bake-oven, and so forth, and to levy heavy fines and
no less heavy taxes, although actual tithes were still something
of an exception. He became the head of a society in which,
under the weight of his authority, the old distinctions between
slaves and freemen became blurred and a new type of dependence grew up instead which came to be known as serfdom.
No precise historical date can be assigned to this development,
but it occurred roughly between the tenth and eleventh
centuries, more or less quickly in different areas. Gerbert's
time must be regarded as one in which the wretched state of
the peasantry was aggravated still further.

Grim the period certainly was, but it will not do to blacken
the picture unduly. There were some glimmerings of light,
heralding the blaze which was to spread throughout the West
from the eleventh century onwards. Here and there attempts
at development were made. Land was cleared; the first dykes
were built along the Netherlands seaboard; castles and villages
sprang up on the frontier of muslim Spain. In some cities, too,
there were stirrings of life, modest as yet but still promising.
Much of this was due to the protection of stout walls (often
dating from the time of the Later Roman Empire), to the

surviving remnants of trade with distant parts and to the enterprise of a few energetic bishops. This was especially so in Italy. Venice was doing business with the Byzantine empire and even with the Saracens, and stretching out to include the islands of the lagoon. In Rome, where the presence of the popes gave a spur to activity, the Lateran was rebuilt at the beginning of the tenth century and successful careers were open to the sons of merchants and craftsmen. Milan, whose inhabitants were noted for their 'natural busyness', boasted paved streets, public baths, hospitals and a foundling hospital; suburbs were beginning to spring up outside the original walls. But examples were also to be found outside Italy. Barcelona already possessed a flourishing commercial quarter centred on the church of Santa Maria close by the harbour where the ships put in. There was Mayence, where 'Frisian' merchants from the Low Countries rubbed shoulders with Jews and men from the far Slavonic frontiers. In Liège bishop Notger (972–1008) built new walls and a great many buildings including an enlarged cathedral of Notre Dame, the college of St Paul on an island in the Meuse, and the octagonal church of St John the Evangelist on a hillock by the river in full view of the cathedral 'so that he to whom Christ on the Cross entrusted the care of the Virgin should see her and keep watch over her'. There were other hopeful signs as well.

UNIFYING FORCES

The community of faith which bound Western Europe together and of which the newly converted peoples became a part was now beginning to be called by a number of different names by various tenth-century authors. This was the expression of a growing self-awareness which can also be seen clearly in several different institutions.

The first of these was the papacy. This had not yet assumed the central position to be conferred on it by Gregory VII in the eleventh century, but it already enjoyed a reputation in strong contrast to the mediocrity of some of its incumbents, appointed at the whim of the turbulent Roman nobility. Some popes were humble, godly men. Others were a public scandal. The worst of these was John XII (955-64), whose biography admitted openly that he 'spent his life in adultery and vanity'. But for all his weaknesses the pope remained the successor of the apostles Peter and Paul and their representative on earth. Bodies of canon law compiled from the ninth century onwards maintain his supremacy in matters of dogma and discipline. Monasteries and churches placed themselves under the protection of St Peter and hence of the Roman pontiff. Secular rulers journeyed to Rome to settle ecclesiastical disputes involving their domains, frequently at the festivals of Christmas or Easter, the solemn celebration of which in the Roman churches left a deep impression on them. Sunifred, count of Cerdagne, who attended the Nativity service in Rome in 951, still remembered it fourteen years later on his deathbed and freed two of his slaves who had been with him on that occasion.

Whenever an unworthy pope showed signs of diminishing the pontifical authority it was left to the regional synods of bishops to take control and make decisions. These met frequently within the framework of an ecclesiastical province, under the chairmanship of the archbishop, and there were also larger assemblies in which important laymen such as kings, counts and barons occasionally took part, since matters were discussed which directly concerned them. The movement for the dissemination of God's peace on earth which grew up at the end of the tenth century was a result of such gatherings. It began with the synods hurling regular protests and anathemas at laymen who violated, plundered or misappropriated Church property. The bishops of Aquitaine, meeting at Charroux in Poitou, added a general condemnation of all those who violated the goods of the poor or maltreated the clergy (989). In the following year the Council of Le Puy made these prohibitions more specific and extended its protection to merchants. The bishop of Le Puy opened the session by reminding his hearers of Christ's Sermon on the Mount and exhorting them to behave like 'sons of peace'. He concluded by making them swear an oath of peace. Measures of this kind, pursued over the ensuing decades, almost certainly though not without a struggle, helped to lessen to some extent the violence and insecurity of regions such as southern France, Burgundy and Provence, where the royal authority was particularly lax.

The tenth century was also the age of Cluny. The monastery of Cluny was founded in 910 by William the Pious, duke of Aquitaine and count of Mâcon, not far from the last-named town. He dedicated the monastery to the apostles Peter and Paul under whose protection – and hence of their successor the pope – it lay. Cluny was to be completely independent of 'the yoke of any earthly power' whatsoever: bishop, king, count – and even its founder himself. The community was to be free to elect its own abbot and dispose freely of its own possessions. It was to be immune from outside pressure, violence and the appointment of unworthy abbots – all of which were suffered by a good many monasteries of the time – and able to revert to the strict practice of the Benedictine Rule. In so far as was humanly possible the ideals laid down by William the Pious were actually put into practice, thanks largely to the zeal, effectiveness and longevity of the first abbots of Cluny, Bernon, Odo, Maieul and Odilon. Before long the house of Cluny had become a model of its kind and more than one lord requested the abbot to come and reform another monastery which had fallen into ruin or lapsed from its rule. These reforms were not always achieved very smoothly and all too often the work so painfully accomplished was undone once the abbot had departed. The final solution was to attach the reformed monastery permanently to Cluny and make the abbot of Cluny its regular superior. In this way a completely new type of organization grew up. Hitherto, although they followed the same rule, the Benedictine abbeys had been completely independent of one another. Now they were formed into a monastic order. By the end of the tenth century this comprised some forty establishments, mostly in France but a few also in Burgundy and Italy. The abbot of Cluny, dividing his time between the centres of this 'monastic empire', involved in numerous spiritual and temporal affairs, was one of the great men of Christendom.

Historians have rightly stressed the importance of the Cluniac movement in the religious life of the tenth century, and in the endeavours towards reformation and improvement which were to affect the Church as a whole in the century afterwards. All the same, the virtues of Cluny should not make us blind to those of other, geographically less widespread monastic associations such as those which sprang up in Lorraine and in Italy. Neither should they make us forget the more random achievements among the secular clergy which in the following century were to be directed chiefly towards the restoration of cathedral chapters. Above all, from the immediate, cultural point of view it must be admitted that the Cluniac reform represented only an indirect advantage. The abbots of Cluny were aiming principally at an ideal of disciplinary and moral reform. They also wanted to see divine service celebrated in their monasteries with the greatest possible correctness and splendour. The monks of Cluny did copy manuscripts as well, but of liturgical works and the writings of the Fathers of the Church. Of culture they seem to have been more than a little suspicious. When Odilon saw in a dream a vision of a precious vase with snakes emerging from it, he regarded this a symbol of classical culture.

Other factors besides the unity of Faith and the great institutions of the Church contributed to the rearrangement of Europe at the end of the tenth century. The old imperial dream of the Carolingians was not dead, and it was left to Otto I as the most powerful ruler in Europe to revive it. If their biographers are to be believed both he and his father Henry I had been hailed by their armies with the classical title of *imperator* after their victories over the Hungarians. Otto I, as a result of his marriage to Adelaida, the heiress to the ancient Lombard kingdom, was also led to intervene in Italy. An appeal from the papacy encouraged him to make a repeat appearance there and on 2 February 962 he was crowned and anointed emperor in the church of St Peter in Rome by Pope John XII and acclaimed by the Roman people. But it was a far cry from the ceremony of Christmas 800. Otto never dominated the whole of Christian Europe as Charlemagne had done. His effective power did not extend beyond his own kingdoms of Germany and Italy, although the combined responsibilities even of these were enough to set his successors a task ultimately beyond their means.

All the same, it is probable that his coronation as emperor may have given Otto at least a degree of moral authority outside his own realms. But even before 962 he seems to have enjoyed a prestige which is reflected in contemporary writings. Flodoard, canon of Rheims, showed no resentment at his intervention in French affairs in defence of the interests of the Church. Family ties – his sisters had married the Carolingian king Louis IV and his rival, duke Hugh – also made him a natural arbiter in dynastic squabbles. The tenth and eleventh centuries were a period very strong in family solidarity, which tended to make up for the absence of any other social framework. Like all great families, Otto's was in the habit of gathering at religious festivals when, in between the church services and the feasting, they would hold family conclaves, presided over by the head of the family, at which everyone's affairs were discussed. The fact that Otto was crowned emperor does not seem to have made a great deal of difference to all this, but rather to have set the seal on it.

Nevertheless, it was not without effect in the long run. Like Charlemagne, Otto I was deeply concerned that his title should be recognized by his brother emperor in Constantinople. His reception was equally cool. The power of the Byzantine emperors was then coming to the full. The throne was occupied by Nicephorus Phocas, an energetic general of a somewhat mystical turn of mind. Negotiations do not appear to have begun immediately. In 967 an embassy from Nicephorus turned up in Ravenna and an exchange of gifts took place. There was a possible basis for agreement in an alliance against the Saracens. However, it ended in discord. Next, Liutprand, bishop of Cremona, who had been sent to Constantinople with a view to obtaining both the recognition of his title for Otto I and the hand of a Byzantine princess for his son, was subjected to all kinds of humiliation. Not until after the assassination of Nicephorus Phocas and the accession of his rival John Tzimisces, another general but a more kindly and peace-loving individual, could the talks be resumed. A fresh mission returned with the princess Theophano, daughter of the former emperor Romanus II, and her marriage with Otto II was solemnized in 972. In the following year Otto I died.

His imperial title had pledged him above all else to act as defender of the Church, and led him to depose the unworthy pope John XII, to exact a promise from the Romans that they would not elect a pope without his approval and to intervene regularly in the appointment of pontiffs. This proved a source of disagreements and difficulties which led step by step to the clash between the Empire and the Papacy. This was not yet. But Otto II had already shown himself unequal to the manifold tasks which devolved upon him, of keeping the Slavs on the Elbe at a respectful distance, maintaining his authority in Germany and Italy, and dealing with the Saracens in Calabria. When he in turn made the all-too-frequent mistake of launching an attack on them in the full heat of summer, he was defeated and survived this crushing disaster by only a few months (983).

He left a son, Otto III, who was still too young to rule. Queen Theophano, who had every excuse for feeling out of her element, was obliged to govern in his name, which she did most ably and efficiently. Theophano died young, and the task was taken over by Otto I's widow, the old queen

Adelaida. At last, in 994, Otto III was of an age to direct the Empire. The son of a Saxon and a Greek and heir to two imperial traditions, the Carolingian and the Byzantine, Otto III is one of the oddest figures of medieval history. He had been soundly educated: he began his studies under a Calabrian Greek, John Philagathos, and a Saxon, the chaplain Bernard later bishop of Hildesheim; and afterwards completed them under Gerbert.

To a much greater extent than his father and grandfather had done, Otto III allowed himself to be carried away by the imperial dignity, to such an extent that it became his chief preoccupation. He made a dramatic show of reverence for Charlemagne. At the feast of Pentecost in the year 1000 he went down with a small following into the crypt at Aix-la-Chapelle where the emperor reposed in state upon a throne. After contemplating him for some time, Otto took the cross from his own neck and several of his garments and had them laid in a sarcophagus. But the Empire he wanted to restore was in reality the Roman, and seals dating from this period bear classical inscriptions, such as the one with an allegorical figure of a woman, representing Rome and the words: *Renovatio imperii romani.* Whenever he had the chance he would go and stay in Rome, where he sat enthroned amid a court run on the lines of Byzantine etiquette, conferring Byzantine titles on certain of his officials and taking his meals alone on a dais rather than with his followers according to the Germanic fashion. From time to time he would disappear on a visit to St Nilus and spend several weeks in his company, living the life of a hermit.

Otto III died before his remarkable personality and imperial dreams had time to affect the destiny of Europe. More than anything else, he was a symbol: the symbol of the prestige which the Byzantine Empire in all its glory could then enjoy even in the midst of Europe. On the cultural level, also, all that was best in the period can be traced to eastern influence, but here the influence was chiefly from the Muslim world.

THE HERITAGE OF THE
CAROLINGIAN RENAISSANCE

THE NEW MAP OF CULTURE

No literary and intellectual life can exist without an infra-structure of schools, centres of book production and libraries. One of the great virtues of the Carolingian renaissance was that it provided western Europe with all these things. But the rulers who inaugurated the movement passed away. In one place the Normans, in the next the Saxons or Hungarians had plundered and set fire to many a monastery and the collection of books that was its pride. How was the Carolingian heritage preserved and kept together through all these threats and disasters?

It is hard to trace a complete and accurate picture of the ravages committed, for example, by the Normans. Their activities would probably emerge as scattered and nowhere total. They infested all western sea coasts as far as and including the Mediterranean. They sailed up rivers and penetrated deep into the heart of the continent. Only a few areas of high ground, such as the French Massif central and its environs, escaped them. A typical story is that of the monks of St Philibert who were driven from their home on the isle of Noirmoutiers and forced to seek refuge first on the Loire and then in Poitou and the Bourbonnais before they and the mortal remains of their patron saint, faithfully carried with them on the stony roads of exile, at last found at Tournus, on the Saône, the 'quiet place' for which they yearned. On the other hand, the armies of the period were not particularly numerous, and except where they camped for any length of time or returned very often they rarely devastated an entire region. In centres such as Soissons or Saint-Amand in Artois the continuity was seemingly not broken, even though they were situated in exposed areas.

Even in places on which the fury of the new barbarians did fall, the survivors laboured with devoted energy to replace their lost treasures and resume their interrupted tasks. Inevitably, the results of their endeavours were patchy in the extreme. At St Riquier and St Vaast at Arras the monks tried to save their most precious books, but the majority were scattered or even perished in other fires. The two monasteries rose again from their ruins and carried on with their work, but it was a long time before either of them recovered the glory of bygone years. Even those places that were spared suffered some upheavals. Early in the winter of 882–3 the aged archbishop Hincmar of Rheims was compelled to flee precipitately in a litter, with the relics of St Remi and a few of his treasures, when the city was threatened by the 'great Norman army'; he died pitiably at his domain of Épernay. In the upshot the episcopal city was not taken but its activity declined. The new bishop, Fulk, was obliged not long afterwards to rebuild two schools, which were almost falling to ruins, one for the canons and the other for the clergy of the surrounding countryside, and to attract well-known teachers. These probably went away again after his death in 900, but not without leaving trained disciples to carry on their teaching traditions.

The abbey of St Martin of Tours suffered several visitations from the Normans, the last of them in 903, but it too survived, thanks to the patience and persistence of its monks. But the patterns used by copyists in the *scriptorium* were destroyed and the traditions of calligraphy and ornamentation lost. The good old days of Alcuin were gone for ever.

In the valley of the Loire the torch was carried on not by Orleans, which shone only with a brief glory under Theodulf, but by the abbey of St Benedict of Fleury higher upstream. Founded in 645, the abbey had a fairly modest history and its reform by the abbot of Cluny would not seem to have fostered an intellectual vocation. However, the abbots had kept its two schools functioning, an external one for secular priests and an internal one for novices. Abbon, given to the monastery as a child, attended both, and later completed his education in Paris and Rheims before returning as head of studies. Abbon set himself to enrich the already well-stocked library. This was especially well provided with grammatical treatises and classical works. Virgil, Terence and Horace stood side by side with Lucan and Juvenal, and the abbey also possessed a manuscript of Ovid which was probably copied at this period. By the end of the tenth century Fleury was, on an intellectual plane, the leading monastery in France.

Ultimately it was the lands permanently occupied by the Normans which posed the hardest problem. The case of England was typical. Nowhere, probably, was there utter devastation. King Alfred was already bemoaning 'the time when everything had not been ravaged or burned and the English churches were filled with treasures and books'. But England was not yet at the end of her troubles. By the beginning of the tenth century all monastic life, apart from two or three convents of nuns, seems to have vanished. It would appear that the poetry of the ruins had a good deal to do with its rebirth, since its main instigator, Dunstan, was the son of a thegn from the vicinity of the old abbey of Glaston-bury, to which its venerable traditions even then drew pilgrims. Dunstan must have pondered as a child on the ancient stones which it would be given to him one day, as abbot of a new Glastonbury, to rebuild. It was also said to have been the sight of a ruined monastery which made King Edgar from earliest youth a staunch supporter of the monastic revival. In this way a few houses reappeared, and in them the whole basis of monastic life had to be recreated. They had to be equipped with libraries and teachers. It was now that the continent of Europe may be said to have paid back to England what it had received from her in the time of Alcuin.

In fact, links with the Continent had persisted even at this period. When Dunstan was exiled by a king less kindly disposed towards monks, he found a refuge for some time at St Peter of Ghent (956). A little while later, monks from Corbie came to teach the monks of Abingdon. But there was no abbey whose influence in England was more far-reaching than that of Fleury sur Loire. It was at Fleury that Oda, archbishop of Canterbury (d. 958), took orders, and there he sent his nephew Oswald to be educated. Oswald, who was later to become archbishop of York, is better known as the founder of the abbey of Ramsey, which was closely linked with Fleury from its inception. The first prior of Ramsey was Oswald's friend Germanus, and for two years the famous Abbon of Fleury came to teach there. The result of all this was a whole new current of intellectual life in England. Finally, when about 970 a need was felt to impose some uniformity on the practices observed in the various English houses, the monks of Fleury and Ghent were called in to help draw up a concordance of rules in which the influence of the reformers of Lorraine and Cluny is evident.

By the end of the tenth century the extent of the achievement was clearly apparent. It was possible for the abbots of eighteen monasteries to attend the king at court simultaneously. Even so, the region which had once been Northumbria, the home of Bede and Alcuin, and was now the Danelaw, was not represented at the gathering. There had been no lack of efforts to re-establish monastic life in the area occupied by the Norsemen and these had met with no real hostility. But in a country barely emerging from paganism it was not easy to recruit local clergy, especially where the old monastic possessions had been taken over by the invaders and consequently could not provide the practical resources necessary to make a new start.

Despite these limitations the cultural life of the English monasteries was resumed with reassuring enthusiasm. *Scriptoria* were working at a speed that was more or less unique in Europe at the time. Before long the newly restored monasteries and churches were equipped with the Bibles, liturgical books and educational works they needed. Manuscripts in general were still written in the old insular hand, which actually reached perfection in the tenth century, but the Carolingian minuscule also made its appearance and had begun its conquest of England well before 1066. The art of illumination began to be revived under influences which can be traced back to the schools of Rheims and St Denis. But the pupils soon outdid their masters. By the beginning of the eleventh century, when books were once more being exported to the continent, the school of Winchester was famous for its work. The gift to Fleury, a little after 1000, of a benedictional written and illuminated at Ramsey becomes something of a symbol. A real literary and intellectual life had begun to make its appearance again in England.

Thus, in contrast to what had happened after the great invasions of the fifth century, the destruction was followed very quickly in western Europe by endeavours to repair the damage. There is no altogether satisfactory explanation of why this burst of energy should have occurred, but even where the ruination was irreparable it must be regarded as the main reason why the Carolingian heritage survived.

Certainly it would be unrealistic at this stage to ascribe anything to the inspiration of the sovereigns. Charlemagne's immediate successors had already abandoned any attempt to pursue his legislation in this field. There is nothing in the work of Otto I and his descendants to recall the great Carolingian capitularies. They did their best to attract learned men to their courts. A handful of clerks from Lorraine and Italy were to be found at the court of Otto I, men like Rathier of Liège, Stephen and Gunzo of Novara; and the king was assured of the services of Liutprand, bishop of Cremona, who had a knowledge of Greek and acted as ambassador to Constantinople. Otto II's marriage to Theophano also introduced into the court a few clerks who were acquainted with Greek culture such as the Italian John Philagathos. Still the most imposing figure was Otto I's brother, Bruno, who as a child had been taught by an Irish monk at Trèves and later became archbishop of Cologne. It was he, more than anyone else, who gave some intellectual interest to the court. Otto I was no more educated than Charlemagne, but he cared much less for anything to do with learning. Certainly his court never possessed the brilliance of Charlemagne's. Otto II was slightly better educated than his father but it was Otto III, fluent in Saxon, Latin and Greek, taught by worthy teachers and finally by Gerbert himself, who stood for the full flowering of this palatine culture. But in relation to the general culture of the time this was an effect rather than a cause.

There is little to be said of the remainder of the courts of the period. The court of western Francia, in particular, was tossed by the tide of events and continually short of money. It was not entirely devoid of culture. Hugh Capet sent his son Robert to study under Gerbert at Rheims. But this had no effect on the general picture of French intellectual life in the tenth century.

It was, in fact, the habits adopted during the Carolingian era, and absorbed into everyday life, by which culture was preserved. There are few instances of a disinterested taste for intellectual pursuits. But it was regarded as natural and even indispensable for every collegiate church (and cathedrals in particular) and every monastery to have its own school and therefore its own library in order to educate its young recruits who were often placed in the care of the community at a very early age. This had been Charlemagne's decree but it had probably never been anywhere near realization at the time, whereas there is some reason for thinking that by the tenth century it had become more or less general and hence that the number of clergy with some basic education was gradually increasing.

Consequently the majority of new foundations, especially monasteries, included the endowment of a school. Here and there a sense of religious responsibility might lead to a broader campaign against ignorance by the provision of external schools, open to clerics outside the community itself and even occasionally including a few laymen. The Italian abbot William of Volpiano, who settled in Dijon with a team of church builders and whose monks stood so much in awe of his inflexible sternness that they nicknamed him *Supra Regulam* (beyond the Rule), organized some teaching for the local clergy. Inevitably these schools formed a kind of hierarchy, some devoting themselves solely to providing children with an elementary education, while others aimed to dispense a fuller and more ambitious programme. Consequently a cleric who wanted to acquire more extensive knowledge might well find himself wandering from one school to the next.

Schools and libraries were still housed almost exclusively in the monasteries and, just as in the Carolingian age, cultural growth was intimately bound up with the growth of monasticism. Even in Charlemagne's time, however, some cathedral churches had played an important part. Secular churches were generally so burdened with parish duties that in order to act as intellectual centres they clearly needed to have a large enough body of clergy in residence and a way of life ordered in some respects according to the monastic pattern but without the same isolation from the world. Even before Charlemagne bishop Chrodegang had tried to introduce something of the kind in the cathedral of Metz. Towards the end of the tenth century there was a considerable increase in moves aimed at strengthening the framework of such chapters, and in particular at endowing them with a sufficient income. To some extent this development was connected with the first modest flowering of city life which has already been mentioned, in that a town with a busy and expanding life of its own was in a position to provide the men and materials to supply the chapter's needs.

But this was never a thing which happened spontaneously. Bishops with strong characters, many of them monastery-educated, were still needed. To cite only one example, Notger, bishop of Liège, who in fact appears never to have been a monk, had worked for several years in the imperial chancellery where he met many eminent men, Gerbert among them. Notger, a Swabian by origin, won the favour of Otto I and was elected bishop of Liège in 972. While accomplishing a good many missions on behalf of his benefactor's successors, he instigated extensive building in his good city of Liège and laid down the basis of the future principality. In his time as bishop, Liège possessed no less than seven collegiate churches; he also extended his protection to the nearby abbey of Lobbes, which was a busy intellectual centre. He took a lively interest in the teaching in the schools of Liège and was responsible for admitting the sons of serfs to the cathedral school. One of them, indeed, was to be the next bishop but two. He had his own pupils whom he would take with him on his journeys. In his time, Liège became one of the most brilliant of the episcopal seats of learning at the turn of the eleventh century.

With this sketch in mind the cultural map of Europe in the second half of the tenth century does not look so very different from that of the Carolingian era. A few houses of secondary importance had grown up in parts of France where there had previously been little activity, such as Angoulême, Aurillac, Brioude, and in particular Limoges in Aquitaine. Ripoll and Silos on the Spanish borders had benefited from the influx of Mozarabic monks, while much further north Mont St Michel was beginning to copy manuscripts. But on the whole Aquitaine and Provence on the one hand and Normandy and Brittany on the other were still large, blank spaces. Along the Loire, in Burgundy and in the region around Paris some of the old centres had survived and new ones had taken the place of those in decline, as we have seen with Tours and Fleury. Auxerre was still active and for one place like Ferrières, which had lost the inspiration provided by Loup, there were Dijon and Cluny to stand for the future. St Denis was falling into decay, but the episcopal school of Chartres was just coming to life. The busiest zone was still the northerly area which stretched from Rheims to St Amand and Cambrai. Across the Channel, the Anglo-Saxon renaissance was in sight.

As in the political field, it is interesting to note that a shift of balance had occurred in favour of the Germanic countries. The effects of the political awakening were especially clear in Saxony where the ravages of the Hungarians had been less serious. The monastery of Corvey, founded by Louis the Pious, benefited from the activities of a number of highly cultivated abbots, and the convents of Herford and Gandersheim saw to the education of the daughters of Saxon noblemen. The monastery of Fulda in Franconia continued to shine as brightly as ever and there was a flourishing episcopal school at Würzburg. In Swabia the monasteries of St Gall and Reichenau were still centres of the foremost importance (although the copying school at St Gall had lost something in the quality of its illumination), and Einsiedeln, founded in 934, was preparing to carry on their work. Most important of all was the rise of Lorraine, where monasteries and cathedrals vied with one another in their achievements. Trèves, Echternach, Cologne and Liège were the most brilliant of these seats of learning. In the north, the movement reached as far as Utrecht and up the Rhine to Worms, Spire and Strasbourg.

That leaves Italy, where the northern cities, such as Verona, Vercello, Cremona and Pavia were by far the most interesting. Rome was somewhat undistinguished. Further south, Monte Cassino was still on the eve of its greatest glory, but Naples and its environs offered exciting contacts with Muslim and Byzantine culture.

MEN, WORKS AND TRENDS

The time of Gerbert looks a great deal less rich in works of any major importance than that of Alcuin. It would be tempting to regard it as a desert with the towering figure of the scholar standing in splendid isolation. Such a view would be unjust. However individual his character may have been, Gerbert was none the less in many respects in harmony with the society which produced him and which he, in turn, influenced.

Not for nothing had the West remained in touch with the classical heritage as this had been pieced together again by the Carolingian renaissance, despite all the troubles, disasters and local failures which had occurred. There had been some diffusion, and sometimes even some deepening of culture. The clumsiness, naïvety and verbosity of so many documents constitutes in its own way a tribute to the fact that it was considered smart to be educated. The charters and declarations of the tenth century are vague and ill-composed but they also betray some fondness for the means of expression. Their authors indulged in endless preambles in order to display their flowery style and acquaintance with the best writers, and in particular with the Bible. The end would be weighed down with frightful curses on anyone violating its decrees, assuring them of the same fate as Judas and the greatest sinners of the Scriptures. It is not easy to picture present-day lawyers prefacing a contract of sale or a marriage settlement with lengthy considerations dotted with quotations from Shakespeare, Molière and Goethe. In all too many authors of literary works the same vanity made itself felt in tortuous conceits and obscure words dredged out of dictionaries. But this was the obverse side of a phenomenon which fortunately also had its advantages.

Just as in Carolingian times, there was a certain amount of reaction against the eager reading of classical authors of a scarcely edifying nature which occurred even in monasteries. The most touching example is that of a young novice named Sister Hrotswitha who had derived an education from a more or less haphazard perusal of the books contained in her convent library at Gandersheim in Hanover, but at the same time retained an endearingly naïve picture of Heaven. Her abbess, Gerberge, the niece of Otto I, encouraged her to write, and even to publish her work. Hrotswitha composed uplifting tales in verse which, though totally lacking in imagination, contained some very striking subjects. One dealt with the martyrdom of Pelagus thirty years previously in Cordova, which had been described to her by a Spaniard. Another told the story of Theophilus, a monk who sold his soul to the devil. This was originally a Greek tale, translated into Latin in the ninth century by the deacon Paul of Naples, and was later to acquire great popularity. It was a forerunner of the Faust story.

Struck by the popularity among clerks of the comedies of Terence, Sister Hrotswitha next conceived the risky idea of replacing them by Christian works which would satisfy the same literary tastes without exposing their audience to the same temptations. Consequently she delivered herself in rhyming prose of such works as *The Fall and Conversion of Mary the Niece of Abraham, The Conversion of Thais*, and others. For all their clumsiness, these pieces are not without a certain sprightliness and sometimes a good deal of comic instinct. Hrotswitha suffered some painful scruples of conscience in the process, since in order to exalt the triumph of Divine Grace over Sin she was obliged to include a number of love scenes. 'Many times I feel myself blushing with shame and embarassment,' she wailed,

for I cannot write in this manner without imagining and describing the hateful folly of the wicked lovers and the unclean delights of such speeches as our ears should refuse even to hear, but if I had avoided such situations out of modesty, I should not have achieved my end which was to show the beauty of innocence in all its glory.

Hrotswitha's temerity did not do her much good. Her concessions to Sin do not seem to have gained her many readers, or to have deprived Terence of many.

Even so, the example of Hrotswitha and Gerberge is interesting because it shows that educated women did exist in Germany. Another example is that of the Bavarian princess Hedwige who learned Greek in anticipation of her marriage to a Byzantine prince. The engagement fell through and she married a German who very soon left her a widow, where-

upon she consoled herself by studying Virgil under the direction of a monk of St Gall and by teaching Greek to one of
the pupils of the monastery.

Classical knowledge also seems to have made some progress
at this period. Some previously little-known works cropped
up in monastery libraries, such as the letters of Cicero at
Cluny and the Tibullus used by Heriger at Lobbes. Of the
works of Aristotle probably little more were to be found in
Europe than some Latin translations of the *Categories* and the
treatise *De interpretatione*. A manuscript of Fleury dating from
the second half of the tenth century contains various treatises
by Boethius on the first and second *Analytics*. This seems to
have been all that was known until the twelfth century, and
was apparently known as the 'new logic' to distinguish it
from the 'old logic' read in the ninth century.

Authors who were brought up on this classical literature
assimilated it so deeply into their system that they would use
the same turns of phrase in their own writing, even in their
most personal moments. This was especially the case with
Rathier, who, besides leading an extremely eventful life,
seems to have possessed an individual character which his
education enhanced rather than suppressed. Born at Liège at
the very end of the ninth century, he was educated at the
abbey of Lobbes; in 926 he accompanied a deposed bishop of
Liège on a journey into Italy. Here his scholarship attracted
attention and, while his master became archbishop of Milan,
Rathier himself received the see of Verona. But his leanings
towards the reform of the clergy, together with his own
aggressive and overbearing character, as well as the troubles
which were rending Italy at the time, forced him to spend
most of his time away from his diocese, either in prison, as a
refugee at Lobbes, or wandering about Italy. In 952 he was
summoned to the court of Otto I, where his merits were duly
appreciated. Bruno appointed him bishop of Liège, but this
proved another position he was unable to keep. He returned
to the king and followed him to Italy, where for some time he

re-occupied the see of Verona. Age had not improved his temper and he spent his last years in Lorraine, bundled from one monastery to another. He died at Namur at the age of eighty-five (974).

As in all else he did, he showed an immoderate fondness for classical authors and even went so far as to praise Plautus and Catullus in his sermons, and the vigour and flexibility of their style came naturally to him. His writings were cluttered with rare words and obscure references, but when he took the trouble to polish them, he was capable of producing a vivid and highly personal style. It is more than anything else this strongly individual sense of personality which makes him stand out from the Carolingian authors and even from those of his own time. In his *Confessional Dialogue* he catalogues his faults and confesses himself unworthy of his mission as a priest, bewailing his self-absorption, and, in the end, not daring to hope for divine forgiveness. Even when he was defending himself against his detractors he admitted sardonic-ally to an uncertain temper, an excessive fondness for books and an insignificant appearance. His tormented introspection never brought him the peace which men like St Augustine finally attained.

In some ways this passion for critical analysis led him to a subtle observation of facts and even to some amazing doubts. In the 'preamble' to a work which never saw the light he re-views the various personalities of a city – nobles and citizens, soldiers and merchants – and makes a detailed study of the particular Christian duties of each one. Meditating on the monastic rule of poverty and chastity, he wonders what would become of the world if all men followed it. His mind was full of confused flashes of insight, but he never used them to work out any practical plans for reform. Like Gerbert, he was one of those men whose minds moved beyond the Carolingian culture that had nourished them, but he lacked the balance, discipline and ability of his more fortunate contemporary.

The flowering of Greek culture and Greek monasticism in southern Italy, the ties formed by Otto I with Constantinople, and the presence of a Byzantine princess on the imperial throne all fostered some familiarity with the Greek language and with Byzantine literature. A certain Leo of Calabria was teaching Greek at Liège under bishop Notger. A long Latin poem stuffed with Greek words called the *Gest of Apollo* was composed in a German monastery and helped to diffuse a Greek tale, *The Story of Apollonius, King of Tyre*, although this had admittedly also been translated into Latin in the fifth century. The Naples area naturally became a focus for borrowings of this kind. The archpriest Leo of Naples made a Latin translation of the story of Alexander, the Greek text of which he had brought back from an embassy to Byzantium in 942. This was a work destined for immense popularity in Europe. Liutprand was another ambassador who acquired a far-reaching secular education at Pavia and entered the Church chiefly as a career. He went to Constantinople the first time on behalf of Berenger of Ivrea, king of Italy, with whom he afterwards quarrelled. He then took himself off to the court of Otto I, where he met a Mozarabic bishop from Elvire, an envoy to Otto from the caliph of Cordova, Abd al Rahman III, who encouraged him to write a history of his times. Liutprand's travels and contacts had indeed qualified him admirably to make this kind of broad survey, but his bitter and resentful turn of mind led him into painful digressions and prevented him writing the work he might have done.

Nevertheless he rose to an enviable position in the entourage of Otto I, who elevated him to the see of Cremona. It was he who translated into Latin the speech made by the emperor deposing the unworthy pope John XII. Five years later his knowledge of Greek got him the job of going to Constantinople to ask for the hand of a princess for Otto I's son. Nicephorus Phocas, who did not recognize the Saxon's imperial title, subjected Liutprand to every possible humiliation, imprisoned him and confiscated the bales of silk which the ambassador intended to take back with him to the West. He was laying himself open to a scholar's revenge. Liutprand was sufficiently conscientious to write an account of his mission, and drew in it a savage portrait of Nicephorus.

> He is a quite monstrous figure of a man, truly a pygmy, with a great head and little tiny eyes, like a mole's, his face distorted by a short, stiff beard, all thick and grizzled, and he is unfortunate in having a scrawny neck, no thicker than a finger. He has a shaggy appearance owing to the length and thickness of his hair. His skin is black, like an Ethiop's. . . . He has a great belly, shrivelled buttocks, long shanks out of all proportion to his height, short legs and stunted feet. He dresses in stinking ornaments, blackened with age, and womanish shoes on his feet. . . . He is insolent in his speech, like a fox in his cunning and a very Odysseus for perjury and lies.

We are unlikely to take a description so clearly motivated by dislike in the least literally, but even so it makes it difficult to read the praises lavished by Greek authors on their basileus with the same simple trust.

Even leaving aside his personal grudges, Liutprand's example makes it clear that contact between the Byzantine Empire and the West was on the whole restricted and somewhat unfriendly. There had been no actual schism between Rome and Constantinople, no fierce doctrinal hostility and no real missionary rivalry since 880, but this calm, which was further encouraged by the degenerate state of the papacy, was largely made up of mutual ignorance. When attempts at renewed contact were made in the middle of the eleventh century the result was disagreement and a schism which has remained until the twentieth century. Economic relations were rather more important, but chiefly in the way of introducing Byzantine art into Europe. In the domains of literature and ideas, therefore, there had been no great advance on the Carolingian era.

More interesting in the present context are the indications of an increased enthusiasm for science. Their significance should not be exaggerated, of course, but all the same they do show that Gerbert was not entirely alone in his time. We have already seen the way in which discussions of the Christian calendar in the Carolingian age had roused an interest in astronomy, which persisted in the tenth century. Heracles, bishop of Liège, had sufficient knowledge to reassure the soldiers of Otto I when they were terrified by a total eclipse of the sun by providing them with a rational explanation (22 December 968). Abbon of Fleury himself wrote a treatise of computation which contained some extremely sensible arguments. The school of Liège was full of enthusiasm for geometry, while Heriger of Lobbes wrote a treatise on the abacus. These studies have been connected with the embassy undertaken in 953 by the monk John of Gorze on behalf of Otto I to the caliph of Cordova. He spent some time in the city and frequented Mozarabic circles and it has been suggested, although there is no actual proof, that he brought back manuscripts.

Here and there were men still taking an interest in medicine. Notker the Physician, who was known as 'Peppercorn', taught basic medicine at St Gall, and Heribrand at Chartres. In England there was the *Leech Book of Bald and Cild*, a weird mixture of magic spells and superstition, but also containing a number of herbal remedies and prescriptions, some of which may have been brought back by pilgrims from Jerusalem. In southern Italy Salerno was developing fast. A Jew named Shabbethai ben Abraham ben Joel, better known as Donnolo, who had been captured by the Saracens of Palermo and had studied there for some time, wrote a Hebrew account of 120 different drugs, mostly vegetable, very few of which are of eastern origin. Salerno also seems to have retained something of its ancient tradition when it was famous for its cures. A number of early eleventh-century works mentioning drugs of eastern origin can probably be associated with this period of renewed activity. By about the middle of the same century the work of Constantine the African, the first great translator from Arabic into Latin, gave the real impetus to the school of Salerno.

One last aspect remains to be considered. The tenth century, like the ninth, undoubtedly possessed some literature in the vulgar tongue, intended to divert the leisure hours of kings and temporal lords. Practically nothing of this has survived. One of the very oldest Germanic poems, the *Ludwigslied*, composed to celebrate the victory of King Louis III over the Normans in 881, goes back as far as the end of the ninth century. Also to the ninth century belongs the Anglo-Saxon *Beowulf*. It was probably in the ninth century, too, that the first Latin version was made of the *Waltharius*, a transcription no doubt suitably edited for the use of monasteries of the amazing adventures of Walther, son of the king of Aquitaine, of Hildegunde, daughter of the king of the Burgundians and Hagen, son of the king of the Franks. It has been regretted that the 'Ottonian renaissance' – clearly a pale reflection of the Carolingian – should not have been accompanied by the production of works in German, or at least, of any that have survived.

What is however certain is that even the most eminent laymen of the time were ignorant of Latin, and that this appeared perfectly natural. No one blamed Otto I for having to use interpreters to speak to the pope or read his letters for him. Otto II had a broader education, but the author who depicts him making confession in Latin does so with a good deal of irony. Nevertheless, there was some dawning interest in mental stimulation among the mighty, and translations into the vulgar tongues were undertaken for their benefit.

The Notker who was known as Thicklips, or 'the German' (950–1022), to distinguish him from two other monks of St Gall with the same name, gives his own account of his work as a translator in a letter to the bishop of Sion in 1017. He translated the Psalms into German for the benefit of laymen and even began on a version of Pope Gregory the Great's famous commentary, the *Morality of Job*. But some acquaintance with the liberal arts being likewise necessary to a proper understanding of the Scriptures, Notker set himself to translate works by Boethius, Aristotle and even Virgil and Terence, only a few of which have survived.

Aelfric was educated at Winchester and wrote most of his works while head of the monastic school at Cerne Abbas in Dorset before 1005. He embarked on a translation of Genesis in response to a request from a pious alderman and wrote the lives of the saints who were particularly revered in English monasteries directly into Anglo-Saxon. Aelfric also composed homilies in the vulgar tongue, in which he was later followed by Wulfstan, archbishop of York. Aelfric is remarkable chiefly for the correctness and smoothness of his language. He had what at first sight seems the curious idea of translating Priscian's Latin grammar into Anglo-Saxon and applying its rules to his native language. To his mind, since reason was universal and common to all men, grammar ought to be the same in all languages. His efforts at least enabled him to give Anglo-Saxon a precision and literary merit it had not previously possessed.

French literature can boast of no works of the same importance. The fragments of a sermon on Jonah and a commentary on the Passion of Christ left by the tenth century are not comparable.

But it would be a great mistake to regard this attempt to make accessible to laymen the treasures hitherto reserved for those with a knowledge of Latin as the beginning of any major development of literature in the vernacular. Even Aelfric seemed anxious to define the limits of his work. The thought of numerous translations of the Bible filled him with nothing but foreboding. To his mind it was much better to make Latin more readily available to cultivated laymen, and it was with this object that he wrote his best-known work, a collection of imaginary dialogues in Latin and Anglo-Saxon, accompanied by a glossary of some 3,000 words. The superiority of Latin as a cultural language was no longer in doubt for Notker the

German, or even for the Saxon monk Widukind who lauded the glory of the Saxons and their duke-king Otto I outrageously – but in Latin.

In fact the arguments about the use of Latin or the vulgar tongues which had been a part of the Carolingian renaissance seem to have lost their edge. In some ways the tenth century may have been a period when nationalism was quietly growing, but no such feelings were carried over into the field of language and ideas. Latin as a literary language still held the forefront of the stage, and if some of the regularity and discipline of Latin grammar rubbed off on a few works in the vernacular, what is more certain is that this supremacy of Latin helped to retard the growth of national literatures. Clerks, wherever they had been born, continued to regard the Church as their country above all other, and its language, Latin, not as a foreign idiom but as the natural means to express their loftiest thoughts. Gerbert's cosmopolitanism and universalism were those of his time.

Chapter 5

GERBERT

GERBERT was not only the most remarkable man of the tenth century, he is also, fortunately, one of the best known. He took great care to keep a collection of all his letters, or at least of those he thought particularly important either in subject matter or literary merit. This collection has survived. It contains 220 letters, all written in his own hand although not all of them under his own name, since his epistolary talents were well known and kings and other great personages asked him to write letters for them. The letters are undated, but a great deal of painstaking research and scholarship, most willingly undertaken, has enabled historians to establish, with only a few minor uncertainties, a probable chronological order.

In addition one of Gerbert's best pupils, Richer, has left a touching and comparatively detailed picture of his master, which takes up a good deal of space in his *History of France*. Richer is not always as accurate as might be hoped, and he allows himself to be drawn into long digressions by his fondness for rhetoric, but all the same he is a useful and valuable witness.

Finally, we still possess a number of treatises by Gerbert which tell us little about the man but make it possible to assess his work.

GERBERT'S EVENTFUL LIFE

We must therefore return to the growing town of Aurillac and the monastery of St Gerald which had been restored to a stricter observance of discipline by Cluny. Of Gerbert's origins little is known except that he entered the monastery as a child. Richer states that he was 'a man of Aquitaine by birth'. A chronicle of Aurillac and the things he himself said agree in describing him as 'of humble origin', having 'neither birth nor fortune in his favour'. Then, and for several hundred years afterwards, the Church was almost the only means of social advancement.

The monastery of St Gerald was able to give him a sound grammatical education; Gerbert retained affectionate memories of his master Raimond, who later rose to be abbot, and sent him letters and books. 'After God', he wrote, 'I owe to him all that I am.' To judge from the pupil, his teaching seems to have been first-rate. It is strong evidence in favour of the culture which had been spreading since the Carolingian era.

In 967 we find the young Gerbert, who must then have been between twenty and twenty-five years old, setting out on the long road to Catalonia. It was the first journey in a life that was to bring him many more, but never back to the scenes of his youth. Aurillac was always to be for him a dream of peace and quiet, never the reality.

The three years from 967 to 970 were the formative years, in which he acquired an intimate knowledge of the subjects of the *quadrivium* which had been so neglected in Carolingian Europe. There have been some doubts as to whether Gerbert spent the whole time in Catalonia. The chronicler Adhemar of Chabannes in the eleventh century asserted that he visited Cordova and later legends depict him studying forbidden sciences and seducing the daughter of his Muslim host, but none of this is altogether to be believed. It is better to stick to Richer's statement that 'Gerbert made deep and rewarding studies in mathematics under the direction of bishop Atto [of Vich]'. Moreover Gerbert does not seem to have acquired the slightest knowledge of Arabic. Above all he could certainly have obtained all the education he wanted in Catalonia. Besides Atto, it is likely that he was taught by that curious individual the count-bishop Miro Bonfill (of Besalu and Gerona respectively), a clever writer who probably had some acquaintance with Greek, and Llobet of Barcelona, the translator of an Arabic work of astronomy from whom Gerbert later requested a copy of the book.

The Catalan monasteries certainly contained more than simply a few refined stylists. Ripoll, next door to Vich, then owned about 200 manuscripts in 'Visigothic' or Carolingian hands. Some of these contained marginal notes in Arabic designed to elucidate obscure passages in the Latin text which prove that their readers must have been more familiar with Arabic than Latin. Probably these were mozarabic monks who had settled at Ripoli. It was through them, and through the ambassadors and merchants who travelled between Barcelona and Cordova, that a great many Arabic works had been introduced and translated in a number of northern monasteries. One very fine manuscript from Ripoll is a *corpus* of Arabic treatises on astronomy and arithmetic. There is therefore no need to imagine Gerbert visiting Cordova.

From time to time Catalan counts, bishops and abbots would travel to Rome in order to lay various matters before the Pope. The request which count Borell and bishop Atto had to put to John XIII at Christmas 970 was a particularly important one. The great see of Tarragona had disappeared at the time of the Arab conquest and the Catalan bishoprics had subsequently been joined under the archbishops of Narbonne. Borrell and Atto were soliciting the creation of a new arch-bishopric centred on Vich. This meant nothing less than a divorce from the Frankish Church which would complete the more or less total political independence already acquired by the Catalan counties. What was in their minds to make Borrell and Atto decide to take young Gerbert with them to Rome?

At all events, their young protégé certainly made a strong impression. According to Richer:

The young man's intelligence and also his desire to learn did not go unnoticed by the Pope and since music and astronomy were at that time almost entirely unknown in Italy, he instantly communicated to Otto, king of Germany and Italy, through a legate, the arrival of a young man so admirably versed in mathematics and so well equipped to teach them. The king at once suggested that the Pope should detain the young man and prevent him by any means returning home.

Borrell and Atto had to leave without Gerbert. They had obtained the desired archbishopric but Atto did not live long to enjoy it. He was assassinated a few months later and the Catalan bishops remained attached to the see of Narbonne.

Since Otto I himself spent the Christmas festival of 970 in Rome, Gerbert probably met the emperor personally. The only favour he asked was to be allowed to go to Rheims in the company of the archdeacon Geran, an excellent teacher of logic, who was also on a visit to Rome as ambassador to the Pope from the king of France. This sacrifice of all other considerations to the love of learning stands to Gerbert's credit, although there are some historians who have depicted him as a schemer.

Gerbert spent nearly ten years in Rheims. He very quickly absorbed all that Geran had to teach him about logic. 'On the other hand', writes Richer, 'when Geran applied himself to the study of mathematics, he was so put off by the difficulties of the subject that he abandoned the pursuit of music.' Once he had become head of the episcopal school of Rheims, Gerbert fortunately had more gifted pupils. Leaving the elementary education of beginners to humbler teachers, he himself concentrated on the teaching of rhetoric and dialectic, before embarking on the *quadrivium* which was really his speciality. The pupils attracted from all parts by his fame included – besides Richer and the future king of France, Robert the Pious – Fulbert, head of the episcopal school, then bishop of Chartres; John, who led a similar career at Auxerre, and many clerks from Lorraine. Rheims seems to have been the first great cosmopolitan school, and others, more famous still, like Chartres, seem to have done no more than follow its

example. The archbishop, Adalberon, whose ambition it was
to make his cathedral a seat of learning, might be well satisfied
with Gerbert. A collaboration based on deep friendship grew
up between the two men.

Gerbert returned to Rome in 980 in the company of
Adalberon. At Pavia, on the way, they met Otto II, with
whom Gerbert appears to have had some acquaintance already.
It was then that an incident highly flattering to Gerbert took
place. The head of the school of Magdeburg, whose name was
Othric, jealous of his reputation and eager to conciliate the
emperor's favour in order to obtain the archbishopric of that
city, had accused Gerbert, on the basis of some incorrect
lecture notes, of a complete ignorance of philosophy. Otto
was delighted to arrange a public contest between the two
men, which Richer reports at some length since it redounds to
his master's credit. 'Having received rich gifts from the august
emperor, Gerbert returned to Gaul with his metropolitan,
covered with glory.'

But being noticed by the emperor had its disadvantages.
Gerbert's most difficult years were about to begin. Never
again would he know the peace he had enjoyed at Rheims, or
the opportunity to devote himself wholly to teaching and to
study. Early in 983 Otto II appointed him abbot of Bobbio, the
monastery founded by St Columban and famous both for its
library and its past cultural history. Now, however, it was
going through a difficult phase, its patrimony wasted and its
community divided against itself, united only in its hostility
to the new abbot. In addition, the abbot, as the king's vassal,
was obliged to give his services as counsellor and provide
military assistance which involved heavy expenses in time and
money. 'O tempora, o mores,' Gerbert complained, 'what
folk I live among!' However he set himself bravely to his task
and determined to remain ever loyal to the tie of vassalage
created between himself and Otto's family.

Nevertheless, when Otto II died suddenly at the end of the
same year, 983, after his defeat by the Saracens, Gerbert no

longer felt able to remain at Bobbio. Inevitably it was to Rheims he turned for refuge. But it was not long before further troubles brought out the man of action in him and he and Adalberon together played a decisive part in the events which followed. Both men fought to help the boy Otto III and his mother Theophano to triumph over the crisis which threatened to bring them down. They fought, too, to bring about the accession of Hugh Capet to the throne of France in 987.

Adalberon's death early in 989 left Gerbert alone in an awkward situation. With complete disregard of gratitude, Hugh Capet saw fit to disarm his adversaries by installing a bastard son of his Carolingian predecessor as archbishop of Rheims. But this archbishop, Arnoul, lost no time in betraying him. Complicated intrigues followed in which Gerbert was unwillingly involved. Finally, after Arnoul had been condemned and deposed by a Council of French bishops, Gerbert was elected in his place, only to find himself at odds with the Pope, who refused to recognize decisions taken without his authority. He defended himself eloquently before several Councils, but to no effect. His opposition to the marriage of his former pupil, king Robert the Pious, with a cousin, deprived him of his last support. Nothing remained for him but to relinquish the see of Rheims, since he could no longer remain there.

The obvious place to seek shelter after this was with Otto III, whom he had defended as a child and who was such an admirer of learning. During 997 – the last year unfortunately for which we have any remnants of his correspondence – the two men grew very close together. 'I am ignorant', Otto wrote,

and my education has been greatly neglected. Come and help me. Correct what has been ill done and advise me on the proper government of the Empire. Strip me of my Saxon boorishness and encourage the things I have inherited from my Greek forebears. Expound the book of arithmetic which you sent me.

Gerbert agreed gladly and promised: 'Greek by birth and Roman by Empire, you may claim as it were by hereditary right the treasures of Greek and Roman wisdom. Surely in that there is something divine?'

Gerbert stood on the brink of a new career, and these were the last, great years. His friendship with the young Otto III was practically unclouded. He went with him to Italy and they enlivened the long journey with endless talk. It was probably then, at the request of his imperial pupil, that Gerbert wrote his treatise *Of Rationality and the Use of Reason.* When Otto III finally gained control of Rome after a rising had undermined the authority of his cousin Pope Gregory V, one of his first acts was to secure Gerbert's election to the arch-bishopric of Ravenna which had been left conveniently vacant owing to the retirement of its previous incumbent (April 998).

Gerbert did not occupy this post for long. In February 999 Gregory V died suddenly and Otto III needed a reliable man to sit on the throne of St Peter, especially since he himself had fallen in love with the ancient capital of the Caesars and decided to settle there. Who was more loyal, learned and altogether worthy than Gerbert? So the humble son of a peasant family in Aquitaine became the heir of the Apostles, taking the name of Sylvester II in memory of the pope who, according to contemporary tradition, had baptized the Emperor Constantine and been entrusted by him with the government of the west. In doing so, he set the seal on a programme of close collaboration.

What would have happened if both men had lived longer? Obviously it is impossible to say. We know some of the acts of Sylvester II, such as the disdainful pardon granted to his old rival Arnoul, now reinstated in the see of Rheims – with the rider that 'your conscience may perhaps be troubled by some remorse' – and the crown despatched to the Hungarian prince Vajk, newly made king and newly converted Christian under the name of Stephen. While Sylvester II guided the affairs of

Christendom from the Lateran, Otto III took up residence on
the Aventine, modelling his court on the ceremonial Byzantine
pattern and leaving it only on hasty visits to re-establish order
in Germany or spend a brief period of retreat in the company
of St Nilus. But the Romans loved neither the German
emperor nor the foreign pope. Early in 1001 both were driven
from Rome by an uprising and forced to wander about Italy,
spending a few weeks in Ravenna and hovering within easy
distance of Rome although the city was still not ready to re-
open her gates to them. At the end of January 1002, Otto III
was carried off by a fever within the space of a few weeks. He
was twenty-two years old. His body was smuggled hastily
back to Germany through hostile country. Sylvester II was
permitted, at the cost of humiliating concessions, to return
to Rome and end his days in peace. In May 1003 he in turn
rendered up his soul to God.

A TENTH-CENTURY HUMANIST

Gerbert was a humanist in the direct line of descent from
the moving spirits of the Carolingian renaissance, but he also
shared the attitudes and prejudices peculiar to his own time.
It is important to take both these aspects equally into account.

Like Alcuin and Loup of Ferrières, Gerbert was tireless in
the pursuit of manuscripts, which indicates that the contents
of libraries were still extremely inadequate. The discovery of
the library at Bobbio with its wealth of classical poets, orators
and philosophers as well as religious authors, was like a miracle
to him. Nevertheless, while at Bobbio he did not forget the
more modest collection at Rheims. 'Let the Pliny be corrected',
he wrote, 'send Eugraphius to us, and have copies made of the
manuscripts which are at Orbais and St Basle . . .' He probably
intended to arrange an exchange of books between Bobbio
and Rheims although he did not have time to put this into
practice. Back in Rheims, he was still secretly bribing a monk
of whose loyalty he was certain:

One thing only I would ask of you most pressingly, which will put you into no danger or hurt and will further strengthen the bonds of friendship between us. You know how eagerly I seek for books everywhere, and you know also how many copyists there are in the towns and countryside of Italy. To work then, unknown to any, and obtain for me transcriptions of the astronomy of Manlius [Boethius], the Rhetoric of Victorinus and the treatise of Demosthenes [Filalet] on ophthalmia. I pledge myself, brother, to preserve an inviolable silence on the service you shall render me. Anything you spend I will repay with interest when and where you instruct me.

After this he was constantly begging for manuscripts, and was able to offer in exchange one of the instruments which he alone knew how to make. Thus, when Remi of Trèves asked him to send a sphere for the teaching of astronomy, Gerbert demanded in return a good copy of the *Achilleis* of Statius. But he was unaware that the poem was unfinished and, believing the copy he received was incomplete, he punished Remi by sending him a sphere only of painted wood and not covered in leather. He disliked lending his own manuscripts and was furious if the borrowers were slow to return them. To the monks of St Peter of Ghent he wrote, paraphrasing Cicero:

How long will you continue to abuse our patience? You talk of charity and are prepared to rob us. . . . You violate the laws of God and man. . . . Give it back!

Even the great sixteenth-century humanists were not more avid in their search for books.

But in one respect Gerbert was different. Alcuin and nearly all the great teachers of the Carolingian age had been primarily grammarians. Gerbert, however, could leave the task of providing a basic grammatical education for the young to elementary teachers, and in his own teaching of the *trivium* placed the accent on logic and rhetoric. By great good fortune we have Richer's word for this. Gerbert dealt with logic or dialectic comparatively fully, including of course the texts of

Boethius and, through him, of Aristotle, discovered in the
tenth century, with an introduction supplied by Porphyry's
Isagoge. Basically nothing was to be added to this syllabus
until Abelard. Gerbert also used the same methods as his
successors up to and including the thirteenth century: a reading of the text, interpolated with commentaries, whether his
own or borrowed from earlier philosophers, and followed by
discussion. With a practicality all his own, Gerbert wanted his
pupils familiarized with all the subtleties of argument and,
writes Richer, 'he entrusted them to a sophist to give them
practice in debating'. This kind of mental acrobatics, artificial
though it may appear to us, taught flexibility and discipline to
still largely uncultivated minds. Gerbert's own treatise *Of
Rationality and the Use of Reason* provides an example of these
exercises. The argument, to quote Etienne Gilson, 'deals with
the logical validity of the proposition that rationality involves
the use of reason in which, contrary to the rules, the predicate
seems less universal than the subject'. Gerbert extricates himself by basing his argument on the Aristotelian distinction
between power and action.

Man always has the power to be a reasonable being since this is a
fundamental attribute of his nature, but he does not always make use
of his reason in his actions. The use of reason is thus an accidental
fact and since the accident may be an attribute of the substance, it is
legitimate to say that the rational being makes use of reason. [Chr.
Pfister.]

Labours of this kind, although they have their uses, are still
a somewhat limited field. Gerbert never rose above this logic.
For him there was no question of constructing an original
philosophy. The time was not yet ripe. What has been called
his philosophy was an eclecticism in which the Christian belief
in Providence was mixed up with classical concepts about the
creation of the universe, freedom and the destiny of mankind.
Even so, there was nothing desiccating about his teaching of
logic because, by linking it closely with rhetoric, he made of
it an art of reasoning and persuasion.

Gerbert did give his pupils a first-hand knowledge of the Latin poets Virgil, Horace, Lucan, Statius, Terence, Persius and Juvenal, whose manuscripts he was particularly interested in finding. He was not unduly concerned to eliminate passages which shocked most people by their superstition and immorality. He taught his followers to write speeches, and his pupil Richer peppers his *Histories* with them, in the manner of Sallust. 'He wished them', Richer says emphatically, 'to express themselves with such art that it might seem that they spoke without the aid of art, which is the supreme perfection of an orator.' These were more than sterile academic exercises. His own effective and well-constructed speeches, for example in defence of his right to the archbishopric of Rheims, the vivid and accomplished letters he wrote in support of the cause of Otto III or of Hugh Capet, were the source of his influence over minds that, while less powerful and practised than his own, were yet sensible of the superiority of a brilliant and logical mind. It is this connexion between his teaching and his actions which strikes us most forcibly today, just as it won him the devotion of his original pupils.

Gerbert was an outstandingly good teacher in a fuller, more profound and more personal sense of the word than a man like Alcuin. He possessed an all-round knowledge (including a scientific reputation which will be discussed in the next chapter) and a natural talent for teaching which led him, for example, to collect the substance of his courses in rhetoric into a table covering twenty-six sheets of parchment sewn together, as well as a tireless urge to increase his own learning for the benefit of his pupils. 'I teach what I know, and what I do not know I learn.' Lastly, there was the shining example of his own genius.

Gerbert's love of classical authors brought him heavily under fire. On one occasion, when he reproached the Romans for their ignorance, the papal legate answered him roundly that: 'Since the world began, God has chosen, not orators and philosophers but peasants and illiterates.' He astonished people by seeking consolation in philosophy rather than in prayer. 'In the greatest torment and trouble only philosophy can offer any comfort.' In his worst moments of anxiety caused by the struggle over the archbishopric of Rheims he would try to find peace in reading Cicero. After Cicero, his model was Boethius, who had written his stoical *Consolations of Philosophy* while under sentence of death. His ideals were 'honesty', moderation and mastery of the passions by the exercise of reason and culture. He pursued this classical gravity even in his literary style which, in its sobriety and conciseness, stands in vivid contrast to the practice of his time.

All this is true, but it should not be allowed to throw any doubts on the sincerity of Gerbert's faith. He proclaimed his absolute orthodoxy in no uncertain terms at the time of his accession to the see of Rheims. He believed in combining faith with reason. 'The Divinity', he wrote, 'made a great gift to men in giving them faith while not denying them knowledge. The just man lives by faith but knowledge must be joined to it, since those who do not possess it are called fools.' Without meaning to overshadow Gerbert (who was not in the least a mystic) it is worth recalling the character of St Augustine who was also brought up on classical culture and who undoubtedly influenced Gerbert. In him Christian feeling and classical wisdom were indissolubly mixed, and to stress one at the expense of the other would be to do him an injustice.

It is therefore not surprising that he should have combined this classical culture with a deep-rooted admiration for the ideal of empire. This was as true of Gerbert as it had been of Alcuin. Both men applied this ideal to their own times through their esteem for one man who stood for the empire incarnate. Gerbert's belief in Otto II as 'superior to all the princes of our time in arms, in counsel and in learning' was in no way feigned. After Otto's death he fell back on the belief in a brotherly coexistence between the Christian kingdoms, facilitated by the family ties between their rulers. Not until the young Otto III had proved his valour against the Slavs and demonstrated his love of learning did he consider the youthful prince's hereditary claims to be justified by his own merits. There could be no Empire without a man strong enough to lead it.

Moreover there could be no question of a universal empire like that of ancient Rome, or even of Charlemagne. The test of time had revealed the irreparable nature of the break which had occurred under Louis the Pious. Gerbert, though he has sometimes been unjustly accused of being a utopian and a dreamer, was perfectly well aware of this. The concept he finally arrived at was of a moral control over the kings by the pope and the emperor acting in concert. Hence, when Robert the Pious wrote to Sylvester II for advice on the ecclesiastical affairs of his kingdom, the letter was passed to Otto III for his opinion. On the same principle, after the conversion of Hungary, Sylvester II preferred to send Stephen a crown of his own rather than join his lands to the kingdom of Germany. Here, by about the year 1000, lay the one real chance that a Roman Empire with some pretensions to universality might yet survive.

GERBERT AND THE FIRST STEPS IN WESTERN SCIENCE

To begin with, Gerbert's scientific work poses some critical problems. How many of the numerous works later attributed to him are in fact his own? What, on the other hand, were his sources and did he confine himself to reproducing facts already to be found in Latin authors such as Boethius in particular, or did he borrow from Arabic science? The work of the Russian scholar Bubnov as far back as 1899 went some way towards settling opinion on the first point. On the second, more recent research on Ripoll and its medieval library has made possible a closer estimate of what Gerbert owed to translations of Arabic works then in the possession of the monastery.

In order to initiate his pupils he had an armourer make for him an abacus, that is a board divided into compartments. It was divided lengthways into twenty-seven sections in which Gerbert arranged his nine figures which were to express all numbers. He made, in addition, a thousand horn symbols with the same figures which could be transposed about the twenty-seven compartments of the abacus in such a way that it was possible to multiply and divide a host of numbers so quickly that, given their extreme abundance, the operation could be completed mentally in less time than it had taken to set it up.

This is Richer's account of Gerbert's most important arithmetical achievement. For the rest, he refers to a treatise written by Gerbert at the request of Constantine, a monk of Fleury, which is also extant.

Gerbert's abacus was quite different from the counting frames used by the Romans, and from anything described in the authentic text of Boethius. A description attributed to this author is in fact a later interpolation. It was basically an Indian system handed on through the Arab world and it seems highly probable that Gerbert was the first to introduce it to the West. Horn counters marked with signs representing the various figures were placed in the columns corresponding to units, tens and hundreds, each time in a particular order: units, thousands, millions, and so forth. In this way a new system of enumeration by position was arrived at. There seems to have been no symbol for zero, the space where it belonged being merely left empty. With this table it was possible to carry out calculations with great speed whatever the length of the numbers involved.

Multiplication was done very much as it is today. The only operation which still presented any real difficulty was division. Gerbert devoted a great deal of attention to this and in 984 he wrote to bishop Miro Bonfill asking him to send a treatise, *Of the Multiplication and Division of Numbers*, by one Joseph the Spaniard. The method most generally employed was that of division 'by difference' which consists in taking into account the round figure (10, 100 or 1,000) immediately above the divisor and the difference between this figure and the divisor.

The modern formula (taking as an example the figure 100) would be:

$$\frac{a}{b} = \frac{a}{100} + \frac{\left(\dfrac{a}{100}\right)(100 - b)}{b}$$

The working involves a series of reductions, as shown by the following table. For example to divide 3,026 by 83:

	thousands			units		
	C	X	I	C	X	I
Difference: 100 — 83 = 17					1	7
Divisor: 83					8	3
Dividend: 3026		3			2	6
$\frac{3000}{100} = 30.$ $30 \times 17 = 510$				5	1	
Take out the three from 3000. 26 + 510				5	3	6
$\frac{500}{100} = 5.$ $5 \times 17 = 85$					8	5
Take out the 5 from 500. 36 + 85 =				1	2	1
$\frac{100}{100} = 1.$ $1 \times 17 = 17$					1	7
Take out the 1 from 100. 17 + 21 = ...					3	8
Incomplete quotients: 30 + 5 + 1 = ...					3	6

Immense mathematical possibilities were immediately opened up. It still remained to overcome the difficulties raised by the lack of a decimal point or any convenient method of indicating fractions. But the first steps had been taken. To some extent it can be compared with the progress made in our own day by the invention of calculating machines.

Gerbert's teaching of geometry was probably less of a novelty for his pupils. Richer has little to say about it and there has been some doubt cast on the attribution to Gerbert of a treatise, *Of Geometry*. He appears to have been content to repeat the facts given by Boethius, taking a special interest in problems involving triangles, and to have been familiar with Euclid and Pythagoras only through Boethius.

In music, too, he produced nothing very remarkable. We still possess one short treatise he wrote for the monk Constantine, and Richer mentions that 'he could make the different notes perfectly clear upon the monochord, dividing their consonances and their symphonies into tones and semi-tones, into di-tones and into sharps and methodically separating the tones into sounds'. There was nothing here that Gerbert could not have found in the musical work of Boethius, of which a manuscript existed at Ripoll. But was he more than a theorist? Did he compose a hymn to St Michael and was he able to manufacture organs as he was later credited with doing? All that can be said is that his practicality and manual dexterity make it seem quite possible. But Gerbert played no part in any of the really interesting musical developments of the ninth, tenth and eleventh centuries such as the first essays in polyphony, codified in the late ninth century by Hucbald, a monk of St Amand, or the attempts at musical notation by neumes which culminated in the first half of the eleventh century in the work of Guido of Arezzo.

Gerbert also took an interest in medicine and was responsible for the copying of medical manuscripts. He seems to have passed on his interest to his pupil. The only journey Richer ever made in his life (and he left a highly picturesque account of it) was from Rheims to Chartres to study under a monk who was an expert in medicine, and he never failed to pepper his *Histories* with more or less lurid accounts of the diseases which killed off kings and great men.

But Gerbert's work in astronomy towered above all this, and it was that in particular which fascinated Richer and amazed his contemporaries. Gerbert's picture of the universe was not a new one: it was the theory of Ptolemy handed down and elaborated by the Arabs. From the Arabs also

Gerbert, with his strong practical sense, borrowed the use of instruments with which to demonstrate the universe and observe the movements of the stars. He personally supervised the making of a wooden sphere, turning on the axis of the poles on which were painted the constellations – Ptolemy, it will be remembered, saw the universe as a total sphere, the most perfect of all. Gerbert also constructed armillary spheres, made up of a number of large hoops showing the parallels (the equator, the tropics and the poles) and the ecliptics. Inside, on the ecliptic plane, 'the circles of the planets' were suspended 'by a very ingenious mechanism'.

Lastly, there was a hollow sphere equipped with a number of tubes which directed the eye to the poles and other accurate points.

Richer is tireless in his praise.

To the general astonishment, he succeeded in making clear this almost inaccessible science by means of certain instruments. ... So divinely constructed was this apparatus that even those who knew nothing of the science could, if they were only shown one of the constellations, recognize all the others on the sphere without the aid of a master ...

Gerbert was asked to make his famous spheres for other schools and took advantage of it to obtain the manuscripts he wanted in exchange.

In the second half of the treatise *Of Geometry* there is a description of the astrolabe. Unfortunately this text cannot be definitely ascribed to Gerbert, but even so it is highly probable that he was familiar with the instrument, which had been perfected by the Arabs, and that he helped to diffuse its use. The astrolabe can be used to obtain a picture of the world by stereographic projection and at the same time as a direction finder. It is in the form of a disc with the celestial and terrestrial spheres with their cardinal points on one side, and on the other a revolving rule to the ends of which are attached copper plates through which a slit has been pierced. Through these slits the eye is directed towards the star to be observed and the position of the rule in relation to the gradations of the disc indicates its height. The whole instrument can be held comfortably in the hand by means of a ring. It is sufficient for the observer to know the position of one point in the sky in relation to himself in order to obtain by the use of the astrolabe a complete picture of the world at any given moment. In this way a great many problems could be resolved.

It would be easy to despise the elementary nature of these scientific ideas which Gerbert in any case was largely content to borrow from his predecessors. But in order to appreciate more fully their worth it is better to look at them in their historical context. What gave Gerbert his originality in a society in love with abstractions was his liking for the concrete and his manual dexterity. It was this which enabled him to comprehend, and pass on to others, knowledge which seemed new and astonishing. It should also be said that it was this basis which made possible all later scientific development.

The amazement and admiration which Gerbert's teaching aroused in his lifetime very soon gave way to malicious incomprehension. Less than a century after his death a legend had begun to grow up which continued to be elaborated until the middle of the twelfth century, when William of Malmesbury produced a highly coloured version of it. According to this story, Gerbert was educated at Fleury, and fled from there to Muslim Spain to study the forbidden sciences. There, having seduced the daughter of his Saracen host, he stole from him, with her assistance, a book which 'contained all that is to be known'. After this he swore an oath of perpetual fealty to the devil and by his wicked devices was able to ensnare the minds of his pupils and achieve a successful career, culminating in the pontificate. In Rome, by the use of necromancy, he managed to discover treasures buried long ago by the Gentiles. He had cast for him a statue of a human head which would answer any questions. When he finally died, he gave orders for his body to be chopped in pieces. The legend died hard. Scholars in the eighteenth century began to uncover the personality which lay behind it. Even so, Victor Hugo in the *Légende des Siècles*, still pictured Gerbert as 'a soul given up to sinister adventures'.

Chapter 6

CONCLUSION

THE tenth century does not enjoy a particularly splendid reputation among historians, who persist in regarding it as a period of general insecurity and feudal anarchy, a 'century of iron'. It is certainly true that it cannot have been a very pleasant time to be alive, except for a powerful minority: the mass of humble folk saw the protection they could look for from the State vanishing away and the burden of lordly demands growing ever greater.

In the cultural field, the brilliant part played by the first Carolingians as initiators found no echo in the tenth century. Fortunately the need was less great than it had been at the end of the eighth. But literary production cannot be compared, either in quantity or quality, with the harvest raised by Charlemagne's efforts. In such fields as Biblical exegesis, the period from the ninth to the twelfth centuries remains a huge blank.

And yet the time of Gerbert was not altogether without significance. The new renaissance of the twelfth century would have been inconceivable but for this long, dark period between it and its Carolingian forerunner – a period of maintenance, deepening and even in some respects of innovation.

The infrastructure of scholarship, the prime importance of which Charlemagne had grasped, had been maintained and now appeared as one of the daily necessities. Although destroyed here and there, it was enthusiastically rebuilt and spread to other regions with the building of new monasteries. The deepening was marked chiefly by a few highly gifted individuals, men like Abbon of Fleury, Rathier of Liège and Gerbert, but it was also enough to free them from the need to devote a part of their teaching to elementary ideas of

grammar. There was innovation, to the extent that first
contacts with the eastern world, then at its cultural height,
fostered an interest in the sciences and introduced some new
thought processes, very elementary as yet but still of basic
importance.

In spite of all this it would be an exaggeration to speak, as
some historians have done, of yet another renaissance in the
tenth century. These developments were not nearly far-
reaching enough to justify such an expression. The legacy
of classical times was a little better known, but in no way
renewed. Intellectual life remained the province of a small
minority which grew little larger, and the monasteries
remained the principal seats of learning. Relations between
England and the continent had been reversed and the Germanic
countries played a more important role. But the time of
Gerbert brought no deep-seated changes either in the kind
of culture, its social roots or its geographical distribution. We
must not try to out-run the still slow and hesitant pace of
history.

PART THREE

The Time of Abelard

ON 15 July 1099 the Crusaders took Jerusalem by storm. After three years of wearying campaigns and bitter, indecisive fighting they reached their goal at last and all feelings of humanity were swamped in them by exultation in the hard-won victory. Drenched in the blood of countless innocent victims, they made their way to the Holy Sepulchre to pray, with tears of joy, to Him who had shed his own blood for mankind.

On 10 July 1099, five days before their triumph, a man died at Valencia in Spain, bowed less with age than with the burden of glory. Rodrigo Diaz de Vivar, famed throughout the centuries as El Cid, cannot have been more than fifty-five, but he was prematurely aged by his hard life. Twice he had driven back from the walls of the Levantine city the Almoravid armies that meant to bring all Spain back under the dominion of Islam. Now his heroic wife Jimena could only carry his body back to Castille, leaving Valencia wide open to the Almoravids.

These were harsh times, full of war and violence which those in authority, especially in the Church, were doing their best to deflect from Christendom by turning it against the Infidel. In this they were partly successful and in the process gave the young forces of Europe a chance to try their strength. It was also a period of great advances in the intellectual history of mankind, one which historians this time are almost unanimous in describing as the twelfth-century renaissance.

In about the same year of 1099, a young man called Peter – later to be known as Abelard – left the country of his childhood and made his way to Paris. He was born about 1079 in the village of Pallet on the road to Clisson a few miles south-east of Nantes, amid green, rolling countryside to which the neat hedgerows enclosing the fields gave a wooded aspect.* His father, Bérenger, although only a humble knight, was able to boast a fairly wide education. He was anxious to pass this on to his children, so they received instruction, probably from a private tutor. His literary studies made a deep impression on Peter Abelard, and he wrote later that he owed his strong intelligence and wayward character to 'the virtues of his native soil or of the blood which ran in [his] veins'. As the eldest son, he would normally have been destined for a military career, but his father had the good sense not to stand in the way of his vocation, and so, in our hero's own words, 'I abandoned the court of Mars to seek shelter in Minerva's bosom'. He studied for some time at Loches but the region had little to offer in the way of further study and he set out for Paris, where he was not long in attracting notice.

First, as we have already done for Alcuin and Gerbert, let us take a look at the setting in which Abelard lived and worked. His death in 1142 came within a year or two of the completion of such important works as the *Eptateuchon* of Thierry of Chartres (1141) and the *Concord of Discordant Canons* of Gratiano of Bologna (c. 1140). The general period to be dealt with is therefore the first half of the twelfth century.

* It is arguable that these hedgerows did not become numerous until the twelfth and thirteenth centuries and that the landscape with which Abelard was familiar as a child more closely resembled an open field. The matter is open to doubt.

Chapter 1

THE AWAKENING OF THE WEST

FROM the middle of the eleventh century the signs of a wide-spread awakening and progress which had long been coming to fruition were becoming increasingly marked. A greater number of peasants were learning to make better use of the land and reclaiming huge areas of forest, heath and marshland. Suburbs were springing up around the old cities and hundreds of new villages came into being. Society was becoming more diversified and life held a few more comforts. There was progress in education and culture, and western Europe was impressively dotted with shrines. Vigorous expansion was taking place on the frontiers of Spain and in the East. Nations were in process of formation, and security increasing slowly. Taken as a whole, all these symptoms, which continued to appear at least until the end of the thirteenth century, suggest to the historian a decisive change in the shape of Europe.

The absence of sufficient accurate documentary evidence – virtually no figures are available – makes it more difficult to grasp this development in its detailed chronological sequence. The picture we have to draw from it now is that of the half century or so of Abelard's lifetime.

THE FIRST STEPS IN ECONOMIC PROGRESS

Inadequate farming techniques, poor yield and inefficient use of the land had condemned the world of Charlemagne – a small minority only excepted – to live with the threat of famine and the reality of malnutrition. Before any futher progress was possible there had to be an improvement in the standard of agriculture.

Supposing we had a time machine to allow us a glimpse of

the countryside at the beginning of the twelfth century, the thing which would strike us most would be the number of forest clearings. Except for a few already reasonably heavily populated areas, most of the cultivated land around the villages was surrounded by more or less dense forest and by stretches of scrubland. On the edges of this the peasants would burn off a patch of green from time to time and raise a harvest or two on the ground fertilized by the ashes before letting it grow wild once more. Now, at last, they were beginning to incorporate their gains permanently into the acreage under cultivation, concentrating chiefly on the hitherto virgin soil of damp hollows and bands of heavy clay. Little by little their labour reduced the waste land to a few straggling plots on the outskirts of the villages, incidentally improving communications with the neighbouring hamlets. By about 1150 this expansion of the old territories was in full swing. For the most part it was the work of anonymous peasants, busy rounding off their own small plots, sometimes unknown to their lord. This kind of clearance was especially common in England.

Elsewhere vast areas of woodland still survived, in the forests of the Paris basin, the Ardennes and Saxony. Here some kind of starting point had to be made for people's endeavours, and this was the task of the lords, who as masters of the land were able to attract settlers with offers of enfranchisement, grants of land, exemption from statutory labour or reductions of the usual tithes. Ultimately, though, they still stood to gain from the improvements made. Many of these villages in clearings had been founded in the eleventh century by churches which offered the tillers the protection of 'God's peace' within the area of a 'sauveté' bonded by crosses planted in the ground. Secular lords and even kings had soon followed their example, eager to have their share of the still unpopulated regions, or to plant villages along the principal roads of their domains.

In other regions the fight against the coastal marshes had begun. The Flemish coast, Zeeland and Holland were turning into busily populated areas, thanks to the many dykes and canals which had been built during the eleventh century, and Dutch settlers were beginning to carry their experience farther afield.

The considerable increase in the surface area under cultivation should not make us blind to other, less spectacular developments, which followed on from it and often helped to make it possible. Much of the soil now being exploited was very rich. The peasants had better tools and were able to cultivate land which had previously been too heavy for men to work, but which in the end often proved to be the richest. This was less a matter of new inventions than of a more general distribution of those already known, and of the increased use of metal to make them more effective. Certainly the plough was now in general use. This asymmetrical implement, able to cut a deep furrow and throw aside the earth turned by the coulter, was a great deal more practical than the old swing-plough for working heavy soils. It also helped to re-fertilize the ground by bringing the underlying humus to the surface. The water mill had been known since ancient times but the irregular flow of rivers in the Mediterranean and the plentiful availability of labour had served to limit its use. Now, along calmer streams and in the more temperate Atlantic climate, they became numerous, grinding the corn much more efficiently than the old mills worked by human or animal power. People were beginning to use them, too, to crush bark for tanning and seeds for oil, and to drive a number of machines. The first windmills also began to make their appearance.

The peasants were also beginning in a clumsy, groping fashion, and with many setbacks, to experiment with crop cycles that were more ambitious than the old two-yearly rotation of autumn-sown crop one year followed by a fallow period the next – a system enforced by the dry Mediterranean summers. On the best soils they successfully alternated spring-sown grain, barley and oats. This was the beginning of the three-year crop rotation which allowed for a greater variety of produce and reduced the non-productive acreage still further. Moreover oats was better food for the horses which were now being used more widely in farming, and which, because they were faster than oxen and could therefore do more, also helped to produce an increased yield.

These advances should not be overestimated. The plough was a heavy implement which needed four, six or even eight animals to pull it, and the mill was still owned exclusively by the lords of the manor or the wealthiest peasants. The improvements in cultivation and in harvests were chiefly to be found in the rich plains of northern Italy and northern Europe.

All the same, the results were there. The peasants were better fed, less afraid of famine and able to bring up more children. Demographic increases led in their turn to the search for more land and better harvests, which might even enable a peasant family, once its own modest needs had been satisfied and the proper dues paid to the lord and the Church, to keep a little over, and this at the cost of comparatively lighter toil. In this way more men were released from the gruelling labour of the fields and freed for other tasks.

One consequence of these changes and of the increased population was the growth of the towns which form such a striking part of the pattern of Europe at the dawn of the twelfth century. New quarters were springing up outside the walled enclosures of the old Roman towns – for so long half-asleep – filled with merchants and craftsmen. Many of them came to settle only for the winter and at the first hint of fine weather they would be off again on their travels in search of custom. Elsewhere, particularly in northern Europe, whole new cities appeared, sometimes according to a deliberate plan of some powerful figure but more often simply growing up piecemeal around a castle, monastery or bridge.

These towns were, it is true, still semi-rural in their atmosphere. Craftsmen would devote part of their time to working in the fields, and the town was at its busiest at the time of the

corn or cattle market. But industries were growing in importance. The textiles produced in the Low Countries and in
northern Italy were beginning to find distant markets. Merchants from Flanders and Artois would turn up periodically
in Champagne, their pack animals laden with fine cloth, or
bring to life the rising fairs of Provins and Troyes. Such
traders were still regarded with some suspicion, but already
they were protected on the roads by the more enlightened of
the nobility. Bridges were being built. The increase in trade
meant more money had to be minted. Kings, lords and
churches delved into their coffers to supply it and brought
out the treasured but little-used stocks of silverware left them
by earlier generations.

THE DEVELOPMENT OF SOCIETY

In different ways and to a varying degree these economic
changes affected all classes of society.

Once again it was the peasants who reaped the least benefit;
and yet even here a good many changes were to be seen. The
ties which bound so many humble tenant farmers to the
masters of the land they farmed were, on the whole, relaxing.
The masters were beginning to make fewer demands in terms
of work done with evident reluctance and to ask instead for
rents which could be used to pay wages. As time went on the
peasant would be free to give nearly all his time to his own
fields, the majority of which would normally be handed
down from father to sons. The poorest, the impoverished
tenants, younger sons and farm labourers, were tempted to
become new settlers elsewhere and in some cases the lord of
the manor would be compelled to agree to an equivalent
'enfranchisement' in order to keep enough workers on his
old lands. In this way a degree of liberty began to infiltrate
the peasants' world in however modest and pragmatic a
fashion.

Taking into account the increase in population, the rise in

the standard of living was probably not very noticeable. Those who benefited were chiefly the few peasants already well enough off to acquire a plough and animals to draw it. It was they who obtained the best harvests and sold their surplus to the nearest town; they who broadened their lands and employed less fortunate hands to labour on them.

The peasants as a whole were still rough, primitive, ignorant and despised. Documents even of a much later date still contain contemptuous references to the 'great coal-black lout' and to the ragged garb of the villein.

Twelfth-century texts make a distinction between the 'citizens' of cities and towns and the labouring masses. A growing number of craftsmen and shopkeepers were employed in providing cloth, shoes and victuals for the ever-increasing urban population, and in building houses and basic furniture. As soon as the mud and snows of winter gave way to milder weather, tradesmen would take to the roads, travelling, for preference, in armed convoys for protection against the robber barons and other bandits who still infested the roads. They carried their own goods far afield or went in search of the other things – salt, wine, precious stuffs or knick-knacks – which were lacking at home, selling their wares in markets or offering them to churches and castles.

In the towns of Italy – ports such as Genoa, Pisa and Venice, or inland cities like Piacenza, Pavia and Florence – this passion for money-making resulted in a genuinely capitalist society. The first steps in commercial practice were developed: the practice of moneychangers receiving deposits from their clients led to a rudimentary banking activity; there were experimental essays in covering the risks of sea voyages to the Levant; and associations were formed between the merchants and the men with capital to back them. But this distinctively 'bourgeois' attitude to life was to be found practically everywhere. His very occupation and the form in which he acquired his wealth in cash and goods made the townsman independent of his overlords and his own family alike, whereas if a lord or peasant wished to dispose of his inheritance he had first to obtain the consent of his entire family. The guilds formed by townsmen for mutual advantage and assistance in their trades and for the protection of their caravans were groups of equals. In the same way they could join forces against their local overlords whenever these refused to fix or lower the taxes levied on trade, release them from the obligations of military service (except in case of dire necessity) or concede them some measure of autonomy in the conduct of municipal affairs or the administration of justice. This was the time of the revolt of the 'free cities' – Cambrai, Beauvais, Laon, Rheims and Sens – against their traditional masters. The great Flemish cities, too, profited from disputes over the succession to the county in order to emancipate themselves. In the south of France and in Italy consulates representing the urban population made their appearance, generally in a more peaceful and progressive fashion.

Already, then, there existed a bourgeois mentality and way of life which was characterized by a new kind of activity, by a liking for risks, the pursuit of gain and the demand for political freedom. It acted like yeast in the blood of a hitherto static society. But except in a few towns in Italy the people themselves were boorish and uneducated. There was as yet no truly bourgeois culture.

The ruling caste was also changing fast. It was chiefly the nobles who reaped the benefit of agricultural progress. The rents paid by their tenants and the profits from the sale of surplus produce piled up in their coffers. The lucky ones were those whose keep overlooked some growing town or important market, a busy main road or even simply very rich farmland. All the same, occasions to spend money were also multiplying fast. By the end of the eleventh century there were many lords who had served their time as Crusaders in defence of the Holy Land or fighting against the Infidel in

Spain. There they came into contact with more refined civilizations, and those who did not die or settle in distant lands came home with a broader range of experience and higher standards of comfort. They set themselves to improve the defences of their castles and also to make them less primitive to live in. They sought out more splendid battle chargers and fuller and more effective armour. They liked to dress in the fine fabrics and bright colours which merchants brought to their homes for sale.

In the best of the nobility this increasing refinement of life was accompanied by a moral and intellectual progress. Not for nothing had the Church directed the warlike ferocity of so many of them against the Infidel, and not for nothing did she bless the sword of a new-made knight and hold up to him the ideal of a protector of the weak and righter of wrongs. Even so, the image was somewhat slow in penetrating.

Nevertheless, these lords were no longer satisfied to fill their leisure hours with hunting and tournaments. They began to show an interest in culture and education. They took a fancy to the poetry sung by travelling minstrels who accompanied themselves on a variety of instruments. The example of Abelard and his father is by no means unique. A number of feudal courts became centres of literary activity.

The Church, too, had been lifted on the tide of change and reacted to it in a variety of ways. Despite the efforts of the eleventh-century reformists to combat boorishness and ignorance and enforce the rule of chastity, the bulk of the rural clergy improved only very slowly. This was because the local priests were recruited inevitably from among the peasantry itself and shared the peasant way of life.

There was more evidence of progress among the secular clergy in the towns. Most cathedral chapters had been re-formed during the eleventh century and college chapters had also been set up in non-cathedral churches. These were financially self-supporting. Their incomes, drawn from urban landowning and taxes on the markets, and swollen further by the donations of the faithful, were increasing steadily. Their cloisters became busy centres of religious education and study. The biggest cities began to be split up into numerous parishes to cater for the growing congregations, whose spiritual demands were often extremely pressing.

Subjected to a great many contradictory pressures, the regular clergy was undergoing something of a crisis and becoming somewhat diversified. Many old abbeys which had once been situated outside the ancient cities had now become incorporated in the expanding urban agglomeration. Some adapted to their new situation by forming themselves into chapters and preparing to play their role in the world. Others went farther and took an active part in economic development. Such was the case with St Denis. Suger, who became abbot in 1122, was a man of humble birth but immense ability. He recouped the abbey's finances and at least tripled its income by establishing a new village here, granting judicious enfranchisement there and imposing a more effective system of tax collection elsewhere. The wealth thus accumulated he expended in lavish charities and even more in rebuilding and beautifying his church. His personal influence can be seen in the impulse which guided ecclesiastical art into new channels. This faultless administrator became the friend and adviser of the Capet monarchs and was made regent of the kingdom when Louis VII set out for the Crusade in 1147.

By the beginning of the twelfth century the order of Cluny had over a thousand houses. Most of these were in France but the order had also penetrated to England, Germany, Poland, Spain, Italy and, thanks to the Crusades, into the Holy Land. Its dominant aim was still the most perfect celebration of the divine office; and to provide a fit setting for the glory of God, the abbots of Cluny encouraged or directed the building of ever larger and more splendid churches. The sculpture which ran riot over their capitals, tympana and porches offers the finest examples of romanesque art at its height. Expenses of this kind could only be met by the most careful administration. This was one of the tasks to which the abbot of Cluny, Peter the Venerable – so called in his lifetime on account of his virtues and his smiling serenity – devoted himself from the year of his election in 1122. He also promulgated statutes intended to revive the strict observation of the Rule, but with the moderation which was one of the traditions of Cluny.

But there was also a new wind blowing through the religious life of the times. Outsiders may easily believe that the appearance of new kinds of monasteries can be explained by the moral laxity of the old. In fact, more often than not it represents the birth of a completely new ideal brought about by the general development of society and ideas. In a world where human relations were becoming a great deal more complex, a world of increased comforts and clearer divisions of labour, many men had a confused yearning towards solitude and absolute poverty.

In most places, therefore, we find men withdrawing either from the world or from monasteries which seemed to them too worldly in their aspirations. They settled in small groups in marshlands or in the depths of forests. Some of these groups lay behind the growth of more widespread movements. Bruno of Cologne, for example, left the cathedral chapter of Rheims, where he was professor of theology, to found La Grande Chartreuse near Grenoble, before ending his life as a hermit in Calabria (1101). In the same year, 1101, a priest from the district of Rennes named Robert of Arbrissel who was famous for the effect of his preaching on young girls, founded a convent for them at Fontevrault. As early as 1075 Robert, a gentleman of Champagne who had risen to be abbot of St Michel at Tonnerre, resigned his position in order to lead a group of hermits at Molesme, not far from Auxerre. After numerous vicissitudes he founded an abbey at Cîteaux, in the wooded marshes of the Saône, where the Benedictine Rule, interpreted in its strictest sense of absolute poverty, penitence, private prayer and physical labour, was restored in full.

But severity of this kind had few attractions and recruitment was slow, until the year 1112 when a young Burgundian nobleman whose parents, like Abelard's, had given him a careful education, appeared at the monastery gates with thirty or so friends and relations. 'From that day on', wrote a friend of the new monk, 'God blessed Cîteaux so that this vine of the Lord bore fruit and spread its branches as far as the sea and beyond.' St Bernard, with his extraordinary personality, was in fact to give the decisive impetus to Cîteaux, before going on to play an outstanding and unique part in the affairs of his time.

By 1113 there were so many monks at Cîteaux that the abbey was obliged to throw off a swarm. Before very long Bernard himself was given the task of organizing an affiliated house at Clairvaux. Statutes also had to be drawn up to establish both the manner in which the rule was to be observed and the relations of the new foundations with the mother-house. These statutes, the 'Charter of Charity', made the new Cistercian spirit very clear. It was a reaction simultaneously against the Cluniac trends and against the rapidly changing world. This was a rigid asceticism characterized by rough woollen garments and food reduced to a bare minimum, but it also meant the rejection of all those trappings which at Cluny were valued as enhancing the glory of religion: elaborately decorated churches, precious vessels and sumptuous vestments. Poverty had to be absolute and Cistercian monasteries must be hidden away 'in places far from the society of men'. The possession of wealth from the labour of others, lordly domains, tithes, mills and bake-ovens was 'contrary to monastic purity'. Manual work, prayer and private meditation recovered a place in the lives of the monks, at the expense of collective worship, which they had lost at Cluny.

A similar state of unrest to that which was driving the clergy to reform and so many individuals to seek for solitude was also at the root of a number of popular heresies. Small groups of heretics had appeared in the first half of the eleventh century in places as far apart as Orleans, Arras and Monforte (near Asti). Then the wave of fervour accompanying the Gregorian reform and the Crusades seems to have channelled these aspirations towards a more purely evangelical life. By the beginning of the twelfth century, when the reform had ended in compromise and the Crusades had revealed themselves a game for knights to play, adherents to the heretical doctrines spread by wandering preachers were once more legion. These preachers were monks or laymen who believed that they had a call to live literally according to the word of Christ: 'Go ye into all the world, and preach the gospel to every creature.' Often their teaching boiled down to a criticism of the Church and the sacraments maintained in the name of some simple and impassioned evangelical ideal. Many of their followers were humble folk and craftsmen.

Peasants seeking better lands, immigrants moving into the new towns, merchants travelling the roads, Crusaders and pilgrims making for the Holy Land, troubadours taking their songs from castle to castle, hermits withdrawing from the world, wandering preachers: all these in their way bear witness to the changing face of western Europe.

THE POLITICAL FACE OF EUROPE

These transformations taking place in the economy, in society and in mental outlook eventually had an effect in the political field also. Rulers were acquiring regular incomes that enabled them to maintain troops of mercenaries and employ paid administrators. As a result there were plenty of petty nobles ready to make a career in their service rather than lead a life of obscurity in their own small castles. Kings could keep relations with their vassals on a more regular footing and weld the feudal hierarchy into the framework of a comparatively efficient and centralized state. The second half of the century opened with the accession of two sovereigns who addressed themselves to this task with perseverance and success. Frederic Barbarossa became the head of the Empire in 1152 and Henry II Plantagenet, king of England in 1154.

But in the time of Abelard all this was still in the future. The factors of disorder and dissipation were still paramount.

In the first instance it was the power of the castellans which was enhanced by the notable advances in the art of fortification: stone keeps set on a broad base to discourage the work of sappers, outer curtain walls flanked by towers and with over-hanging galleries to protect the defenders. It is true that for a long time yet the humbler lords would continue to build wooden towers, but those who had grown rich through the control of a market and those who had abundant serf labour at their disposal were able to build themselves massive fort-resses that could withstand a lengthy siege. Any sign of weak-ness in the central power was reflected in an increase in the number of such castles. 'Each mighty man raised his castles and held them against the king. . . . They cruelly oppressed the poor people of the land by forcing them to work on them. When the castles were finished, they filled them with devils and perverted men . . .' Thus the Anglo-Saxon Chronicle of Peterborough, describing the state of 'feudal anarchy' existing in England around 1140 – and this was England, where the Norman conquest of 1066 had left a strong, organized society but which the play of circumstance and the baronial mentality was reducing once again to disorder.

Another cause of trouble was the Quarrel of the Investi-tures. This cannot be gone into in detail here, but it had a number of consequences which have a direct bearing on our subject. Some people in the eleventh century had been shocked by the way in which the clergy was often closely dependent on the secular powers. This dependence seemed a source of evils and abuses at all levels, from the parish priest who was appointed by the lord of the manor from among his

serfs, to the bishop chosen according to the dictates of king
or baron, and even to the pope himself, whose election only
the intervention of the emperor had been the means of
wrenching from the hands of the factious Roman aristocracy.
The men installed in holy office in this way were not always
necessarily bad but all too often what their masters wanted of
them, more than anything else, was a docile cleric, a loyal and
effective vassal, since with the bishopric or abbacy went land.
Regarded purely as a fief, this pledged the beneficiary to ties
of vassalage. As a result the income from domains which had
once been given to God for the purpose of good works would
now be partly deflected to the payment of taxes and to maintaining knights, while the prelate himself was obliged to
occupy himself with the duties of a vassal, attending court to
advise and pay homage to his lord and leading his proper
complement of knights into the field. In the last resort, the
ideal prelate was a man like Turpin, the archbishop of Rheims,
in the *Chanson de Roland*, a mighty wielder of the sword
(against the Infidel, of course): 'the priest never sung mass
whose prowess in the field could equal his'.

Violence was not the only fault which, the reformists were
saddened to note, was widespread among the clergy. Intrigue,
bribery and corruption for the sake of obtaining Church benefices were other things they denounced, as well as the traffic
in holy objects which they stigmatized under the name of
simony, after Simon the Magician, who tried to buy from the
Apostles the power to work miracles. As 'nicolaism' (the
word is drawn from a reference in the Apocalypse) they
attacked the incontinence of priests who lived with a concubine or even married in church, and whose sons afterwards
claimed their parish as a hereditary right according to the
custom of the time. Here and there pious bishops strove to
reform their clergy, but a negligent or less zealous successor
could reduce their efforts to naught. It was not enough to
treat this as a moral problem. What was needed was a structural reform that would free from secular control a Church

united in a common unceasing effort to achieve moral and intellectual progress. The feudal ceremony of investiture which sealed the possession of a fief stood as a symbol of the Church's subjection. It was no longer acceptable for clerics to be invested in their ecclesiastical functions by laymen.

By about the middle of the eleventh century these reformist ideas had spread throughout the Roman clergy as a whole. Circumstances favoured the emancipation of the papacy. A decree passed in 1059 reserved the election of the pope to the college of cardinals which had grown up gradually around him. The remainder of the clergy and the people of Rome had merely to ratify their decision, while the rights of the emperor were subject only to a vague passing reference. This was the starting point of the Quarrel of the Investitures. To us today it would appear that any improvement in the moral and intellectual level of the clergy must come from a general progress of civilization, no less than from a structural reform. People at the time obviously lacked the hindsight which enables us to form such an estimate.

All temporal powers stood to lose in this struggle in so far as it was aimed at depriving them of a measure of control over their subjects. But none were so deeply involved as the Empire. This was firstly because the emperor, at least since Charlemagne, had assumed a general leadership of Christendom in which there was little distinction between specifically political, moral or religious issues. By virtue of this concept, special ties existed between the emperor and the pope as the joint heads of the Christian nations. This was why Otto III had been in a position to appoint Gerbert as pope. Furthermore, emperors who had the wellbeing of the Church at heart had several times in the course of the eleventh century intervened in Rome to obtain the deposition of unworthy popes and secure their replacement by educated and virtuous pontiffs. At the time enthusiastic churchmen had bestowed on them such titles as 'Lord of churches' or 'Christ's representative'. But was this a normal state of affairs? And what would happen when there was a man less enlightened and well-intentioned at the head of the Empire? This was exactly the situation which arose at the death of Henry III in 1056. The decree of 1059 was in fact aimed deliberately at his successor, the child Henry IV.

On the other hand, the emperors, at least since Otto I, unable to rely on the loyalty of their own dukes and counts, had made it their deliberate policy to lean on their ecclesiastical vassals. They used them in their administration and obtained the bulk of their armed forces from them. It was vital for them to be able to depend on utter devotion from their bishops and abbots, and to have control of the elections which were canonically the task of the clergy and faithful of the individual dioceses in the first case and of the inmates of the monastery in the second.

The struggle reached its height during the pontificate of Gregory VII (1073–85). It leaves dramatic pictures graven on the mind: of Gregory VII and Henry IV mutually deposing one another with impressive ceremonies; of the German king (he was not yet emperor), deserted by his bishops, presenting himself at the gates of the castle of Canossa, where the pope had shut himself up, and remaining there for three days barefoot in the snow to implore the mercy of his enemy (1077); and of Gregory VII driven from Rome and expiring in exile at Salerno under the compromising protection of his rude Norman allies (1085). In fact, the most striking thing about this conflict is, right from the start, its apparent irreconcil-ability. The two adversaries, both equally convinced of the justice of their cause, were utterly committed and it seemed as though the fight could only end with the absolute defeat of one of them.

Yet this was not so, although it took more than half a century of fighting and wrangling before the compromise, originally evolved in England and France, was finally adopted and ratified by the Concordat of Worms in 1122. This compromise was based on the carefully drawn distinction between the temporal and spiritual functions of bishops and abbots. The emperor respected the freedom of elections and gave up the investiture (which in Germany was performed by handing over a ring and a cross); but he continued to confer the temporal domains, 'by the sceptre', and could demand the fulfilment of those duties to which the prelate was committed 'by law'. The solution was more than simply a balance of power. It marked the culmination of a great intellectual achievement, of which there will be more to say farther on.

In any event, this conflict had dealt such a blow to the imperial power that at best it would be a very long time before it recovered. On a number of occasions the rest of Christendom had come down heavily in favour of the regular pope and against the anti-pope elected by the emperor. The vague claims to universal supremacy – a distant echo of the might of Charlemagne which even Otto III had still been able to cherish – were finally dissipated. The kingdom of France in particular emerged with its independence greatly strengthened. Not for nothing, either, had the popes and the supporters of reform awakened the German and Italian prelates to a sense of their own vital independence, and appealed to the great temporal lords, who were only too glad to put a check on the emperor's power. The Concordat of Worms was followed in Italy, and to an even greater extent in Germany, by thirty years of chaos and unrest in which the only law was that of the *Faustrecht*, or 'might is right'.

Under such conditions, the real future of Europe lay in certain developments which took place on a much more modest scale. France at that time was little more than a rather loosely knit confederation of great fiefs. In some of these the holders, assisted sometimes by circumstances and always by their own energies and abilities, had succeeded in establishing themselves firmly in power. This was the case with, for example, the Counts of Flanders or the Plantagenets of Maine and Anjou, whose conquest of Normandy and accession to the English throne would soon make them one of the most powerful families in Europe. In the Île-de-France, too, a great, greedy glutton of a man was devoting himself wholeheartedly to the thankless and never-ending task of punishing the robber lords of his domains and razing their castles to the ground. He never flinched from danger, was the first to enter the blazing keep of Mouchi, and the first to hurl himself into the water at the crossing of the Indre. He earned the gratitude of the churches and of the common folk who suffered under the tyrants. Suger sang his praises splendidly, and for all his faults Louis VI may be regarded as one of the architects of the 'Capetian dawn'. But his work remained a fragile thing, at the mercy of human weakness.

Now let us take a look at the frontiers of Christendom. It is probably here that we shall find the most striking examples of small but strongly welded states. In the north of Spain the exigencies of the fight against the Saracens, and the large sums paid out by them in tribute, equally assisted the counts of Barcelona to impose their authority over the mosaic of fiefs which later constituted Catalonia. In 1137 a dynastic crisis put count Raymond Bérenger IV on the throne of Aragon and not long after this the compilation of the various articles comprising the legal code, known as the 'Usages', of Barcelona displays an admirable attempt at codification and organization.

The kingdom of Sicily, standing at the crossroads of three worlds, the Western, Byzantine and Muslim, constituted, to quote Edmond Jordan, 'one of the most remarkable political creations of the Middle Ages'. In the second half of the eleventh century Sicily had been overrun by the descendants of the Norman mercenaries who had settled in southern Italy some fifty years earlier. The man really responsible for pulling together this assortment of territories was Roger II Guiscard. His administration was faced with the task of dealing with an extremely varied population thrown together by a complex history. His chancellery promulgated laws in Latin, Greek and Arabic, and he himself employed Muslim mercenaries, showed a great fondness for Arab ways (even going so far as to maintain an official harem), and protected Arabic-speaking poets and scholars who rubbed shoulders at his court with Latin writers. The creation of a just and efficient administration and the publication of a sound legal code, the Assises (1140), show him to have possessed in full the spirit of organization which was the distinguishing feature of the Normans of whatever country.

Christianity and Islam also came face to face in the east. After the capture of Jerusalem in 1099 the Crusaders had turned their conquests in Syria and Palestine into a somewhat precarious collection of feudal states. Unfortunately the unusually propitious circumstances which had made this possible were short-lived. A new Turkish power was emerging, centred on the principality of Aleppo, which by taking Egypt ultimately succeeded in encircling the Latin states. From the early years of the twelfth century these states were subjected to increasing military pressure, which was reinforced by a wave of religious opposition. The brotherhoods of soldier-monks which had been created in Jerusalem for the purpose of receiving and protecting pilgrims were obliged to transform themselves into the Military Orders – the Templars and Hospitallers – which slowly drained the resources of the West while at the same time offering the noble world an ideal of religious chivalry. But even this was not enough, and the fall of Edessa revealed the extent of the danger. A second Crusade, preached with fiery eloquence by St Bernard in 1146, endeavoured to avert the peril, but without great success. And yet, although the losses sustained on these expeditions were in future to give pause and there would be no repetition of the fantastic enthusiasm of those early days, the image of the Crusade remains one of the most widespread and definitive elements in the background of western Christendom, in which Abelard lived and struggled.

Chapter 2

THE ENRICHMENT OF CULTURE

LITERARY RENAISSANCE AND THE BIRTH OF LITERATURE

THIS time there can be no doubt about it. The classic work of the historian Charles A. Haskins is justly entitled *The Renaissance of the Twelfth Century*.

In it, he paints many pictures which are oddly reminiscent of those we have already seen in the Carolingian age, differing only in scope and achievement. The dedicated work of innumerable copyists was enriching the libraries of monasteries and now, to an even greater extent, of city churches. The Carolingian minuscule, practically unchanged since the ninth century, was spreading into Spain and being adopted in Rome, to reign supreme over a huge area in which, apart from some slight national peculiarities, it achieved a startling degree of uniformity. To quote Charles Higounet:

Italy had a fondness for rounded characters and fairly large modules; Germany had a heavier and more angular script than other regions; England retained its liking for thin, spiky characters; Spain followed France which in turn remained closest to the Carolingian tradition.

The Latin classics were known and loved in much the same way and in much the same order as in the ninth century: Virgil and Cicero well to the fore and Ovid sufficiently acceptable to be copied, somewhat surprisingly, at Cluny.

This literary background was by now thoroughly assimilated. The best Latin authors of the twelfth century give the impression of writing in their mother tongue. To them, Latin was no longer simply a matter of academic exercises, more or less clumsy and conventional – although such things continued to be turned out by less gifted students. But these poets were really expressing their own thoughts and feelings in a language which came naturally to them, and for a comparatively wide audience. In fact the twelfth century was one of the finest periods of all Latin poetry, the diversity of which was also becoming more marked. Developments in the use of various metres are reassuring evidence of a spontaneous life of its own. There is an increasing use of rhyme, contrasting with the general practice in classical verse. Above all, such a variety of genres! A complete inventory would be impossible, and we shall confine ourselves here to citing a few examples.

Religious poetry deserves pride of place both on account of its abundance and the intensity of its inspiration. It is religious both in subject matter – whether descriptions of biblical scenes, accounts of the lives of saints, or illustrations of morality or dogma – and also frequently in its purpose: offices for the saints, hymns and liturgical dramas (especially commemorating the death and resurrection of Christ). The twelfth century stands out from the mass of religious poetry as a whole largely on account of its quality, since it produced nothing particularly original. Many works are anonymous and it is not even always easy to assign them to one century rather than another. Some outlived their own time, like the poem 'On Contempt of the World' by the Cluniac monk Bernard of Morlaas, which was used long afterwards as the basis of a series of hymns. Some are still sung today, although the English text cannot convey the full rhythmic splendour of the Latin:

> The world is very evil;
> The times are waxing late:
> Be sober and keep vigil;
> The Judge is at the gate.
>
> . . . .
>
> Brief life is here our portion;
> Brief sorrow, short-liv'd care;
> The life that knows no ending,
> The tearless life, is There.
>
> . . . .

> Jerusalem the Golden,
> With milk and honey blest,
> Beneath thy contemplation
> Sink heart and voice oppressed:
> I know not, O I know not,
> What social joys are there;
> What radiancy of glory,
> What life beyond compare.

Happily, the poet's fervour is not lost here, as it all too often is, in a welter of complex imagery and allegorical meanings.

Hildebert of Lavardin, who was bishop of Le Mans from 1097 to 1125 and ended his days, like Alcuin, at Tours, though in the capacity of archbishop, also wrote a great deal of moral and theological verse. But the works which speak most directly to us today are those in which he expresses more personal feelings, such as the melancholy and resignation he felt as an exile in England, where he was taken by the English king after the capture of Le Mans by the English. More famous still are his poems extolling the glories of ancient and latter-day Rome.

> Par tibi, Roma, nihil, cum sis prope tota ruina;
>   Quam magni fueris integra fracta doces.
> Longa tuos fastus aetas destruxit, et arces
>   Caesaris et superum templa palude jacent.
> . . . .
> Urbs cecidit de qua si quicquam dicere dignum
>   Moliar, hoc potero dicere: Roma fuit!
> Non tamen annorum series, non flamma, nec ensis
>   Ad plenum potuit hoc abolere decus. . . .
> Urbs felix, si vel dominis urbs illa careret,
>   Vel dominis esset turpe carere fide!*

* Even in ruins, Rome, you are unequalled; battered, you still show how great you were in your prime. Now old age has spoiled your splendour and low in the marshlands lie the house of Caesar and the temples of the gods. . . . Fallen is the city of which, if my words would do her justice, I can only say: she was Rome. Yet not the passing years, or fire, or sword, could ever quite put out her brightness . . .

Oh happy city, had she been spared her masters, or had those masters deemed it shame to have no faith.

Later, the city of St Peter is seen as destined for a future greatness more splendid even than that of ancient Rome. Hildebert makes the city say:

Vix scio que fuerim, vix Rome Roma recordor – *

Even in his own time, the fame of the 'divine Hildebert', the second 'Homer', had spread far afield. Leaving aside the verbal exaggerations, this is a judgement we can fully endorse.

But there are free and joyous poems too, with an immediate appeal to the modern reader, which cut right across any lurking image of the Middle Ages as a period of restrictive piety. What these poems are praising is the pleasures of this world and they do so with a wholehearted vigour often verging on obscenity.

> Meum pectum sauciat
> puellarum decor,
> et quas tactu nequeo,
> saltem corde mechor. ...
> Secundo redarguor
> etiam de ludo.
> Sed cum ludus corpore
> me dimittat nudo,
> frigidus exterius
> mentis estu sudo,
> tunc versus et carmina
> meliora cudo.
> Tertio capitulo
> memoro tabernam. ...
> Meus est propositum
> in taberna mori,
> ut sint vina proxima
> morientis ori;
> tunc cantabunt letius
> angelorum chori:
> Deus sit propitius
> huic potatori ...

* I scarcely know who I was, I, Rome, have all but forgotten Rome

> voluptatis avidus
> magis quam salutis
> mortuus in anima
> curam gero cutis.*

Without going so far as to canvass for a social reform quite foreign to the spirit of the age, these poems are sharply satirical of the privileged classes such as knights and prelates.

> According to knowledge,
> Demonstrably right,
> A lover from college
> Will outdo a knight

is the conclusion reached by two damsels after putting the matter to the test. And the *Commentary on the Holy Gospel According to Silver Mark* deals unkindly with the greed of pope and cardinals.

The authors of these verses, collectively known as Goliards, are somewhat mysterious. All too often legends, spread by themselves as much as by their enemies, take the place of any certain facts. We know they were mostly poor, wandering scholars, or occasionally men of some position who had their reasons for not seeking undue publicity. The poet who refers to himself as the Primate has been identified as a canon of Orleans who flourished around 1140, and 'the Archpoet' as a secretary to the arch-chancellor of Frederic Barbarossa. Poetry of this kind, against which the ecclesiastical authorities militated

---

* I am cut to the quick by a girl's beauty, and if I cannot touch her, at least I can have her in my heart. The second charge is I'm a gambling man. But when I'm left without clothes to my back, my outside is cold but my mind is seething, and that's when I make my best songs and verses. The third charge that comes to mind is the tavern. . . . I intend to die in a tavern, where there is wine by my dying lips, and a chorus of angels shall sing joyfully: God be merciful to this drunkard. . . . Greedier far for pleasure than salvation, my soul is dead. So I may as well look after my skin.

See Helen Waddell's *Medieval Latin Lyrics* (Penguin Classics) for a splendid verse translation of these lines from the Archpoet. – TRANSLATOR.

persistently and, in the end, successfully, burgeoned particularly in the shadow of the episcopal schools of northern France.

Historical writings – in prose, for the most part – also abounded in the first half of the twelfth century. These works fall into the general pattern of forms which had been traditional at least since Carolingian times, and many are remarkable for their sense of character, narrative skill and stylistic elegance. Favourite subjects of the time were stories of the lives of saints or of the discovery or translation of relics. To us there is something wearisome in this monotonous catalogue of virtues; so much credulity is irritating. We can be grateful to Guibert of Nogent, the son of a petty nobleman from the region of Beauvais turned monk, for displaying some honest doubts in his little book *On the Relics of Saints*. He reacts to the information that two heads of John the Baptist had turned up, one in Constantinople, the other at Saint-Jean d'Angély, by concluding that either the saint had two heads or one of them is a fake.

The growth of communications often produced a much greater wealth of information in the *Annals*, those year-by-year accounts of events which had come to their author's knowledge. In this connexion, the annals of St Albans in England and those of a number of Italian cities are especially worthy of note. There was a revival of the chronicle of the universe, a combination of religious history and the progress of the temporal world right up to the most recent events. Otto of Freising, a student of Paris and later the man responsible for introducing the new logic to Germany (and the uncle of Frederic Barbarossa), was the author of a valuable and highly readable chronicle culminating in the coming of the Antichrist and the ending of the world. Orderic Vitalis, although he never left his monastery at St Evroul in Normandy, collected an abundance of material in his *Ecclesiastical History* and treated his subject with great psychological insight.

There were also a number of works devoted to great men and outstanding events. The Crusades, those fantastic adventures in foreign lands, were as we can well imagine a particularly fertile source of inspiration. In addition, William of Malmesbury wrote accounts of the English kings and bishops which are remarkable in their impartial concern for the facts and in their quest for a connecting link between events, while Suger, the abbot of St Denis, wrote a very nice life of Louis VI – the Fat. Autobiography, which in a few clumsy examples had begun to appear as early as the tenth century, now began to blossom. Here we find Guibert of Nogent again, leaving us an account of his life that is both refreshingly intimate and full of smiling indulgence. The best-known work of Abelard falls into this category.

But this is not a history of Latin literature in the twelfth century, and the reader would have every right to protest at a protracted list of names. All the same, something must be said of the art of letter-writing, sermons, and loftier subjects like law and philosophy, all of which were traversed by a new current of life which is apparent in other ways besides sheer quantity. There is a maturity of outlook and purity of form, and even a very personal voice makes itself heard from time to time. The academic stage was past and now the movement was to appeal to an increasing number of individuals.

But in the literary field the renaissance of the twelfth century was without issue. In the centuries that followed, people continued to write a good deal in Latin, and in good Latin at that, but the substance of what they wrote has little interest for us. This is not only because it was too static but also because in future the emphasis in the schools was to be much less on grammar and rhetoric than on dialectic as the gateway to theology and philosophy. There was a definite reason for this. The teaching of literature as such became gradually stereotyped, relying exclusively on anthologies of extracts culled from various authors and reducing the art of writing to the repetition of mechanical formulae.

Moreover, many works from the thirteenth century and after have ceased to give the impression of being thought directly in Latin. They are like a garment, covering ideas originally conceived in another language. This was a real transition, which began to operate around the middle of the twelfth century. Previously a knowledge of Latin had been to some extent synonymous with education itself. The *illitteratus* was the man who was ignorant of Latin. Now a whole new public had grown up, the product of a certain improvement in material conditions, social habits and intellectual curiosity, which, while unable or unwilling to learn Latin, was none the less eager for more cultured uses of leisure. This movement began with the nobles but was quickly taken up by the townsmen.

The growth of literature in the vernacular happened most speedily in places where a relaxation in the power of the Church was reflected in a falling off in the quality and quantity of Latin. In the south of France, for instance, where the effects of the Carolingian renaissance had scarcely penetrated, scribes were finding it more and more difficult to write official documents in Latin. The words of the spoken language, the *langue d'oc*, so called from the latin *hoc* which was used in affirmation, came much more readily to their pens. Around the year 1100 it had become current practice to write all such documents in the vernacular. But the real gems of the language are a number of lyric poems written in an already highly polished form and dating from the end of the eleventh century. The joys they celebrate are more than simply the crude delights of physical passion, but include the sensations, sufferings and rewards of a carefully cultivated, and sometimes hopeless love. This was an entirely new concept of love, not specifically Christian, since it showed small respect for the bonds of matrimony, but none the less refined and in many ways denoting a much greater respect for women. The linguistic transition was in fact accompanied by a parallel change in sensibility.

Also dating from the last years of the eleventh century is the French epic, the *Chanson de Roland*. Here the old story of the defeat of Charlemagne's nephew at Roncesvaux is presented with all the associations guaranteed to appeal to an audience of fighting men, the pride in countless deeds of valour against the Saracen, the unshakeable loyalty of the knight to God and his lord, and the love of the '*douce France*' that was their native land. The knights of southern France and England listened eagerly, and a German translation was also widespread in that country, taking its place alongside the memory-haunted tales of Gudrun and the Nibelungen which had been handed down since the time of the great invasions. In the Germanic lands histories were still being written in the vernacular. The Anglo-Saxon Chronicle, dating from the time of Alfred the Great, was kept up until 1154, when Anglo-Norman, the language of the new aristocracy, finally carried the day. Also about the middle of the twelfth century we find the beginning of the *Kaiserchronik* at Regensburg, written in high German.

The increase in the written use of the vernacular would not have been possible without the determination of the authors in question to fit it for this new dignity. This was more than simply the wish to rid it of peculiarities of dialect. All these literary languages, though still in their infancy, underwent a series of modifications of considerable interest to a systematic and comparative analysis which contrive to give them a more or less 'modern' air. In this way they were equipped to meet the new demands upon them. At all events a step forward had been made and the existence of cultures using languages other than Latin became increasingly widespread.

THEOLOGICAL THOUGHT

The achievements of the Carolingian renaissance had been, on the whole, fairly well preserved throughout the troubles of the tenth century. But if the net result had been to produce only an increasing familiarity with the great Latin authors of antiquity, coupled with a purer, more elegant and self-assured manipulation of their language, it would not have led the Christian West to a great deal that was new. Fortunately the methods of reasoning and expression forged by this contact were to be violently put to the test by problems arising from the growth of civilization itself. The word 'violently' is important because it was precisely the dramatic impact of the problems in question which stripped these intellectual techniques of their scholarly and somewhat artificial associations and turned them into a tool which men continued to feel an imperative need to perfect and sharpen to ever-greater effectiveness.

Their efforts were directed especially to the fields of law and theology. Given the mental stage of society at the time, it was more or less inevitable that this should be so. Let us therefore try to define some of the advances made in both these subjects – without, let me make it quite clear, claiming to provide a complete history of law or theology in the twelfth century.

In the case of theology, the eleventh century had really marked the beginning of a new era. After the patristic age there had been a definite decline. Some theological arguments had arisen in the ninth century, but at a fairly low level, while the best theology of the tenth had come down to 'an intelligent reading of the Bible and a few Fathers'. The eleventh century saw the first attempts to apply the dialectic evolved by men like Gerbert to the contents of Revelation.

The term 'dialectic', it should be said, was then understood in its Aristotelian sense of a method of correct reasoning from statements considered simply in terms of likelihood – a logic of probability as opposed to scientific necessity. Of course there were those who became so besotted about this dialectic that they transferred their faith in these processes of reasoning to the statements themselves, and in some authors this enthusiasm becomes childish and ridiculous; but there were others who seemed to be questioning certain fundamental dogmas, and they enjoyed an immense reputation.

One of them was Bérenger of Tours, who was born in that city about 1000, rose to be head of the episcopal school there, and died in 1088. Bérenger professed the utmost faith in human reason.

No one, short of wilful blindness, will dispute that reason is incontestably the best guide in the search for truth. It is the nature of a great heart always to have recourse to dialectic, and to have recourse to that is to have recourse to reason, and whoever does not do so denies that which honours him the most, since his reason is the image of God in him.

Bérenger based this last assertion on the book of Genesis. He himself applied dialectic chiefly to the mystery of the Eucharist, demonstrating that since the accidental attributes of the bread – colour, taste, consistency etc. – remained, its substance also remained and could not therefore be said to have been replaced by that of Christ, which could only be added to it. Bérenger seems to have been making a clumsy stand against an over-literal interpretation of the Real Presence, rejecting the idea of 'transubstantiation' put forward by Paschase Radbert* without seeing that it was capable of interpretation on a more spiritual level. His concepts were condemned more than once. Bérenger agreed to more orthodox professions of faith which he then in part retracted. This reflects the ambivalence of his whole attitude.

A good deal younger than Bérenger was Roscelin, a native of Compiègne and a master of dialectic who was brought to trial in 1092 by a Council which failed to convict him of heresy. After this he lived for some time in England and later returned to France, where he taught in various places. Abelard heard him at Loches. He died in 1120. The best way to grasp his particular intellectual contribution is probably by means of his total rejection of the absolute 'realism' of Plato. For Plato,† objects perceived by our senses were no more than reflections of the Ideas which were the only true and enduring Reality. Consequently individuals had no reality of their own but were merely the visible reflections of the Idea of Mankind. Roscelin, on the other hand, thought that when we utter the word 'man' we are implying only two realities: the individual human

* See p. 100.
† See p. 122.

being to whom the word applies and the word itself (*nomen*) in its own physical reality as speech. Hence the term 'nominalism', which is used to describe his position.

This can be seen as simply a harmless verbal quibble. But Roscelin pursued his theories in, for example, his analysis of the mystery of the Trinity. According to him, the Trinity could not exist outside the three persons which composed it, and any assertion to the contrary would mean confounding the members. One of his opponents pointed out that this would lead Roscelin to the perilous conclusion that: 'if custom allowed, it could be truly said that there are three gods'. It would be more accurate to say that for Roscelin the Trinity was made up of three persons and hence of three distinct substances possessing one power and one will. Roscelin almost certainly intended no unorthodoxy. In one of the few examples of his writing to have survived, a letter to Abelard, in which he was moreover extremely free with his abuse, he demanded: 'Surely we should at least be granted freedom to pray to God, the three in one, in whatever manner we understand Him to exist.' But, interpreted in the light of his nominalism, Roscelin's theory was a disturbing one.

Consequently a movement arose which was aimed at refuting both these masters. One of Bérenger's principal opponents was Lanfranc. Lanfranc was an Italian from Pavia who became a monk and then abbot of the Norman monastery of Bec, whence he was summoned by William the Conqueror to take over the see of Canterbury. His attitude was still largely one of negative criticism. Argument at least made it possible to define terms, establish a vocabulary and move on from there to constructive developments. This progress can be seen clearly in the greatest of all eleventh-century theologians, St Anselm.

Skipping a generation, Anselm's career forms an astonishing parallel to Lanfranc's. Born, like Lanfranc, in Italy (about 1033, near Aosta), Anselm joined him at the monastery of Bec, where he became head of the school and later abbot. Finally he succeeded Lanfranc as archbishop of Canterbury from 1093 until his death in 1109. He lacked Lanfranc's political and administrative talents but far outshone him as a theologian. He is remembered particularly for his proofs of the existence of God, although there is nothing to be gained from going into these here, any more than the other ideas developed by him in his numerous treatises. What is important in the present context is certain aspects of his intellectual approach. At the time these were even more influential than his ideas themselves.

The most striking thing at first sight about this refuter of Roscelin is that he seems to have shared to the full the latter's faith in the power of reason. He shows the measure of this faith in the *Monologion*, which he wrote for some monks of Bec who had asked him for a treatise on the existence and essence of God in which everything would be proved by reason and nothing based on scriptural authority. It is true that Anselm began – in contrast to some dialecticians – by stating that it was first necessary to base oneself firmly on faith, since it was the Revelation and our faith in it which provided the essential elements for the use of our reason. We do not understand in order to believe, we believe in order to understand. This is one of St Anselm's most celebrated pronouncements.

But this said, it is a duty to reflect on the information given. Men will never exhaust the whole truth, and the Fathers, who were mortal, did not have time to say everything. It is therefore up to us to carry on their work and to make use of our reason in so doing. As Étienne Gilson wrote: 'It is all as though it were always possible to arrive at an understanding, if not of what one believes, at least of the necessity for believing.' St Anselm even tried to prove the rational necessity of the Trinity and the Incarnation, an undertaking of such temerity that it was to deter even Thomas Aquinas. But in refuting Roscelin, St Anselm took care to insist that he was not attacking the supporters of dialectic, only 'the heretics of dialectic who consider spiritual substances no more than a breath'.

Attempts at rational explanation may be accompanied sometimes by a certain aridity which can be shocking to believers. There is nothing of this in St Anselm. All his thought is bathed in an intense piety and his works take the form of long meditations, sometimes supported by dialogues, in search of ideas by which the soul may raise itself to God. 'Lord, let me penetrate through love that which I taste through knowledge.' The phrase sums up the admirably balanced nature of his approach. His treatise on Redemption is punctuated by burning exhortations:

O Christian soul, soul raised up from a fearful death, O soul ransomed and delivered from a wretched servitude by the blood of God, awake, remember thy resurrection, think on thy redemption and thy deliverance. ... Savour the goodness of thy Redeemer, burn with love for thy Saviour!

Equally moving is the long prayer to the Virgin in which St Anselm sums up Marian theology prior to St Bernard.

St Anselm's technical innovations were no less remarkable than the quality of his work. Other theologians of the period leaned heavily on the authority of the Scriptures and the Fathers, and their writings resemble a series of quotations linked by a commentary. Even Abelard was still using this method. Anselm certainly studied his sources, but he had assimilated them to the point where they became the very flesh of his own thought. What we find in him is therefore a chain of private reasoning. His work is a 'rational exploration of dogma', far in advance of his time, and already looking forward to the thirteenth century. It was, as De Ghellinck has called it, 'a real leap forward'. Anselm worked with an apparent effortlessness which has led to many comments on his 'stunning dialectical virtuosity' and, at the same time, with an extreme conscientiousness which led him to frequent revisions.

In many ways St Anselm was ahead of his time, and even of Abelard himself, although his influence was certainly less widespread. This was because he was less strongly aware of the things which preoccupied his contemporaries. He worked in monographs and separate treatises concerning individual points of dogma, whereas they felt the need to have this knowledge systematically arranged and classified into a properly graded whole. This was the form taken by the work of another Anselm, the head of the episcopal school at Laon, at the beginning of the twelfth century. On the other hand Anselm of Bec rose serenely above the divergences and even contradictions revealed by a careful examination of the usual authorities. His contemporaries, as we shall see, did not get off so lightly, and hunted earnestly for a method of interpretation which would extract them from their difficulties. Much of Abelard's influence was due to the fact that he concentrated on doing exactly this.

REFLECTION ON LAW

Just as in theology, if not to an even greater extent, the early Middle Ages marked a definite regression in legal thinking. In ancient Rome the legal sciences had been remarkably highly developed. From a study of the laws in force in Rome and the areas under her dominion, jurists were able to isolate the fundamental principles whose application then allowed for further improvements in the system itself and more effective solutions to practical problems. The emperor Justinian in the sixth century A.D. had employed a commission of experts to collect, codify and harmonize the impressive bulk of Roman law and legal writings. The results of their labours are known by the title of *Corpus juris civilis*. Its most interesting section is the *Digest*, containing a collection of the opinions of earlier jurists, while the much simpler *Code* is a straightforward account of former imperial constitutions.

At the same time as this monumental work – which is still the basic source for studies in Roman law – was being put together in Byzantium, the situation in the West was degenerating fast. Each race of invaders possessed its own body of unwritten custom which, however, they made no attempt to impose on the 'Roman' inhabitants of their new kingdoms. A number of barbarian kings even thought it worth while to commission abridged versions of Roman law. The best known of these is the *Breviary* of Alaric promulgated at Toulouse in 506. It was a greatly inferior work to the Code of Justinian but it had its uses. At the same time the example of Roman law and the new demands of a sedentary existence led the barbarian kings to establish the customs of their own peoples in writing. These were the so-called barbarian 'Laws', covering the period from the fifth to the ninth centuries.

In this way a curious situation grew up in the West, characterized by what has been described as the personality of law, whereby the law invoked varied according to the status of the individual involved. The first question asked was: to which law do you appeal? As time went by and the descendents of the invaders gradually merged with those of the original inhabitants, and as the growing ignorance on the part of the judges consigned both Roman and barbarian laws to oblivion, their role was taken over by regional customs, i.e. by the traditional usages of particular areas, which varied from place to place.

At the same time – and this is the most important thing for the present purpose – a concept of law was taking root which, while Germanic in origin, also found an odd ally in religion. According to this theory all law had its origin in God. Law was therefore immensely old and the way in which it manifested itself was through the human conscience. Laws cannot truly be made: they are discovered by means of the collective conscience of its representatives, and of ancient documents. The promulgation of regulations which violate tradition and the sense of justice can have no legal validity: the ancient laws survive in spite of these 'evil ways' and 'innovations', and demand their abolition. It might be thought that such a concept would have fixed the law in a rigid pattern, but in practice memory, especially in the absence of written records, allowed a good deal of latitude, and people often believed that they were returning to the good old ways when what they were actually doing was to adapt custom to the new needs. But this was an instinctive development. There could no longer be any question of a legal science as such.

This was the general picture, although it varied in detail in different countries. In Anglo-Saxon England, the written laws were still common knowledge and had even been amplified by the passing of new statutes. Some loyalty to the Visigothic laws was still in evidence in the ruins of Christian Spain, and extended to the population as a whole. In Italy, in particular, despite the intellectual decline and the Lombard invasion, Roman law – always excepting the *Digest*, which was clearly beyond the comprehension of the period – was still taught in the form in which it had been fixed by Justinian. Pavia, the capital of the Lombard kingdom, was also a centre of active studies in jurisprudence. The specialists assembled at the royal courts adopted Roman methods in drawing up collections of Lombard laws, writing commentaries on them and adapting them to suit practical requirements. By the eighth century the school of Pavia had begun to draw students from everywhere in the West. Also in Lombardy, in about 1050, such men as Lanfranc, afterwards archbishop of Canterbury, and Yves, afterwards bishop of Chartres, who were to play a leading part in the affairs of their time, were receiving their legal education.

The development of canon law is no less revealing. The Church could not avoid incorporating into its statutes a number of customs which were to a greater or lesser extent forced on her by the barbarian kings, sometimes through the medium of the episcopal synods, and more or less justifiable. The result was to produce considerable variations and confusion in the rules enforced by the European clergy. If these were to be clarified at all it was first necessary at least to collect these rules into some kind of order. Such collections therefore made their appearance, especially after the sixth century, generally compiled either chronologically or according to origin (Councils General, Roman synods, papal letters, and so forth). But this system meant that a great deal of research had to be done every time anyone wanted to know the law on a particular subject, such as baptism, marriage or the celibacy of the clergy. Consequently men began to compile organized case-books, the best-known of which is the *Decree* of bishop Burchard of Worms, written in the first half of the eleventh century. Even the best of these collections suffered from serious defects. Many included texts of dubious origin, such as the numerous Irish canons which had been brought to Italian monasteries by monks from that country. Frequently they quoted their sources in a garbled and incomplete form, with scant regard for accuracy. None of these collections is complete and the authors may be suspected of having selected from among the countless texts at their disposal very much as the fancy took them. Still more serious were the summaries which twisted the original text, interpolations, canons attributed to imaginary Councils – and even deliberate falsifications.

This was the background against which the Quarrel of the Investitures developed. It was simultaneously the symptom and the cause of an intellectual revival. Each phase of the struggle, every move made by either of the participants, brought forth a fresh crop of pamphlets and treatises intended to justify the position of either the pope or the emperor and criticize that of his adversary. Such of these writings as have survived now fill three fat volumes of the *Monumenta Germaniae historica*. They deal with a wide variety of questions, including the proper rules to be followed in observing the celibacy of the clergy, the proper rules for accession to ecclesiastical offices, and whether these could be conferred by the temporal powers. From here they went on to discuss the exact functions of priests, abbots and bishops, and on the other hand, the precise nature of temporal power. That this power was held from God was not in dispute, but was it directly from God or through the Church as intermediary? What should be the relationship between the temporal and spiritual powers? Could the latter exercise any constraint? How far, and under what conditions, could it use excommunication to expel the recalcitrant from Christian society? Could it even pronounce the deposition of a king who betrayed his mission? And what was the exact position of the papacy within the Church? This is by no means an exhaustive list.

Consequently there need be no limits to the ambition of a cleric capable of applying the methods of reasoning and expression learned in the schools to the burning arguments of the day. An enormous body of thought and persuasion was produced and a great many very different solutions put forward, some of which sowed the seed of much future development. In the end all this did enable a compromise to be reached which resulted not only in a balance of power but also in a more subtle and accurate definition of ecclesiastical functions, as they then appeared, and one in which the spiritual and temporal aspects were more clearly distinguished. This is an excellent example of the progress of ideas accompanying and facilitating the solution of a conflict between two powers.

But this was not all. Every statement made in the course of the debate had to be supported by appropriate authorities. The emperor's supporters, for example, set out to establish the antiquity of the custom by which their master held rights of investiture over ecclesiastical benefices, by means of quotations drawn from the Old Testament. Gregory VII retorted by an attack on custom: 'Should you think fit to oppose us with custom, remember that Our Lord said not "I am the custom" but "I am the truth".' This penetrating observation was later to provide the basis for a whole theory of custom, setting limits to its authority and submitting it to the control of reason.

However, Gregory and his supporters were also out to

prove that the reforms they proposed were by no means innovations but merely a return to normal practice. At the instigation of the pope, and possibly even before his accession to the pontifical throne, a great deal of research had been set in motion into the archives of the Holy See and in the libraries of churches in Rome and southern Italy. This research, and sometimes merely a more attentive reading of already familiar texts, brought to light an impressive amount of material which was later incorporated in new collections of canon law, such as that by Yves of Chartres, or the *Britannica* (so called because it is now housed in the British Museum). This included papal letters, ancient customs of the Roman Church, canons of Councils General (of which only a minute portion had hitherto been known), as well as hitherto unknown patristic texts – St Cyprian was discovered and St Augustine better known – quotations from the 'Pontifical book'* and the three-part chronicle of Cassiodorus. Thus, to quote the historian Paul Fournier, 'for the first time history delved into the collections of ecclesiastical law'. Lastly, there were the texts of Roman law, and it seems probable that a text of the *Digest* was discovered in the course of these researches. This time neither the will nor the ability to use it was lacking. In fact it is in the *Britannica* that we first come across the ninety-three quotations from the *Digest* which later appeared in the works of Yves of Chartres.

This reinstatement of all that was best in Roman legal science was not without its consequences. It was accompanied by a veritable renaissance in the study of Roman law, in Rome itself, in Pavia, in the old imperial capital of Ravenna and, most of all, in Bologna. It is in Bologna, in about 1065, that we first hear of a fine jurist named Pepo; but the greatest glory of the city was Irnerius, who was born about 1060. Little is known of his life except that he was in the service of the countess Mathilda of Tuscany, an ally of Gregory VII,

* A kind of official history of successive pontificates.

and later of the emperor Henry V. His career as writer and professor at Bologna can be followed until at least 1125. He taught Roman law, elucidating each passage by useful comparisons and encouraging discussion among his pupils. He was the author of various commentaries or glosses and his chief work was entitled *Questions on the Subtleties of Law*. His disciples, known as the glossarists, carried on his work and some later became advisers to Frederic Barbarossa, whose ambition was to base his power – among other things – on this restoration of Roman law. Like Irnerius himself, the glossarists carried their tendency to take principles to their logical conclusions, their liking for consistency, their passion for classification and acceptance of subtlety to a fine art which in general was happily allied to a genuine good sense. By the end of the twelfth and during the thirteenth century the students of Bologna had helped to multiply the centres of study of Roman law throughout Europe.

We have dealt successively with the advances made by theologians and by jurists, but in fact these disciplines are inseparable from one another. One instance will serve to demonstrate this. In the course of the Quarrel of the Investitures, the serious question arose in Germany especially as to whether priests who had been condemned by Rome on charges of simony or incontinence, and even excommunicated, could continue to exercise their functions. A great many did so, and were even encouraged in this by their bishops. Whether the sacraments administered by these men had any value became a subject of fierce controversy to thousands of Christians, roused against their bad shepherds by the Pope. People trampled on the host because it had been consecrated by a married priest, refused the last sacrament and even baptized their own children. Students of canon law found themselves obliged to consider the nature of the sacraments, whether their validity depended on the worthiness of the person who administered them and, beyond this, on the nature of the priesthood itself, all of which were theological problems.

In addition, both theologians and canonists came up against the one major problem which by the year 1100 had become particularly urgent. Whatever subject they were dealing with, they had numerous references at their disposal which were all too often divergent and even contradictory. A lack of critical and historical sense allowed them to set an equally absolute and general value on all the canons of various Councils and all the writing of the Fathers of the Church, with the result that they found themselves caught up in endless insoluble arguments. Burchard of Worms complained bitterly in the preface to his collection of canon law that this confusion was bringing ecclesiastical law into discredit. In the controversies raised by men like Bérenger or Roscelin and in the disputes surrounding the Quarrel of the Investitures, these divergences assumed a dramatic importance. Men had to choose and to justify their choice. The supporters of Gregory VII, for instance, would only accept the canons of councils approved in their own day by the Pope. Yves of Chartres, at the end of the eleventh century, put forward a number of rules designed to ease the necessary compromise.

In the prologue to his own collection of canon law, he warned his readers:

do not immediately break out into reproaches against me if the authorities I have quoted appear to contradict one another. The doctors of the Church contradict each other no more than the doctors of the body who adapt or modify their remedies according to the intensity of the disease, and the person of the patient. ... For in reading them it is necessary to take into account the circumstances in which they wrote, the time and place and those for whom they were writing.

Above all, Yves of Chartres counselled making a distinction between those rules which should be strictly interpreted according to the letter of the law, and those which could bear some leniency and be bent to a more merciful interpretation.

It was probably from Roman law, with its classic distinction between justice and equity, that Yves drew this basic principle which was to be applied in their policies by popes like Urban II and which was materially to aid arrival at a compromise. This was a considerable step forward, but the general question of reconciling differing authorities still awaited systematic treatment.

CHURCH AND CULTURE

As long as monks had existed there had also been a strong movement aimed at directing them away from the paths of secular learning. The fear that they would become absorbed in it at the expense of their religious life was only too natural. Alcuin, while confessing the attractions it had had for him in his youth, advised his pupils not to abandon themselves too readily to the poetry of Virgil. Gerbert found himself confronted with God's expressed preference for peasants and illiterates. In the face of the trouble caused by applying dialectic to dogma, it was inevitable that this current of opposition should be reinforced in the eleventh century. Among the many writers who declared themselves strongly against any recourse to dialectic, St Peter Damian deserves a special place.

Peter Damian was an Italian monk who was a counsellor to several popes and tireless in his abuse of philosophers and philosophy. According to him, all human science was an invention of the devil who at the creation of mankind had appointed himself professor of grammar:

'Ye shall be as gods, knowing good and evil.' (Genesis III 5). There, brother. Would you learn grammar? Learn to decline 'God' in the plural!

Elsewhere he finds a telling image to show the uselessness of the study of letters for the knowledge of God: men do not light a lamp in order to look at the sun. But it would be unjust to judge Peter Damian on these hasty considerations alone.

He himself was quite capable of scholarly reasoning and his part in the intellectual life of the eleventh century, little of it as we know, is coming to seem an increasingly important one.

The figure of St Bernard occupies a similarly dominating position in our attitude to the twelfth century. The foundation of the Cistercian order, which was closely connected with the work of St Bernard, has already been described in some detail. Now we can take a look, against the background of the Cistercian ideal, at the reasons which were to make St Bernard an opponent of Abelard.

St Bernard was a fine scholar whose writings are to be admired as much for the eloquence of their style as for the vigour of the thought they contained. He had a profound, personal experience of the state of religious ecstasy and has left a highly detailed account of these mystical experiences and the means to reach them. His contribution to Marian theology is outstanding. Moreover he recognized that a knowledge of dialectics and philosophy could be extremely useful on occasion, but he insisted that these must always take second place. 'Peter, Andrew, the sons of Zebedee and their fellow disciples, were not chosen in a school of rhetoric or philosophy, and yet it was through them that the Saviour accomplished his work of Salvation.' And again: the apostles 'did not teach me to read Plato and unravel the subtleties of Aristotle, but they have taught me how to live, and that is no small science.'

In any case, the interest displayed in the secular sciences always seemed to him suspect:

There are some who wish to learn only in order to know, and this curiosity is unworthy of a man; others wish to learn only in order to be thought clever, and that is shameful vanity; others learn in order to trade their knowledge, to gain money or honours, and this traffic is dishonourable.

Especially he denounced the growth of these tendencies in monks. The general decline in the intellectual level of Europe

had naturally led them to turn their monasteries into sanctu-
aries of culture. But at a time when this culture was again on
the increase, and when the bulk of profane studies was becoming so enormous as to invade the whole lives of those who
were concerned in them, and where, moreover, the practice
of these subjects put the truths of the Faith in doubt, it was
fitting, in this as in other things, that the monks should be
recalled to the strict observation of the Rule laid down by St
Benedict. The monk's role was not to teach but to weep and
pray.

There was a good deal to be said for this point of view. In
fact, the monasteries were beginning to play a smaller part in
the spread of culture.

THE NEW SPREAD OF CULTURE

Guibert of Nogent, who was born in 1053, has left us a
valuable testimony to the real mutation which was taking
place in the field of education around the year 1100. 'In the
days immediately before, and even during, my own childhood', he wrote in about 1115,

the lack of schoolmasters was so great that it was all but impossible
to find any in the villages and they were hardly to be met with in the
cities. If by chance any were to be discovered, their learning was so
scant that it could scarcely be compared to that of the mere wandering
scholars of today.

This familiar passage indicates a rise in the standards of
masters and pupils as well as an increase in their numbers. It
marks, too, a kind of social transference. By the middle of the
eleventh century culture was still half shut up in the monasteries. What struck Guibert was the possibility of finding
teachers in the places where an increasing proportion of the
population was now concentrated – in the towns and villages.

The link between social evolution and the development of
education is therefore established. The early progress in

farming techniques which fostered demographic expansion and gave the individual peasant an increased yield, also released a growing number of men from work in the fields. The division of labour became more marked and a more complex social order emerged, in which an increasingly important part was played by intellectual occupations. Legal experts were needed to conduct the growing numbers of courts and deal with cases of greater complexity, and to run the notaries' offices which were springing up all over the southern regions. Feudal lords and sovereigns wanted educated clerks for their chancelleries and for local administration. In the cities there was a shortage of municipal scribes, and even tradesmen now required a minimum of education. The number of doctors was growing everywhere. Moreover, all this no longer concerned the clergy alone. Even outside the Church the acquisition of some degree of culture began to seem more and more natural.

All the same, the various royal courts cannot be said to have played an outstanding part in the general spread of culture. Some did encourage it by example, without becoming actual centres of learning themselves. The court of the new Norman kings of Sicily was a shining example in this respect. From 1130 to 1154 Roger II, who was himself able to read and write Latin and probably understood Arabic as well, inaugurated a dynasty of unusually enlightened patrons. We should remember, too, the feudal courts of southern France, whose manners extended, as a consequence of the marriages of Eleanor of Aquitaine, to the royal courts of France and England. But any such guiding role as in the great days of Charlemagne was no longer even conceivable.

Furthermore, the urban schools were only slowly and hesitantly coming into existence, and freeing themselves with some difficulty from ecclesiastical influences. They were situated in the areas of the greatest urban development: in Italy, where teachers are mentioned most frequently in the towns of Tuscany, and in the Low Countries, where the fire which destroyed the church and school of St Pharailda at Ghent towards the middle of the century gave the citizens an opportunity to open their own schools – though not without provoking the clergy into instant denunciation of this 'insolence of the laity'.

It was within the framework of the Church itself that the shift in the balance of society was most strongly felt. The monasteries ceased to play the leading part in the maintenance, enrichment and diffusion of culture which had been theirs since the sixth century. From this time on, very few of them would throw open their schools to pupils not formally dedicated to a life spent within their walls. St Vincent of Metz and St Trond in 'Lorraine' still possessed external schools, and there were certainly a number of other exceptions to this intellectual decline. The great abbey of Monte Cassino shone with the last glimmers of a splendour which had reached its height in the eleventh century. Cluny, thanks to the many-sided personality of Peter the Venerable, rose for some time to an intellectual peak which formed no part of its real vocation. In Lorraine the movement started in the time of Gerbert had grown to such proportions, and there was such collaboration between the monks and secular priests, that a number of monasteries such as Lobbes and Gembloux continued to play their part in a well-endowed intellectual scene. Normandy, after the Scandinavian occupation of the tenth century, had reverted to a condition very like that of Carolingian Europe, but for some time the presence of those two remarkable Italian teachers, Lanfranc and Anselm, made the abbey of Bec a quite outstanding centre of learning, although the monastery's comparative isolation has been seen to have limited the effects of St Anselm's teaching. Moreover, these were the exceptions. Elsewhere the libraries had ceased to grow, or even to be much used, and the copies made in previous centuries had begun to gather the dust from which they would be unearthed by the humanists of the fifteenth century. Intellectual life had reached a standstill. St Gall, Corbie,

Bobbio, Fulda, and all the long list of glorious names were all so many burnt-out fires.

Intellectual activity, which had deserted the ancient monastic foundations, spread out to incorporate cathedral schools and city chapters. Charlemagne, in the past, had urged these to aid in the spread of learning just as much as the monasteries, and his appeal cannot be said to have gone unheard. But with the coming of new life to the ancient cities, their churches had found a steady increase in their material and intellectual resources alike. They, and they alone, were in a position to throw open their doors to the host of students drawn by the prospective careers now available to educated men, or simply by the thirst for knowledge.

As in all periods of swift academic expansion – and in spite of the declared optimism of Guibert of Nogent – the problem lay rather in the number and quality of the teachers. Few were the schools able to boast of an uninterrupted succession of eminent professors over any length of time. All too often students would be attracted for a time by the presence of one such teacher, only to drift away again when he left. The schools, moreover, could only specialize in the subjects on which the masters' reputations were based. It was not until the end of the century that the teaching body had grown sufficiently to allow of a more equitable distribution among the schools, and meanwhile a process of selection was in force. The historian Haskins has summed up the situation in a classic observation: 'In 1100 the school followed the teacher, by 1200 the teacher followed the school.' Laon, in the early years of the twelfth century, provides an excellent example of a school whose brilliance was as short-lived as it was dazzling. Its great teacher, Anselm, was probably already in his decline when Abelard dealt him the final blow.

Among the centres which succeeded in maintaining a more constant level of achievement, Chartres and Paris deserve a special mention. Chartres had almost certainly had its episcopal school since the ninth century. Gerbert's pupil, Richer, travelled there to attend lectures in medicine, the only journey he ever made in his life. It was another pupil of Gerbert's, bishop Fulbert (1008–28), who turned it into an important centre of literature and philosophy, and Chartres retained a lively concern for matters of grammar and style even after the influence of new teachers had directed its studies chiefly towards philosophy and the scientific aspects of the classic *quadrivium*. A Breton, Bernard of Chartres, as a chancellor from 1119 to 1126, was responsible for introducing the Platonic note which characterized the school and at the same time greatly enhanced its reputation. All his works have been lost. His fame today rests entirely on the fervent admiration of his pupils, one of whom, an Englishman named John of Salisbury, did not scruple to call him 'the most abounding spring of letters in Gaul in modern times'. These pupils also made their own contribution to the development of a Platonism which, in the imperfect state of knowledge concerning the work of that philosopher, could be at best only rudimentary. The Norman, William of Conches, and the Poitevin, Gilbert of la Porrée (both of whom died around 1154), were the most brilliant exponents of a system to which Platonic philosophy and mathematics both made their own contributions – however humble – and which also made some attempt at a rational explanation of the origins of the world on the basis of the Biblical facts.

With Abelard came the definitive triumph of Paris over Chartres. By the beginning of the twelfth century the episcopal school which had been founded on the Île de la Cité already enjoyed a considerable reputation. Several teachers split off from this school and gathered their pupils on the montagne Sainte-Geneviève around the monastery of that name, on the site of what was later to become the Quartier Latin. In 1108 the college chapter of St Victor was established on the side of the same hill by William of Champeaux, the master who, as we shall see, was to be so cruelly – and somewhat unfairly – ridiculed by Abelard. This school was directed for some time by a young Saxon, Hugh of St Victor, the author of an admirable treatise on the sacraments. In addition to great breadth of vision – 'Learn everything,' he told his pupils, 'and then you will see that nothing is superfluous.' – Hugh was possessed of an unshakeable determination to direct all these various branches of learning first and foremost towards a better understanding of the Scriptures. In this respect St Victor marks a new era in the history of Biblical studies. Hugh and his pupils concentrated on establishing the most reliable text of the Bible and fixing its literal meaning before searching for allegorical interpretations, and they had no scruples in seeking enlightenment by talking to the Jews. Among the students of St Victor were Bretons, Normans, Englishmen, Scots, Germans, Norwegians and Italians. Abelard was by no means the only scholar who contributed to the fame of Paris.

As in the teaching methods employed, this shift of emphasis to the city churches brought about some alterations in detail, but no overwhelming change in the intellectual map of Europe.

In spite of the respectable contribution made by a few episcopal schools such as Bamberg, Freising and Canterbury, Germany and England were the most sparsely populated areas of this map, but they did produce a number of brilliant individuals, most of whom were educated in France. Indeed, northern France was at this time going through a particularly interesting period. Both politically, with the Capetian revival, and artistically, with the first steps towards the gothic style, the centre of gravity was in the Île-de-France, but the region of the Loire and 'Lorraine' on its eastern borders also remained areas of great activity. The new, rich current of ideas now sweeping throughout Italy from Sicily to Bologna and from Salerno into Lombardy is also worth mentioning, and the increasing scope of intellectual contacts in Spain, which will be examined in some detail further on.

All the same, the teaching methods which became current at this period cannot be called altogether new. A fairly clear impression of what took place can be obtained from John of Salisbury's description of what he saw in operation at Chartres. All teaching was primarily by means of 'lectures'. The teacher, whether he was reading from the Scriptures, classical poets or orators, or from collections of Roman or canon law, would pause frequently in order to elucidate the text before him in three ways. First he applied himself to a grammatical analysis (*littera*), next he would expound the meaning conveyed by an initial reading (*sensus*), and finally he would explore the deeper levels of thought which might be concealed under its apparent meaning (*sententia*). He would then check to find out how much of this intellectual nourishment had been assimilated by his pupils, of whom a considerable effort of memory was required. This could be eased to some extent by a variety of mnemonic techniques, such as summaries in the form of question and answer, simple memorable verses, or synoptic pictures, but memorization was nevertheless unavoidable because of the scarcity of books.

From here on, the twelfth century marked a new stage of development. The commentaries began to be arranged in a consistent whole and classified according to a logical plan. They incorporated set 'questions' on specific points, inter-pretations of difficult texts and the reconciliation of several divergent texts. It was in this field that Abelard achieved his most notable work.

Chapter 3

ABELARD

ABELARD's life is known to us in an intimacy of detail of which medieval documents afford few examples. At a moment of crisis in his career, and possibly with some idea of recapturing the attention of his public, Abelard himself wrote, in the form of a letter of consolation addressed to a friend, an extremely frank autobiography. The *Historia calamitatum*, the 'story of my troubles', is undoubtedly a highly subjective account and as such should be approached with caution, but Abelard seems to have been more inclined to judge himself harshly than to attempt to justify his conduct. Moreover, we also possess an exchange of letters between Abelard and his mistress Heloise which are so beautifully written – with such freedom of expression and so close to us in feeling – that there has even been some doubt as to their authenticity. But it seems certain that these passionate letters were actually written by Heloise and Abelard. Finally, this evidence is usefully completed by recollections of Abelard left by a number of his students.

For the first time, therefore, we are able not merely to record the more or less accurately established facts of a life, but to conjure up the feelings, emotions and calculations which filled and guided it. In addition, there is the never-to-be-neglected opportunity of frequently allowing the actors in this life-story to speak for themselves.

We left the young Abelard on the road to Paris after spending some time studying under Roscelin at Loches. In Paris he studied dialectic as a pupil of William of Champeaux, whose strongly Platonist ideas were in direct conflict with those of Roscelin. William was a famous teacher and the audience he drew to the cloister by the cathedral surrounded him with respectful admiration. Peter Abelard soon shattered this atmosphere.

Well received at first, I soon became a great nuisance to him because I persisted in refuting certain of his ideas and because, not fearing to dispute with him on very many occasions, I sometimes had the upper hand. This temerity also aroused the indignation of those of my fellow-students who were considered the first, an indignation that was all the greater because I was the youngest and the last comer.

Deciding he had learned enough, our hero was now eager to teach in his turn. This was not easy, since he had to obtain an authorization which William applied himself earnestly to getting him refused. But no great man is without his enemies, and it was probably with their help that Abelard was able to teach in the royal city of Melun (probably 1102 or thereabouts). He was an instant success. Pupils flocked to hear him and William found himself somewhat deserted. Before long Abelard transferred his school to Corbeil, nearer Paris, 'so as to be able to redouble my attacks more conveniently'. He flung himself into this task with youthful abandon, overdoing it to the point where he was soon in need of a complete rest. He returned to his family at le Pallet, 'ardently regretted' by his pupils. William of Champeaux must have heaved a sigh of relief.

A few years later, however, Abelard returned, completely recovered, and took his seat once more in the lecture room of the master who had meanwhile become canon of St Victor (1108) but was still teaching in the episcopal school. Another clash was inevitable. Publicly challenged on his solution to the problem of universals, William was obliged to modify his views and became a general laughing stock. He had no alternative but to resign. His successor at the cathedral school very wisely allowed his troublesome pupil to teach in his place. But the fight was not over. William secured the dismissal of this exceedingly diplomatic master and Abelard was obliged to return to Melun. Later he settled on the montagne Ste Gene-

viève. His pupils followed him everywhere. William disappeared into a monastery and ended his days as bishop of
Châlons-sur-Marne.

This marked the first stage in Abelard's life, and his first
success. Shortly afterwards he went home to le Pallet where
first his father and then his mother entered religion. Abelard
was present at the ceremony. Then came the question of what
he should do next. His secular education was complete. There
remained the study of theology, a subject which, as we have
seen, was still in the throes of creation. One name dominated
all others: that of William of Champeaux's former master,
Anselm of Laon, already an old man. Abelard set off for Laon,
still spoiling for a fight.

I therefore approached the old man who owed his reputation more
to his great age than to his talents or culture. All those who came to
him seeking his opinion of a subject which perplexed them went
more perplexed than ever. If one were content with listening to him
he seemed admirable, but if he were questioned he showed himself to
be nothing. For verbiage he was admirable, but his reasoning was
empty. His flame filled the house with smoke instead of illuminating
it. . . . Having learned this, I wasted no further time at his school.

No doubt Anselm was past his prime, but the little we know
of him suggests that Abelard's verdict was not altogether fair.
Anselm's pupils had accused him of shirking attendance at the
master's lectures and Abelard allowed himself to be provoked
into laying a bet that he would produce a commentary on a
particularly obscure prophecy of Ezekiel. To their great surprise he did so, with a success which left them utterly divided.
Anselm's most loyal and intransigent supporters persuaded
the old man to expel the audacious scholar from his classes,
and Abelard made his way back to Paris.

This was undoubtedly the most brilliant period of his life.
He was now completely qualified and able to include theology
among his subjects. One witness has described how scholars
drawn by his youthful fame flocked to hear him from England,

Brittany, Anjou, Poitou, Gascony, Spain, Normandy, Flanders and Germany. Abelard was not boasting when he wrote that

My two courses were attended by ever greater numbers of eager listeners; what profit they brought me, and what glory, you already know. ... But fools are always puffed up by prosperity. ... From this time I believed myself the only philosopher on earth.

It was now the year 1118. Abelard was nearly forty. Hitherto he had led a life devoted to study and one, beyond all doubt, of blameless chastity. Now he was assailed by 'the devil that walketh abroad in the noonday'. This particular devil took the enticing form of the niece of a canon of Notre Dame, whose name was Fulbert. Heloise was then seventeen years old and, if our hero is to be believed, extremely beautiful; but she was remarkable chiefly for the extent of her education. It was this that Fulbert asked Abelard to complete. Did Abelard, as he asserts, conceive from the very first the idea of seducing the young girl? At all events, he refused to accept any payment for his lessons and asked only that he might lodge in Fulbert's house. The trusting Fulbert agreed and even urged Abelard to punish his pupil in case of need, according to the custom of the schools. 'In short,' Abelard wrote,

we were first united under the same roof and then by a single heart. Under a pretence of study, we gave ourselves up wholly to love. The lessons furnished us with the means to those mysterious communings dictated by the vows of love. The books were open, but our words were more of love than of philosophy, and there were more kisses than explanations. My hands wandered more often to her breast than to our books and our eyes turned lovingly on one another more often than on the texts before us. The better to avert suspicion I would sometimes go so far as to beat her, blows given in love and not in anger, by fondness, not hatred, and sweeter than all balm. What more can I say? In our passion we experienced all the phases of love, and every refinement known to the imagination of lovers we exhausted. The more novel these delights were to us, the more we prolonged them with a frenzy that could never tire.

For the girl this was love, absolute and at first sight, which made her abandon herself utterly to her lover's will. However cold-blooded he may have been to begin with, he too was soon invaded by the fever of his senses and devoured by a consuming passion. He wrote love poems which have unfortunately not survived. 'Most of these verses, as you know, have become popular in many lands and are still sung by those who find themselves under the spell of the same feelings.' He neglected his work, to the great disappointment of his students. 'I no longer gave my classes with more than a lukewarm indifference . . . all I did was to repeat my old lectures. . . .' In the face of such evidence the lovers could not hope to keep their secret for long. Fulbert, naturally, was the last to notice. In a fit of righteous anger he drove his guest out of his house, but the meetings continued in secret and Heloise conceived a child. Abelard promptly abducted her and sent her to one of his sisters in Brittany. There Heloise gave birth to a boy who was given the curious name of Astrolabe.

Abelard offered to make amends by marrying Heloise. Having taken only minor orders, he was canonically at liberty to marry. All he asked was that the marriage should remain a secret 'so as not to damage my reputation'. It was Heloise, always ready to forget herself for the sake of her lover, who opposed the plan.

Abelard has recorded her arguments:

But let us say nothing of the hindrance a wife would prove to your philosophical studies, and think of the position a lawful alliance would place you in. What connexion can there be between academic work and the conduct of a home, between a pulpit and a cradle, books or tablets and a distaff, the pen or stylus and the spindle? Is there any man who, when he is meditating on the Scriptures or philosophy, can bear the crying of a new-born baby, the singing of the nurse who lulls it to sleep, the coming and going of servants, men and women about the house and the constant smells and uncleanliness of children? You will say that the rich do it. Yes, no doubt, because they have rooms set aside in their palaces or great houses, because with their wealth money is no object and they do not know the everyday worries. But the condition of philosophers is not like that of rich people and those who seek a great fortune or whose lives are given up to the things of this world rarely devote themselves to the study of Scripture or philosophy.

Practical considerations were not the only ones she named. A philosopher, like a man dedicated to religion, ought to live in continence or at least avoid tying himself by marriage. Heloise recalled the examples of Socrates, who was tormented by his wife, and of Cicero, who refused to marry again. These arguments may surprise us today but they were certainly very strong in the time of Abelard. This was the ideal of a life of heroic continence held by the masters and pupils Abelard saw around him. He had failed to keep faith with it but at least he wanted to keep his marriage a secret. Heloise knew the secret could not be kept. She concluded stoically:

Indeed, the name of wife appears more forceful and more holy, but I have always preferred that of mistress or, if you will forgive my saying so, of concubine and prostitute. For the more I humble myself for you, the more I hope to find favour in your eyes and, by mortifying myself thus, to bring no hurt to the splendour of your fame.

Against the advice of Heloise, Abelard married his mistress, and the difficulties she had foreseen very soon followed. In spite of the care they took to live apart and meet only in secret, the news soon spread. Fulbert, anxious to publicize the fact that reparation had been made, was probably instrumental in this. With the utmost heroism Heloise swore an oath that she had never married Abelard. To save her from abuse, he sent her to the convent at Argenteuil where she had been brought up.

When they heard of this, her uncle and her family or relatives thought that I had deceived them and had put Heloise in a convent in order to be rid of her. Beside themselves with anger, they got together and one night as I was resting at home in a room apart they bribed one of my servants to admit them and subjected me to the most barbarous and shameful revenge . . . they cut from me those parts of the body with which I had committed that act of which they complained, and afterwards fled.

His physical sufferings and his shame – which was further increased by the countless nasty Biblical references to eunuchs which flooded to his mind – were made all the worse by the lamentations of his students, who immediately flocked to their master's house. 'In this condition of misery and confusion it was, I confess, a sense of shame rather than a vocation which drove me to the shelter of the cloister.' Heloise had already preceded him there, acting on his instructions and probably with the object of making quite sure she would never be another man's.

There were those, as I recall, who would have spared one so young from the yoke of the monastic rule, as from a torment too great to bear; they pitied her fate but her only answer, through her sobs and tears, was to utter the lament of Cornelia: 'Oh noble husband, so little formed for such a marriage! Had my fate such power over a head so lofty? Wicked that I am, was I to marry to bring about your undoing? Accept in expiation the punishment I willingly go to!' With these words she advanced towards the altar and received from the bishop's hands the consecrated veil and publicly professed the conventual oath.

Heloise was then twenty years old, more or less, and for love's sake she embraced a lifetime of seclusion and asceticism.

Abelard himself entered the royal abbey of St Denis of which Suger was to become abbot a few years later. For some time he remained there in a state of prostration. Then, in response to requests to resume his teaching, he did so at a priory attached to the abbey, at Maisoncelle in Champagne. The pupils who flocked to hear him proved that his misfortunes had in no way diminished his reputation, and with this encouragement he set himself to write down the substance of his teaching. The result was the *Treatise on the Unity and*

Trinity of God, an application of dialectical methods to one of the most pressing theological problems of the day.

It led him into fresh trouble. The Treatise was far from perfect, it was occasionally imprudent and not altogether understood, and a number of theologians found it highly alarming. At the instigation of two former pupils of Anselm of Laon, Abelard was brought before a Council at Soissons, presided over by a papal legate (1121). Despite the protection extended to him by a number of prelates, Abelard was found guilty and sentenced to have his book burned and retire once more to his cloister. Eluding the mob stirred up by his enemies to stone him, he returned once more to St Denis.

But he was fated never to be left in peace anywhere. It was not long before he made himself thoroughly unpopular with the monks by rebuking them for their irregular lives – which in fact in 1122 Suger was to begin reforming. One particular incident precipitated the disaster. It was at the time the undisputed belief that St Denis, bishop of Paris and founder of the abbey (probably in the third century), was one and the same as Dionysius (or Denis) the Areopagite, the Athenian converted by St Paul, who was, moreover, credited with the authorship of the philosophical treatise solemnly presented to Louis the Pious by the Byzantine ambassador in 827.* We may smile at such confusions, but in the twelfth century nearly every church in France boasted a supposed foundation by the immediate followers of Christ or the Apostles. It was a dangerous belief to contradict. Abelard committed the error of showing the monks a passage from Bede which disproved the identification. Indignantly they drove him out.

Abelard was finally allowed to retire to a deserted spot near Nogent-sur-Seine. He was given a piece of land on which to build himself a hermitage of mud and wattle, and there he settled with a single clerk. But his retreat soon became known. Students hastened to beg him to resume his lessons. Abelard yielded and a village of tents and hovels sprang up rapidly

* See p. 102.

around his hermitage. 'My disciples ... were more like hermits than students.' The money they provided rescued him from poverty and enabled him to rebuild his hermitage in stone. 'It was called the Paraclete in memory of the fact that I had come here as a fugitive and, in the midst of my despair, had found some rest in the consolations of divine grace.' His repose was brief. Again the accusations of heresy pursued him and he sank into an intense depression.

Struck with horror, as though beneath the threat of a thunderbolt, I expected at any moment to be dragged before councils or assemblies as an heretic or unclean person. ... I fell into such despair that I thought of leaving Christian lands and going among the infidel where, at the cost of some small tribute, I might buy the right to live a Christian life among the enemies of Christ.

In this extremity he must have heard with some relief the news that the monks of St Gildas of Rhuys had just elected him their abbot. St Gildas, situated on a peninsula facing Quiberon on the south of the bay of Morbihan, was not so very far from the region where Abelard was born. None the ess, he soon came to regard his sojourn there as a fearful exile.

It was a barbaric land with a strange tongue and a rough and savage people, while the monks lived with a lawlessness that was notoriously rebellious to all check. ... And there, on the shores of the fearful, roaring Ocean, at the extremities of a land which forbade me all possibility of further flight, I repeated often in my prayers: From the ends of the earth have I cried unto Thee, O Lord, in the torment of my heart.

Abelard did his best to re-establish discipline in the monastery, where nearly every monk had a wife and children, and to rescue it from the clutches of the local tyrant, with the result that one day brigands were set to ambush him on the road, and on another occasion the wine in his chalice was poisoned.

In the midst of all these horrors there was an unexpected piece of comfort. Suger, who was just embarking on his work of reorganization, had unearthed a charter proving that the priory of Argenteuil belonged to St Denis. Heloise (by now the prioress) and her companions were obliged to leave (1129). When Abelard learned of this he offered them the Paraclete; the gift was confirmed by Pope Innocent II, in Abelard's presence, on the occasion of the consecration of the high altar at Chartres. He was free to visit the Paraclete and to see Heloise once more.

It was at this time that he wrote his *Story of My Troubles*. The text came to the eyes of Heloise and was the start of a touching correspondence between them.

To her master, or rather her father; to her husband, or rather her brother; from his servant, or rather his daughter; his wife, or rather his sister; to Abelard, from Heloise.

These are the opening words of Heloise's first letter and they stress, with some subtlety, the painfully equivocal situation to which fate had condemned them. She admits that reading his story has reopened all her wounds. She recalls her past feelings for Abelard and sets herself to justify it. Finally, she asks the help of his pious teaching.

After ten years she was still passionately in love. Her second letter reveals how far:

Those lovers' delights we enjoyed together were so sweet to me that I cannot find it in my heart to condemn them, or even wipe out the memory of them without pain. Whichever way I turn, they are always in my sight, they and their desires. Even while I sleep, their illusions pursue me. Always, even in the most solemn moments of the mass, when prayer should be most pure, the obscene images of these pleasures still enthrall my poor soul so that I give myself up to this depravity rather than to prayer. I, who should bemoan what I have done, sigh instead after that which I have lost. And not only those things we have done, but the very times and places in which we did them together are so graven in my heart that I see them all again with you and am not free from them even in my sleep. Sometimes even the movements of my body reveal the thoughts that are in my soul, and they betray themselves by involuntary words. I am so unhappy and with what justice I repeat the lament of a soul in torment: 'Wretched that I am, who will deliver me from this living death?'

Could it really have been the abbess of the Paraclete, justly famed for her wise guidance of her community, who wrote this astonishing letter? Surely she must have been suffering from some desperate – and possibly temporary – mood which drove her to an exaggerated expression of her feelings? Abelard, at all events, was horrified. With a pressing gentleness he did his best to recall Heloise to a more exalted love.

My own love, which enwrapped us both in the bonds of sin, was no more than concupiscence. It does not deserve the name of love. I slaked my miserable desires with you, and that was all I loved. You say I suffered for you. It may be true, but it would be more just to say that I suffered because of you, and even that despite myself! I suffered, not for love of you but by the violence that was used against me, not for your salvation but to your despair. But Jesus Christ suffered for your salvation, suffered for you of his own free will, Jesus, whose sufferings are the cure for all ills, takes away all sufferings. I beseech you then to give to him all your grief and compassion.

So far as we know, Heloise never agreed in so many words to follow Abelard's suggestion and sublimate her human love in God. Her letters in future were confined to requests for advice on the guidance of her community, but beneath the nun's veil, her single love and a truly classical stoicism remained the masters of her soul. As prioress, however, she proved careful not to ask her sisters 'to be more than Christians', not to attach too much importance to outward forms and to follow the counsels of 'reason' and 'discretion'. In this way her cultured and disciplined mind did become a real part of her religion.

As for Abelard, he managed to get himself released from the impossible abbacy of St Gildas and, while taking on the spiritual direction of the Paraclete and preaching here and there, was able to resume his teaching in Paris. John of Salisbury recounts how in 1136 he travelled to France to continue his studies and listened to Abelard who was then presiding on the montagne Ste Geneviève, a famous doctor and admired by all. There, at his feet, I acquired the first elements of the art of dialectic and, according to the feeble measure of my understanding, drank in with all the eagerness of my soul everything that fell from his lips.

In writing, too, this was a fruitful period. Abelard endeavoured to revise and clarify the thoughts expressed in his earlier work, but these activities, and the success which attended him, were not long in bringing fresh trials.

The trouble started when a Cistercian named William of St Thierry wrote a treatise refuting thirteen so-called errors of Abelard's. In particular, William attracted the attention of St Bernard, whose energy and moral influence were then at their height. At first there were interviews in which Bernard tried in vain to persuade Abelard to modify his teaching or give it up altogether. In the end Abelard asked for a public debate, counting on his unparalleled command of dialectic to convince his opponents of the futility of their accusations. Bernard seemed to agree. In fact, he shunned the very idea of an argument in which, for all his broad learning and mental agility, he would be beaten in advance. When Abelard appeared before the Council held at Sens at Pentecost 1140 on the occasion of a visit by King Louis VII, the assembly, cunningly prepared by Bernard, turned itself into a tribunal. Convinced that anything he said would be misinterpreted, Abelard preferred to maintain a haughty silence, greatly to the disappointment of such supporters as he nevertheless possessed among the Council. He declared that he acknowledged no judge but the Pope. The Council hastily condemned nineteen propositions drawn from his writings and had their verdict ratified by Rome.

Unshaken, Abelard determined to go to Rome to defend himself. It was a trying journey for a man broken by age and suffering. He set off, stopping at various monasteries on the way. At Cluny he was received by Peter the Venerable and was won over by the tact and kindliness of this truly saintly man. He agreed to repudiate everything in his writings which might have conflicted with the Faith, and in addition to resume his writing and to teach the monks of this most revered of all monasteries. Through Peter's good offices it was even made possible to arrange an interview of reconciliation with Bernard. At last Abelard was able to live for a few months in peace. Here he wrote his last works, including the *Dialogue Between a Philosopher, a Jew and a Christian*, in which the latter shows that, far from denying the truths which they themselves uphold, the Christian faith contains and enriches them. Abelard died in harness in April 1142, at the age of sixty-three, in the Cluniac priory of St Marcel near the Saône to whose more peaceful and healthy surroundings the solicitous care of Peter the Venerable had transferred him.

The same solicitude followed him even after death. Peter was anxious that he should be the one to tell Heloise of the death of her beloved, and he did so in words of immense delicacy:

And so, dear and reverend sister in God, he with whom, after your carnal union, you were united by the better and stronger bonds of divine love, with whom and under whom you served Our Lord, he, I say, as before in your own, is now warmed in the bosom of our Lord who, at the day of His coming, when the voice of the archangel and the trumpet of God shall sound out of heaven, shall keep him and restore him to you by His grace.

More than this, Peter himself accompanied Abelard's remains to the Paraclete where he was buried, and dictated a form of absolution which was placed on the tomb.

Heloise lived on for another twenty-two years. She died in 1164, having reached the same age as Abelard, and was buried at his side in the crypt. In the fifteenth century their remains were transferred to the great church of the Paraclete, only to be disturbed again by the Revolution. Today they lie together in the cemetery of Père-Lachaise in Paris.

ABELARD'S WORK AND ITS SIGNIFICANCE

It is not merely for the purpose of allowing the reader a few pages of light reading that Abelard's life has been recounted in such detail. It is a life which throws light on a whole period and a whole society with which it was in so many respects bound up. It shows us the life of the student, travelling from one city to the next to pursue his studies, and hastening sometimes immense distances to sit at the feet of a famous teacher. It shows us the position of the teacher, tied by the dual necessity of obtaining a licence to teach, generally from a bishop, and getting together enough pupils to earn himself a livelihood. We can feel the excitement running through this small yet rapidly expanding intellectual world, the intoxication with which they handled these still unfamiliar mental tools, and the heroic, almost ascetic light in which they viewed the philosopher and his function. We see a few women among them, for it is unlikely that Heloise was unique, and find some evidence of female emancipation which can be connected with the new poetic accents of the *langue d'oc* and with the importance which the cult of the Virgin began to assume in Christian sensibilities at this stage. We can also see the extent to which these intellectuals had been nourished on classical traditions: Heloise cited Socrates and Cicero and quoted from the *Pharsalia* as she took the veil.

Lastly, this account makes clear the extraordinary appeal Abelard undoubtedly exercised, and suggests some reasons for it. To his pupils he was a teacher without parallel, with his loathing of stale formulae, his boldness and originality of thought, his readiness to face up to a problem in all its implications and carry it to the logical conclusion, and finally his sheer intellectual agility and the vigour and clarity of his explanations. Abelard threw his whole personality into his teaching. Perhaps it was from his father the knight that he inherited his pugnacious temperament, which made him constantly on the look-out for an argument, endlessly, and

not always justly, at odds with the old masters, and ever ready
to involve himself in public disputes. Certainly his eager,
impatient search for an explanation for everything was a far
cry from the prayerful meditation of a man like Anselm of
Bec or even from the cautious and moderate Peter the
Venerable with his deep sense of mystery.

Nevertheless Abelard always displayed a distinct yearning
for orthodoxy. When his views were condemned he protested
that he had been misunderstood and not that he was right and
his adversaries wrong. One of his letters to Heloise defines his
attitude in no uncertain terms:

> I would not be a philosopher to contradict St Paul, nor would I be
> an Aristotle to cut myself off from Christ, for there is no other name
> under heaven by which I may reach salvation. The rock on which I
> have built my conscience is the same as that on which Christ built
> his Church.

But to some extent he was the victim of his own nature.
This made him a symbol of intellectual revolt during his
lifetime and has continued to make him something of an
enigma to historians.

So many different pictures have been drawn for us of this
son of Bérenger. Most of all, it is his unhappy love affair
which has captured men's imagination. Villon, in the fifteenth
century, remembered '*la très sage Héloïs*' in his *Ballade des
dames du temps jadis,* and so did the nineteenth century, with
its passion for legends of romantic love. But the nineteenth
century also recognized Abelard's intellectual gifts and even
saw him as a free-thinker, defending the rights of reason
against St Bernard – a rationalist born out of his time. Our
own day has added the picture of a 'progressive' Abelard,
ranged alongside the citizens struggling for their independence
in contributing to the collapse of feudalism and the 'pontifical
theocracy'. But in all these views certain aspects of his
personality are magnified to the point of caricature and
certain aspects of his work artificially cut off from the whole.

Yet even the most scholarly and responsible of historians are still prone to argue over Abelard's real beliefs. Was he a heretic, or merely guilty of some theological errors? Or was he, as he himself claimed, merely misunderstood? Supposing him to have been a heretic, how can we explain the fact that so many bishops, even popes, should have defended him or been influenced by him? And supposing he were not, must his enemies stand convicted of malice and injustice?

If we try to discover some of the reasons why so many doubts about him have persisted, we shall see more clearly why it is important to approach his work with caution.

The first thing to remember is the state in which we now have this work. The Council of Sens ordered it to be completely destroyed. Some of his works are known to us only through a single copy which must have travelled a long way even in 1140 to be out of reach of authority, while others are merely more or less faithful reconstructions made by his followers. All we possess is a few spars from the wreck.

This lack of documentary evidence is all the more serious because Abelard was constantly revising and rewriting his work. His writing was closely bound up with his career as a whole, and his teaching and indefatigable argumentativeness led him to alter or add to his writings as new ideas or further information came his way. There was undoubtedly a development in his thought, but in order to follow it we should have to study every stage of his work; and this is just what we do not possess. Moreover, so much rewriting makes it almost impossible to establish any certain chronological pattern for his work, since that which has survived is undated. There is no point in assuming that Abelard's work progressed from the simple to the more complex, because even at a very late stage he was still composing handbooks for beginners. Consequently any attempt at reconstructing his work chronologically must be largely hypothesis.

It would be of some help if all this had been satisfactorily edited. To quote one example, there is this sentence which occurs in the *Introduction to Theology*. 'We do not believe because God has said so, but because we are convinced that it is so.' This would seem to be an admirable plea for the rights of reason against faith, and the passage has been extensively used by historians anxious to portray Abelard as 'the standard-bearer of free-thought'. It has also involved those who maintain Abelard's orthodoxy in complicated mental contortions in order to explain it. But the manuscript on which this passage is based is corrupt; another copy discovered at a later date shows that the copyist had omitted part of the sentence and in so doing had totally reversed Abelard's meaning. This was originally part of a commentary on a passage of Gregory the Great and what Abelard actually said was that it was possible to have faith without merit and that this was the case when 'we do not believe because God has said so, but because we are convinced that it is so'. It is an example which may help us to appreciate the thanklessness of the task facing textual critics.

Even when Abelard's text has been established and dated, real problems of interpretation still remain. These are partly due to the terminological confusion which frequently dogs pioneers in any field. He will use the same word in a number of different senses within the same work, but this is only obvious from the most detailed examination. Nor is he always careful to explain his intentions or the standpoint from which he is writing. To take yet another example: in the same *Introduction to Theology* Abelard defines faith as 'opinion concerning things which are not apparent'. Now the word 'opinion' (*opinio, existimatio*) was used in the sense of a vague, indefinite awareness, containing a certain subjective element and therefore questionable. St Bernard finds fault with him for 'apparently considering either that our common faith is worth no more than an opinion, or that it is open to anyone to make a selection from the truths we are offered just as the fancy takes him'. In fact Abelard was not attempting to define the Faith as such, or to assess how much it was justified. All he was trying to do was to describe the psychological processes which come closest to the intellectual act on to which it is grafted. Following Aristotle, Abelard maintained that the only certain knowledge we can arrive at unaided is that of the concrete facts provided by actual, individual objects. It followed that in matters of Faith our reason faltered and divine Revelation should be our only guide. This is the very opposite of rationalism. And yet St Bernard's misinterpretation is not hard to understand and must have been made by more than one of Abelard's pupils; only in their case it would have been accepted wholeheartedly. Its effect upon orthodox theologians is understandable.

These remarks have been intended primarily to encourage caution and as a warning against looking for the most original and outstanding aspects of Abelard's work where these are not in fact to be found. In order to assess his real contribution we must take another look at his development as far as it can be deduced from the most probable chronological estimate of his work.

Abelard was first a pupil of Roscelin and afterwards of Roscelin's most implacable adversary, William of Champeaux. St Anselm had accused Roscelin of moving in the direction of tritheism. This may have been so but it did not solve the dialectical problems he raised, while at the other extreme the answer worked out by William was no more satisfactory. Did this mean dialectic should be abandoned altogether? Abelard found in this the material for two complementary themes which ran through all his work: a criticism of the errors committed by dialecticians and a reinstatement of dialectic when properly understood. He also evolved his own solution to the problem of universals and tried to apply it to the elucidation of the mystery of the Trinity. The result was the *Treatise on the Unity and Trinity of God* which was condemned at Soissons.

Abelard set to work once more. He had confined himself to presenting his arguments; now he endeavoured to base these on the texts of the Scriptures and the Fathers. The first version of the *For and Against* (*Sic et non*), comprising a collection of quotations drawn from his own readings grouped according to subject – now lost – can probably be assigned to this period. Thus armed, he returned to and expanded the subject matter of his treatise in his major theological works, entitled *Christian Theology* and *Introduction to Theology*. While putting the finishing touches to the latter during his last period of teaching in Paris (1135–40) he also wrote a *Morals* and produced a final version of the *For and Against*, which was expanded to include a great many more texts.

This brief summary makes it clear that Abelard was extremely concerned to support himself more and more firmly on the 'authorities' of the Fathers of the Church. No previous author had read or quoted so extensively, and those who came after him were constantly delving into the abundant treasure so conveniently stored up for them by his efforts. There can be no doubt that for Abelard himself this was more than simply a useful tactic to be employed in combating his adversaries: it was the result of a profound belief.

In those fields where we are able to pursue it, the development of his thought seems to have been increasingly directed away from rationalism. At first, following certain theories of St Justin and St Augustine, he thought that the pagan philosophers had been able to reach some of the truths of Christianity and attain some more or less confused foreknowledge of the Incarnation and the Trinity. Not that he believed they had done this by the power of reason alone and without the aid of Revelation. Abelard felt that the rectitude of their thought and the moral strictness of their lives had earned them the right to a kind of personal illumination to assist the progress of their reason. Later he appears to have abandoned these adventurous ideas which diminished – though to no very great extent – the need for Revelation.

We must now attempt to define the exact nature of Abelard's achievement. First of all there is his work as a philosopher. To begin with, Abelard succeeded in presenting and even formulating in its entirety a complete exposition of the problem of universals, and in offering a solution. This solution was admittedly somewhat questionable, but it was strongly argued, carried to its conclusion and, above all, new. This is not the place for a full discussion of Abelard's theory, but it is worth remembering the words of one excellent judge that 'there may perhaps be strong grounds for maintaining that, paradoxically enough, the first Latin work to put forward any new ideas in philosophy dates from the twelfth century A.D.' (Étienne Gilson). Abelard's achievement is all the greater since he possessed only a very incomplete knowledge of the works of Aristotle, on which he might otherwise have leaned. Sufficient stress has already been laid on the lack of powerful and original thought from which the time of Alcuin and even Gerbert suffered to such a marked degree, to warrant describing this as a considerable step forward. That it was due to a man of exceptional genius is true, but his example remained. To recall another happy phrase of Étienne Gilson's: 'Abelard, as it were, set an intellectual standard below which it would afterwards become unthinkable to fall.'

As a theologian, Abelard's work was also considerable, if admittedly suspect. By attempting to postulate the mystery of the Trinity correctly and by laying man's responsibility for his actions more in their intention than in their consequences, he was running into difficulties from which he was unable wholly to extricate himself. He has, however, one remaining merit, which is that of having been the first to produce a complete and ordered synthesis of theology. This was his goal and he achieved it. The text of the *Introduction to Theology* opens with a strong statement of his intentions. 'The sum total of man's salvation lies, in my opinion, in three things, which are faith, charity and the sacrament.' The whole pattern of the book follows from this. Under faith are listed all the terms of Christian dogma. Charity comprises the arguments devoted to moral precepts, virtues and vices. Lastly, there is the sacrament, a systematic account of the sacraments of the Church. No previous author had succeeded in presenting a doctrinal synthesis to equal it. Abelard was the first to apply to it the name of 'theology', which had previously been used, among other things, to designate the study of the Scriptures or of divinity. Another expert judge, Father de Ghellinck, has called this 'a real turning point in the history of theology'.

Finally, there is Abelard's teaching in method, the rules of which he laid down in his *For and Against*, and which he himself applied in his other work. Like many others before him he came up against the divergencies and contradictions which, to all appearances at least, were to be found in the Scriptures and the work of the Fathers. His own extensive reading and his piercing intelligence even enabled him to make some notable additions to the list. On the other hand, with characteristic energy, he went far beyond all previously suggested attempts at reconciling them. In this connexion it is worth quoting almost the whole of his preface to *For and Against*.

He begins by saying that because the writings of the Fathers may seem to us to vary or even contradict one another, this is no excuse for judging them hastily or regarding what they say as untrue. We should rather take stock of our own inadequacy and reflect that they were guided by the light of the Holy Ghost while we are not. We must therefore look elsewhere for the reasons for contradictions which exist only in appearance.

First of all, certain authors have used words in an unusual sense, or even in a number of different senses. This may be a literary device: did not Cicero counsel the avoidance of uniformity as the mother of boredom? It may also be a means of communicating more effectively with an audience, by adopting its own vocabulary even where this is not strictly correct: did not St Augustine advise doing just this? Moreover, there is always some difficulty in getting to the root of another person's ideas. This latter was a difficulty which Abelard himself, with his complaints of being misunderstood, was in an excellent position to know.

Another necessary precaution is to make quite sure that the writings in question are not apocryphal. A great many works have been attributed to a venerable author in this way simply in order to acquire the benefit of his authority. Account must also be taken of the errors made by copyists, and here we must resort to the best manuscripts. We read in the Gospels of St Matthew and St John that Christ was crucified at the sixth hour, whereas according to St Mark it was the third. In fact Mark too had really said the sixth hour and the apparent contradiction was to be explained by a confusion in the Greek characters.

What is also certain and must be taken into account is that the Fathers themselves occasionally revised and modified certain passages. St Augustine, for instance, corrected himself several times when his knowledge of the truth increased. It is important to distinguish between when an author is expressing his own personal views and when he is merely recording those of someone else: St Augustine, St Hilary, and others besides, interpolated in their works passages from Origen or from notorious heretics. We must be careful not to attribute to them things which may be merely quotations. There is moreover the habit of using colloquial expressions even though these do not correspond to the facts. We do this in our own conversation. In the same way, because Joseph was regarded as the father of Jesus, although this was not so, the Virgin said to her Son: 'Thy father and I have sought thee sorrowing.' (Luke II. 48.)

Even taking all these observations into account, divergences still remain. In the case of the rule laid down by one of the Fathers, we must examine his intentions, whether he was stating a categorical law, or speaking in the way of a dispensation, or merely offering general advice. (In this we can see the distinctions drawn by Yves of Chartres at work.) Finally, even if there can be no question of any error occurring in the

Gospels, the Fathers, with the best will in the world, might have been mistaken sometimes, especially in matters not directly concerning the Faith. Did not the prophets themselves err when the prophetic spirit deserted them? God permitted this in order to recall them to humility. Was not St Peter himself mistaken, even after Pentecost, on the subject of circumcision, and was not St Paul compelled to correct him? St James, too, wrote that: 'if there is one whose words never give offence, then that man is perfect. Even at my advanced age, I lay no claim to such perfection, and how much more then when I began to write as a young man.' A certain hierarchy must therefore be acknowledged among the authorities. Just as Isidore of Seville once advised that, in case of conflict between the canons of two different councils, it was best to choose the more ancient and venerable, so one must always know how to exercise a certain amount of selection.

Men should not therefore be deterred by the apparent contradictions in the authorities, or refuse to face up to them. Their basic agreement cannot be in doubt. We have God's word for that. A method of establishing this agreement exists and should be used. This was the object of the apparently contradictory quotations which Abelard assembled on all questions of theology in his *For and Against* without himself actually offering a solution in so many words. What had been a source of difficulties became in this way the subject of a systematic exercise. It was an intellectual triumph.

This is the real meaning of the *For and Against*, and not, as has sometimes been thought, a wish to discredit the authorities by displaying their contradictions. It is true that the basic principles of Abelard's method were neither wholly new nor altogether perfect. The quotations still had to be placed more accurately in their context, taking into consideration the historical conditions under which the works in question were written. Nevertheless, it was certainly an advance.

When Abelard lay dying at St Marcel the intellectual movement to which he had made such a decisive contribution was reaching its peak.

In about 1140 an Italian monk about whom practically nothing is known except his name, Gratiano, was completing his *Concord of Discordant Canons*. This was a real step forward in the history of canon law. The contents were not merely classified in the most satisfactory order possible, but the divergences between the juridical sources were systematically examined in the case of each subject and resolved according to the method used in *For and Against*. This raised canon law to the dignity of a science and made it a law unto itself. The success of this work was immense, and all later authors based themselves upon it.

In theology itself a number of works of this period reveal the direct influence of Abelard. However they may have been divided in other respects, it is possible to discern a connexion between Abelard and Peter Lombard, a Parisian master of theology who composed, around 1150, a collection of *Sententiae* which proved to have a brilliant scholarly future. It would be an exaggeration to say, as one of Abelard's biographers has done, that Peter Lombard was 'Abelard successful . . . Abelard as a bishop'. In fact Peter's *Sententiae* are a vast, systematic and reasoned exposition of the truths of the Faith, and he did not follow Abelard's plan or his dialectical method. He did however benefit from Abelard's efforts to establish a balance between faith and reason and to provide a rational explanation of revealed doctrine. On a number of points he even adopted Abelard's ideas. Finally, it was at least partly to Abelard and to Gratiano that he owed his skill in combining several different doctrinal traditions into a richer synthesis.

ALONGSIDE ABELARD

SUCH, then, as far as we can tell, was Abelard's role in the intellectual development of the twelfth century, with its greatness, its fertility, and the sacrifices which followed from the stress laid on dialectic among the liberal arts. In many respects Abelard dominated his time just as Alcuin or Gerbert had dominated theirs. But was he wholly representative? To answer this question in the negative is in no way to diminish him. The farther we go along the road travelled by European culture, the more conscious are we of a richness and diversity too great for any one personality, however eclectic, to contain it all.

What must now be taken into account is in fact an entire movement which grew up alongside Abelard and, as it were, just out of his reach. First let us recall everything that has been said so far about the treasures of science and philosophy accumulated in the Near and Middle East in classical times; about the way in which these traditions were preserved or rediscovered in Byzantium, and, to an even greater extent, in the Arabic world; about the growth of centres of this same learning in Muslim Spain and lastly about the way in which Gerbert, having absorbed it himself, was able to take a new step forward by passing on some fragments of its treasures to western Christendom.

But Gerbert was an isolated figure, far ahead of his time. The memory of his teaching was preserved by a handful of scholars but gradually faded out. The ties which had been established with Arabic science were not pursued. In this respect the eleventh century was a blank, however numerous the contacts between Latins, Arabs and Mozarabs within Spain itself. The century which opened with the death of

Al Mansur, the great scourge of the Spanish Christian states (1002), and closed with the capture of Jerusalem by the Crusaders (1099), saw rather the growth of the *camino francés* – the pilgrim route of Compostela – of the *Chanson de Roland* and the idea of the Crusade itself. Not that these differences invariably drew a curtain of hatred between the two camps. There is plenty of evidence to show that a good deal of peaceful coexistence was going on at the same time. A more likely explanation is that the Christian West was not yet in a condition to assimilate the treasures now within its grasp, and so the way opened by Gerbert remained untrodden for nearly a hundred years after. Abelard himself, when he learned of the existence of Aristotle's *Metaphysics*, deplored the absence of any Latin text; and yet, even in his lifetime several pioneers had embarked once more on the labours which ultimately resulted in the full revelation of Greek and Hellenistic thought, enriched by contributions from the Hindus and Arabs to Christian Europe.

For Byzantium and the Arab world the eleventh century was a period of considerable disturbance. Like Europe in the fifth century, the East was experiencing its great invasions: the Seljuk Turks captured Baghdad in 1055 and, while preserving the Abbasid caliphate as a polite fiction, proceeded to embark on a programme of expansion which carried them into Byzantine Anatolia, where they crushed the basileus' armies at Manzikert in 1071, and then went on to wrest Syria and Palestine from the equally decadent Fatimid caliphs. But it was not long before the power of the Seljuks also began to fall apart. It was this – temporary – confusion which gave the Crusaders their opportunity.

At the same time, the Arab Empire literally collapsed in the middle. Towards the mid-eleventh century the Fatimids let loose the marauding tribes of the Hilali on the Maghreb with the object of keeping them out of upper Egypt. Their ravages were such that the Maghreb did not recover until the nineteenth century.

Further west the triumphs of al Mansur were a thing of the past and the cracks in Muslim Spain which they had for some time concealed were widening fast. The caliphate of Cordova had lost all authority and become a mere pretext for the squabbles of rival claimants. In 1031 it disappeared altogether, giving place to the *reyes de taifas*, princes of Arab, Berber or even Slav stock who surrounded themselves with refined and luxurious courts and called in Christian contingents to settle their quarrels for them. In this weakened condition Spain lost Toledo, ceded to the king of Castille in 1085, and was saved from rapid Christian reconquest by the Almoravid intervention. This had its origin in groups of hermits (*al murabitun*) from Mauretania, practising a simple and austere form of Mohammedanism, who after stirring up support among the warlike tribes advanced with them into Morocco, founded Marrakesh in 1062, unified the Maghreb as far as Algiers, and then, in 1086, finally landed in Spain in response to an appeal by the king of Seville. Their troops, manoeuvring in close formation with drums beating, inflicted defeat after defeat on the Christian knights, who were used to headlong charges which then broke up into hand-to-hand fighting. Even so, the tireless persistence of the king of Castille proved able to contain them while they were caught up in the struggle against the Muslim princes of Spain, 'faithless libertines, corrupters of the people, and unworthy to rule'. The Amoravids did not gain complete control of all Muslim Spain until 1110, and not long afterwards came the first stirrings of unrest among the Almohad communities of the Maghreb which, in less than a quarter of a century, were to bring about their downfall.

It was this troubled period of the eleventh century that saw the most brilliant flowering of 'Arabic' science. This was the time of al Biruni, of Ibn Sina (Avicenna) and Ibn al Haitham, all of whom may be considered among the most remarkable minds of all time. Even so, while it rose to astounding heights, this intellectual life could not but suffer in the long run from the effects of this instability and increasing lack of unity. The slowing-down process was further contributed to by the considerable orthodox reaction in the East, where official theological colleges, the *madrasas*, were being created, just as in the West, where the freedom of the Spanish courts scandalized the new masters. But, as yet, this was no more than a slowing down and there was still a great deal of activity, especially at the two extremities of the Arab world. In Persia, this appeared in a succession of works in the Persian language, dominated by the towering figure of the poet and mathematician Omar Khayyam (d. 1123). Spain, the last country to experience this wave of intellectual excitement, was also the last in which it maintained its full strength. There are too many names to mention here, but we cannot ignore those of the astronomer al Zarqali, who worked in Toledo at the time of the Christian reconquest; of the medical family of Ibn Zuhr at Seville; and of the geographer al Idrisi, who was born at Ceuta, educated at Cordova and spent part of his working life at the Norman court of Palermo. What is more important, however, is the extent to which this activity was becoming decentralized. To begin with it had been centred on Cordova, now it was spread among a number of cities, including Toledo, Seville, Saragossa. Also important is the part played by the Jews, some of whom had come from the East, where they were no longer allowed sufficient freedom. This picture will help us to understand the geographical distribution of intellectual contacts between the Arab and Christian worlds at the time of Abelard.

The Crusades were at one time thought to have played an important part in the development of these contacts. This view has now been discarded. Neither Syria nor Palestine figured any longer among the real centres of cultural activity, and the Crusaders, in any case, were no scholars. Some of those who settled in the East did acquire oriental outlooks, while others brought back with them to the West a taste for luxury and even hygiene; but all this hardly went beyond the ordinary details of everyday life. All the same, it is easy to exaggerate a reaction against earlier views, and we should not forget that Adelard of Bath travelled, as we shall see farther on, from Antioch to Tarsus, and that in Syria itself a good many translations were being made. One of these, of the *Al Malaki*, the medical encyclopedia of Ali ibn Abbas, was produced at Antioch by a Pisan by the name of Stephen in 1127. But Stephen had developed his interest in the study of Arabic sciences at Salerno and in Sicily, and the inspiration which led Adelard to embark on his travels came originally from Spain.

Italy in the late eleventh and twelfth centuries was in an intellectual ferment. Bearing in mind what has already been said about the juridical research undertaken during this period, we also find, just as in the Quattrocento, a notable increase in the number of direct contacts with Greek culture. Sicily, for long a part of the Byzantine empire and then ruled for several hundred years by Arab emirs before falling under the control of Norman princes, was clearly a special case as far as contacts of this kind were concerned. It is to the credit of these latest conquerors that, uncultivated as they were, they were nevertheless quick to realize this. Already Roger II Guiscard had commissioned a religious history from a Greek monk and a treatise on geography from al Idrisi. This trend was carried on and amplified by Roger's successors and is especially interesting because it was echoed among the Normans of France and England with whom constant links were maintained.

Further north, the medical school of Salerno was reaching the peak of its achievement. This may have had its origins in local traditions, as Salerno had been a noted health resort since very early times, but a much stronger impetus was certainly given by the work of Constantine the African (d. 1087), the translator of a number of Arabic works, and later of his pupil John the Saracen (d. *c.* 1103), who in addition to his own translations produced treatises on urinary diseases and on fevers. The use of human corpses for dissection was still regarded with abhorrence, but at Salerno at this period extensive research was carried out on the anatomy of the pig, which was supposed to resemble the internal structure of human beings.

Even Rome played an unexpected part in the general activity. It was in Rome that the Jewish philologist Nathan ben Jehiel was born and to Rome that he returned after his travels in Sicily, Italy and France, to complete his basic dictionary of the Hebrew language, the *Aruk*, which he enriched with interesting comparisons with the other Semitic languages, Persian, the Slavonic dialects, Latin and Italian, in about 1101.

In northern Italy the ties formed with Constantinople by Liutprand of Cremona in the tenth century were steadily maintained. The increasing volume of Italian trade with Byzantium was partly responsible for this. In the first half of the twelfth century we can find many scholars such as Moses of Bergamo, an earnest grammarian who lost all the Greek manuscripts he had bought for his collection when the Venetian quarter of Constantinople was destroyed by fire, or James of Venice, who at an unspecified date (possibly 1128) was responsible for a direct translation of Aristotle's *Second Analytics*, or Burgundio of Pisa who was active in Constantinople from about 1136 and whose translations of medical and theological works were used, among others, by Peter Lombard.

Recently reconquered Spain was however the most fruitful region for such exchanges. In 1106 the Jew, Moses Sefardi, was baptized at Huesca and took the name of his patron, king Alfonso I of Aragon. The newly christened Pedro Alfonso was a genuine scholar, whose conversion was probably due to Cluniac influences. At all events, he was soon travelling to Christian lands. Around 1110 he was in England as physician to king Henry I Beauclerc. But his chief claim to fame is as an astronomer, although only fragments of his work now remain. The British Museum has the preface to one of his treatises, in which he gives greetings to 'all the peripatetics of our holy mother Church, and all those who have fed on the milk of philosophy and diligently practised the study of science throughout France'. He attached great importance to the dissemination of scientific knowledge, and for a start produced his own list of the liberal arts, from which grammar was omitted on the grounds that it is different for every language and therefore cannot lay claim to the dignity of a general science. Its place was taken by medicine – a vast change of attitude since the Carolingian era.

Hearing that Latin students of astronomy were prepared to travel vast distances in search of instruction, Alfonso offered them the benefit of his own experience, which was extremely reliable, since it was based on constant observation. Whatever the reputation of individual masters, he maintained that observation was a basis that should never be neglected, or we should be like the goat who went into a vineyard to satisfy his hunger and ate only the green leaves instead of taking advantage of the ripe fruit.

The study of astronomy, he urged, ought not to be frightening since it was neither as difficult as some people believed, nor contrary to religion, as was claimed by others. What was harder was to overcome one's own pride and become a pupil in a new subject when one was already an acknowledged master. But then we must think of the glory this discipline shed on the scholars who showed themselves worthy of it.

They are moving lines, and they herald the dawn of modern science. We may smile today at the small knowledge of these twelfth-century men, but in more than one respect they already possessed a truly scholarly attitude of mind. They had a respect for facts learned by observation, together with a desire to excel themselves and to pass on their results to others.

This time Alfonso's progress did not go unnoticed or even remain an isolated phenomenon. He found many disciples in England, and chief of these was Walcher, the prior of Malvern, a monk who originally came from Lorraine. Walcher had not needed Alfonso to inspire him with a love of astronomy. He had already acquired an astrolabe with which to observe the eclipses (in Italy in 1091 and in England in 1092), and used his results to formulate lunar tables. He was therefore overjoyed to find a teacher to help him in his studies. What he learned is reflected in his treatise *Of the Dragon*, in which he describes methods of calculating the positions of the sun, the moon and its 'nodes' (the points of intersection in its orbit with the angle of the equator), and of forecasting eclipses.

Less well established, although highly probable, is the extent of Alfonso's influence on Adelard of Bath. Adelard was a deservedly famous personality about whom we now know almost nothing. He was born in Bath and probably studied in France, at Tours, before going on to teach at Laon. He was therefore a good example of the traditional culture dispensed by the cathedral schools. This is as he appears in his dialogue *Of the Same and the Diverse* in which he shows, in argument with his nephew, the superiority of the liberal arts over earthly passions, fortune, power and pleasure. He was sufficiently conservative to indulge in a jibe at 'these new Platos and Aristotles who are born every day'. But then he began to travel, to Italy and Sicily and later to the East, where he spent seven years, and visited Cilicia, Syria and Palestine. He must also have spent some time in Spain or else he inherited the teachings of Alfonso, for his translation of the astronomical tables of al Khwarizmi shows the corrections made at Cordova. In 1126 he was back in Bath and lived for at least another sixteen years in which time he had some connexion with the court and may have been employed at the Exchequer. His travels had a considerable effect on his ideas, and his best-known work, the *Natural Questions*, shows him among his friends after his return answering their questions and giving them a highly flattering picture of the Arab world. It is true that the work contains very little that is specifically Arabic, or even particularly new, apart from a quotation from Aristotle's *Physics*, of which this is the earliest known Latin version. But besides his translation of al Khwarizmi, Adelard produced another of Euclid's *Elements*, also taken from the Arabic.

The most interesting thing about Adelard is his attitude of

mind. His curiosity was indefatigable and, in the oddity of the questions it led him to ask, sometimes very funny. Why, he wondered, are the fingers of the hand all different lengths? Why can babies not walk from birth? He was also alert for new observations and experience. He noticed that a blow struck at a distance is seen before it is heard. He jotted down his impressions of an earthquake in Syria. He tried the experiment of hanging up a vessel full of water with small holes pierced in the bottom and a single hole with a plug in it at the top and observed that the water would only drip out if the hole at the top was open and bubbles of air were able to rise to the top to fill the space. In a good many cases the ideas which Adelard deduced from his observations have been confirmed by modern science, among them his belief in the continuity of the universe and the indestructibility of matter. 'And certainly in my judgement nothing in this world of sense ever perishes utterly, or is less today than when it was created. If any part is dissolved from one union, it does not perish but is joined to some other group.' He also had a fair idea of gravity and knew that if a hole were drilled through the centre of the earth, an object thrown into it would come to rest midway.

His ideas of scientific method are equally interesting. He grasped what was to be one of the great weaknesses of all scientific work for centuries to come: the lack of instruments which would make it possible to go beyond the limits of the unaided senses. 'The senses are reliable neither in respect of the greatest nor the smallest objects. Who has ever comprehended the space of the sky with the sense of sight? . . . Who has ever distinguished minute atoms with the eye?' He exalted the processes of reason in the face of teachers whose authority was accepted with blind faith. His words to his nephew have been often quoted:

It is difficult for me to discuss animals with you. For I learned from my Arabian masters under the leading of reason; you, however, captivated by the appearance of authority, follow your halter. Since what else should authority be called than a halter? . . . Wherefore, if you want to hear anything more from me, give and take reason. For I'm not the sort of man that can be fed on a picture of a beefsteak.

In this there was nothing that was not perfectly consistent with Faith, since the assertion that everything followed a rational sequence did not mean a refusal to see it as the effect of the divine will.

Adelard of Bath also exercised a very wide influence. Some twenty copies of the *Natural Questions* have survived, and the scientific tradition which he and Walcher helped to form in England persisted and reached its apogee in the thirteenth century with Robert Grosseteste and Roger Bacon, both of whom quoted Adelard. In contrast to the Continent, where there was a greater devotion to philosophical studies, England early revealed a scientific bias.

Now to return to Spain. Pedro Alfonso had been baptized at Huesca, and it was in the region of the Ebro, too, that a number of translators were at work around the second quarter of the twelfth century. At Tarazona, some sixty miles west of Saragossa, the bishop installed after the reconquest of the city commissioned one Hugh of Santalla to translate a dozen scientific works; but astrology figured largely in the list, and Hugh himself seems to have been a somewhat undistinguished scholar.

It has been noted that these translators working in Spain fall into three distinct categories. First there were the Jews and Mozarabs, like Pedro Alfonso. Next came the Spanish clerks, whose only recommendation was a knowledge of languages, among whom Hugh must be counted. Lastly there were the foreign scholars, drawn by the thirst for knowledge. These included two men from very different environments who met on the banks of the Ebro in about 1140. One, Hermann of Carinthia, was probably of Slav origin and had studied at Chartres before learning Arabic. The other was an Englishman, Robert of Chester. Together they translated works of astronomy and meteorology. They were planning to tackle the

Almagesta of Ptolemy when they were diverted by other work. After this their paths diverged. Hermann, after a spell at Leon, was in Toulouse in 1143, where he completed both his translation of Ptolemy's *Planisphere*, which he dedicated to his master, Thierry of Chartres, and a philosophical work which was the first in Europe to be really influenced by Arabic cosmology. Robert went to Pamplona and later to Segovia. He returned to London in about 1147. His principal works were the translation of al Khwarizmi's *Algebra* and tables of astronomy adapted to the meridian of London.

Further east, in Barcelona, an Italian, Plato of Tivoli, assisted by a Jew named Abraham bar Hiyya, was devoting himself between 1134 and 1145 to translations from Arabic and Hebrew. Their *Book of Plans*, an excellent treatise on practical geometry, must now be assigned to the year 1145 and not, as was previously thought, to 1116; but even so it is still the first Latin work to offer a complete solution to a quadratic equation. As early as 1138 they had been jointly responsible for the first Latin translation of a Ptolemaic work, although this was admittedly a minor one, the *Quadripartitum*, or *Treatise in Four Parts*. Other works which have been attributed to them are more doubtful, but in the two fields of geometry and astronomy these authors have considerable importance.

No mention has yet been made of Toledo, which had become the capital of the king of Castille in 1085 and whose 'school of translators' has been often praised. In fact, the first Latin archbishop of Toledo was on somewhat unfriendly terms with the Muslims in the city, who blamed him for breaking his sworn word and turning their great mosque into a cathedral. His successor, Archbishop Raymond, seems to have shown rather more interest in the possibility of intellectual exchanges in his city. Avendeuth the Israelite and Dominic Gonzalez (*Gundisalvi*) dedicated to him the results of a collaboration in which the former translated from Arabic into Castilian and the latter, a Spanish clerk, from Castilian into Latin. John of Seville, a somewhat elusive character who may have been a converted Jew and of whose work we know only a part, probably worked in Toledo; and it was in Toledo also that another Italian, Gerard of Cremona, settled towards the middle of the century. Gerard's ambition was to learn Arabic in order to translate Ptolemy's *Almagesta*; but he was not content with this, and so many translations are attributed to him that he must have had an entire team of translators working under his direction. This was the beginning of a new phase, which lasted well into the second half of the century. Interest began to be directed much more towards philosophical works, and the personality of Aristotle himself, about whom Abelard complained of knowing so little, began to emerge.

This was an interchange on a much broader scale than anything which had taken place in the time of Gerbert, and this time there was to be no further interruption. A new interest in the sciences was becoming apparent nearly everywhere in Europe, and was especially evident, as we have seen, in England and in Italy. It appeared, too, in Marseilles, where in 1140 we find one Raymond adapting the astronomical tables of Toledo to the local meridian, and in Narbonne, where not long afterwards Abraham ben Ezra was inaugurating a series of translations from Arabic into Hebrew for the benefit of the Jewish communities of Languedoc and Provence. Even the swift decline of the school of Chartres which occurred during the second half of the century was further evidence of this, since Chartres suffered from competition with Paris, where Abelard had been responsible for a rapid advance in dialectics. But its pseudo-scientific speculations were also superseded by the works introduced from Spain.

It is not easy for us to assess the exact significance of this renewed contact with Arabic science. Even more than a body of information and methods of work, it brought a new spirit and a more realistic approach to the physical universe, which had previously been regarded chiefly as an imperfect copy, a world of symbolic appearances masking the true Reality. A whole new and unexplored area was opening before men's minds. But there were still too many factors against this 'revolution' to allow it to have its full effect.

First it must be stressed that the versions produced at this period were very far from fulfilling our modern requirements of a good translation. It appears that each word of the original text had to be rendered by the exactly corresponding word in the language into which it was translated. Consequently the words were placed in exactly the same order without much reference to the context or the peculiarities of individual idiom. The result was often a series of misconstructions if not of completely incomprehensible nonsense. The more intermediary stages the translation went through – from Greek into Latin by means of Syriac and Arabic, for instance – the greater the chances of error. Translations made directly from the Greek therefore had a real advantage, but these were still comparatively rare. There were however some translators who distinguished themselves by a severer standard of accuracy. John of Seville would suggest emendations when the text as literally translated seemed unsatisfactory. Moreover, some general progress was discernible even from one decade to the next.

It must also be admitted that the products of Arabic science were not always viewed in Europe in their loftiest and most fertile aspect. It was not only the pure, disinterested thirst for knowledge which drove so many savants to Spain and to work so hard when they got there, nor was this alone what made their writings so valuable. Much more important was a naïve desire to acquire power over the hidden forces of nature by wresting her secrets from her. This has already been seen in the way pride of place was given to astrological works. Even those authors who are most reticent on the subject of actual magic do not commit themselves to the point of categorically denying the possibility. For a long time, right up to the seventeenth century at least, this tendency remained deeply ingrained in all European scientific research of the kind, concerned less with the regular and normal workings of nature and its laws than with the 'occult virtues' of bodies – those which are not immediately apparent to the senses or to the reasoning which is based on them. It was a tendency which was to encourage numerous experiments made, more or less haphazardly, in the hope of discovering the secrets of nature. As early as the thirteenth century it led Roger Bacon to make his famous prediction of marvels, such as the aeroplane and submarine, which modern science has realized and placed at the disposal of mankind. Unfortunately it also produced an unhealthy intellectual equivocation which in too many cases deflected men's endeavours from a truly scientific approach.

Finally, whether we like it or not, we have to admit that the genuine scientific curiosity which dominated the work of men like Gerbert, Pedro Alfonso or Adelard of Bath did not remain in the forefront. The work of Peter the Venerable is worth mentioning here. As abbot of Cluny, which possessed a number of subsidiary houses there, Peter visited Spain in 1141 and saw the translators at work in the Ebro region. This gave him the idea of using their skills to obtain a complete and accurate Latin text of the Koran. By disseminating a knowledge of the Muslim religion which was somewhat loosely regarded as a Christian heresy, he felt that it would be possible to combat it with intellectual weapons at least as efficiently as by waging physical war on its adherents as the Crusaders were doing. Somewhat unwillingly Hermann of Carinthia and Robert of Chester abandoned their scientific works for a while and placed themselves at his disposal. Completing his team with the addition of a Muslim and a Mozarab, Peter got his translation finished and made unsuccessful efforts to bring it to the notice of St Bernard, who was preoccupied with other, more urgent, business. Only Peter was sufficiently far-sighted to realize the danger which so many works coming from a more cultivated world represented for the Church, and, on the other hand, to see that once the Muslims' errors had been properly established it would be possible to take full and fearless advantage of what they genuinely had to offer and even perhaps to win them over to the True Faith. Peter himself wrote a refutation of Islam, two books of which have survived, in which he courteously invited the Saracens to a frank discussion, acknowledging their qualities and virtues, stressing all there was in common between their religion and true Christianity, and urging them to the logical effort of mind which would lead them inevitably to Christ.

Peter the Venerable's belief in discussion was quite remarkable for his time, but it was a solitary phenomenon. On the other hand, the truly scientific attitude of earlier times was soon submerged in a welter of philosophical systems. Hermann of Carinthia was already concluding his work with a philosophical treatise. In the second half of the twelfth century the works of Aristotle (or those attributed to him), the commentaries of Arab thinkers like al Farabi and al Kindi, and finally the contemporary systems of Ibn Rushd (the famous Averroes) and the Jew Maïmonides came definitely to the fore. In this way the trends coming from Spain strengthened those which Abelard had launched with such vigour. More pragmatic scientific considerations did not entirely disappear, but they did become less important and somewhat marginal, even in a geographical sense, since most of this work was carried out in England.

Chapter 5

CONCLUSION

In conclusion, it should not be forgotten that the time of Abelard was one of a new and original flowering in Western art. This was the period which produced some of the finest masterpieces of romanesque art. The building of the nave and transept of St Sernin at Toulouse, the chevet of which had been consecrated in 1095, dates from the first half of the twelfth century, and romanesque sculpture, with splendid achievements at Moissac and in Toulouse itself already to its credit, was reaching a new peak. In Burgundy alone the three years from 1130 to 1132 saw the consecration of the great church of Cluny, the romanesque church of Vézelay, and the cathedral of Autun. Close by, at Fontenay, the new Cistercian architecture was providing a model of austere simplicity (1139–47). But already the first experiments in gothic art, at Durham around the year 1100 and at Morienval in the Île-de-France between 1122 and 1130, were beginning to appear. They led with astonishing swiftness to the creation of such vast edifices as the choir of St Denis, the work of Suger, which was consecrated in 1144 and to the commencement of work on the first great French gothic cathedral at Sens in 1140. A new and vigorous spring of creative power was welling up.

We are dwarves perched on the shoulders of giants. Though we may see more and farther than they, it is not because our sight is keener or our stature greater but because they bear us up and raise us by their own gigantic height . . .

This often quoted tribute by Bernard of Chartres to the ancients, the study of whom formed the basis of all culture, is also a splendid display of optimism.

It is true that the growth of schools in the twelfth century itself presented a problem which was only resolved by a great deal of groping in the dark. The enrolment of students, the conditions under which they were to live, their courses of study and examination procedures all necessitated some move towards a more formal organization which, in the thirteenth century, was to produce the universities.

It is also true that twelfth-century authors are generally blamed for relying too much on book learning and an excessive respect for authorities. The criticism is amusing, coming, as it does today, from those responsible for our own university discipline, which is all too often bowed under a massive weight of bibliography. But it is well known that both first-hand observation and the study of documents benefit if they are backed up by a cultural experience, which must be derived to some extent from books. The founders of our European culture would have been foolish indeed to ignore the accumulated treasures of centuries of work and thought. Psychologically, too, they were understandably fascinated by it.

Lastly, some will regret the shift of interest which occurred in the mid-twelfth century away from the literary preoccupations which had previously predominated but which were now to remain somewhat in the background until the fifteenth century. It is regrettable also that this interest was not re-directed wholeheartedly to the scientific questions beginning to emerge from contact with the East, and in that the eyes of Abelard's successors dialectic assumed what may seem to us a disproportionate importance. But there is nothing to be gained from trying to rewrite history as it ought to have been. The very force of circumstances made men in the twelfth century feel the need for more subtle instruments of reasoning, for a rational choice between the often contradictory principles offered by the texts available to them, and for concepts based on a finer and more definitive analysis. To their minds the acquisition of a sound method of rationalization was the key to all future progress. To quote Adelard of Bath:

Aristotle, with his sophistical wit, would entertain himself by using the arguments of dialectic to maintain a false statement to his hearers while they defended the truth against him. The truth is that once they are assured of the aid of dialectic, all other arts may tread firmly, while without it they stumble and reel about.

The fact that this decision should have been taken so consciously in the twelfth century should provide us, in our search for the historical conditions of intellectual progress, with all the more food for thought.

We may therefore agree with Bernard of Chartres that by the middle of the twelfth century the first, infant stage in the history of European culture had been passed.

Conspectus

THE early growth of European culture was clearly bound up with, if not actually dictated by the growth of the entire social and economic structure of Europe. Even the very modest improvement in agricultural methods which enabled the peasants of these regions to reap better harvests and released them to some extent from the pressures of hunger and malnutrition, played an essential part in bringing about some demographic expansion and in freeing manpower – and minds – for other activities such as craftsmanship, finance or even more strictly intellectual labours. The rebirth of towns in the twelfth century provides the most visible evidence of these benefits; and this, in its turn, led to others.

This is closely paralleled by the changes we have seen taking place over the periods dealt with in this book. In the time of Alcuin a tiny minority of clerks responded to the wishes of an exceptionally enlightened ruler by founding, often in monasteries buried deep in the countryside, the *scriptoria*, libraries and schools which enabled a modest start to be made. Nearly two centuries later, in the time of Gerbert, the social environment had not altered substantially but the number of monastic seats of learning had certainly increased and the seeds of a few urban centres were to be seen springing up, while the role of the temporal rulers had ceased to be all-important. In the time of Abelard the change had taken place. The number of people engaged in intellectual activities was now considerable, the possibility of independent careers was open to them and the influence of urban seats of learning was from now on decidedly more far-reaching than that of the courts.

Nevertheless, we must beware of taking too narrowly exclusive a view of this chain of events. Economic and social development had made possible a division of labour. Through the legal and political problems it entailed it had also encouraged intellectual labours and imposed a certain system of priorities; but even so the mind still developed along its own lines. The various aspects of human evolution are connected, but each retains its own specific character.

At the risk of oversimplification: intellectual progress from the ninth century to the twelfth may be said to have taken place at three main levels. The first of these is the basic one of language, of linguistic analysis and literary expression. The scholars of the ninth century did their best in their endeavour to revive the correct and graceful manipulation of the language of a distant past that had nothing in common with their own times. They were, first and foremost, grammarians and versifiers. Three centuries passed before the full fruit of their labours appeared. By then Latin had reverted to the role of a scholarly or ecclesiastical language, and literary expression was fast turning to new and hitherto undeveloped idioms. Grammar became once more an elementary subject entrusted to the humblest teachers: when, that is, its very standing as one of the liberal arts was not challenged.

The second level was physical observation, concrete experiment, technical advance and pure science. To us today the observation of natural phenomena occurring all around us, and some search for facts and causes, is a simple and obvious activity. Then, however, it was a minor, even incidental aspect of study. It does not help to blame religion for concentrating men's minds on another world: their religion did not necessarily force them to turn their eyes away from divine creation; on the contrary, voices were later to be heard advocating the contemplation and study of the wonders He had worked, as a way to the full adoration of the Creator. A much more important reason for the slow start was the prevailing mental attitude which, among a number of possible interpretations, still preferred that of St Bernard to that of St Francis. Though, as we have seen, quiet progress was being made in the

fields of agriculture and craftsmanship, the effects of which
were beginning to transform the conditions of life, all this had
very little connexion with the scientific heritage of antiquity
which was gradually being revived in Spain and Italy. Though
this first move towards a scientific renaissance was in itself
heavily encumbered with magic and superstition, we may
nevertheless be tempted to see in it an element of promise.
Thanks to it, the time of Gerbert rose somewhat above
mediocrity. But the most spectacular and rewarding work
of the twelfth century was directed along different lines.

The third level at which progress was made was in reasoning
and philosophical thinking. This progress was at first, and for
a long time, very slow. To us the political and philosophic
notions of the Carolingian era appear to have been still in their
infancy. Gerbert, later on, was chiefly remarkable for his
rhetorical strength. And yet the changing world was presenting problems which had somehow to be resolved. In a welter
of confused ideas and fumbling logic, men clung instinctively
to an ill-digested mass of sacred texts and references whose
divergences and contradictions seemed to their despairing
minds to be ever more obvious and serious. As a result their
basic urge was to achieve control over the laws of reasoning
and selection, and to sharpen their intellectual tools. There
can be no doubt that dialectic was of prime importance in
the time of Abelard.

And yet, in the course of this briefly summarized development, many problems have cropped up which any psychologist or sociologist would certainly pounce on: the initial steps
and gradual spread of writing; the elaboration of teaching
methods; the role of literature, didactic at first or concerned
with escapism and marvels, and only gradually beginning to
describe emotions and develop a feeling for psychology; the
progressive mastering of the intellect as a tool. The list is
endless.

What should also be stressed is how much this progress
owed to the diversity of this emergent Europe, and to the

mutual co-operation and emulation which grew up among its various elements. This was more than just a progressive fusion between Romans – between the already varied and very unequally romanized peoples of ancient *Romania* – and 'Barbarians', the invaders whose own origins and destinies were by no means one. This first amalgamation gave way, little by little, to another between the new units which were beginning to show some of the characteristics of our modern nations.

A word must be said about the part played by each of these components. First, the old Mediterranean lands. Italy provided Charlemagne with some of his best helpers; from the eleventh century onwards she rediscovered the genius for law which Virgil had celebrated in classical times, and made extensive contacts with the Eastern world. From Spain after the Arab conquest a flood of books and scholars found refuge in the West, bringing new and fertile knowledge, while later still *Hispania* became the scene of outstanding collaboration between Muslims, Jews and Christians.

In the north there was Ireland, that last, strange refuge of classical values which were then brought back to the continent by tireless Irish missionaries. The old, half-romanized Britain became the land of the Angles and, from Alcuin to Lanfranc and Anselm, formed close and amazingly fruitful ties with Rome, while from the twelfth century onwards contact with Spain led to the growth of a promising scientific tradition.

It is essential to mention the importance of that privileged area which lay between the Loire and the Rhine, where the real bonds of Europe were forged; where so many monasteries and later cities flourished; and where the breath of inspiration blew strongest. And if the men responsible for this activity were originally foreigners, they none the less raised a rich harvest.

Beyond the Rhine lay Charlemagne's vast creation, Germany, where the first seeds of intellectual life had been sown by Hrabanus Maurus. The time lag would take hundreds of years to make up, but meanwhile Germany contributed countless individual talents to the European pool.

The birth of European culture came about in a series of renaissances, an odd, loping march forward in which men kept their eyes firmly on the past, on the revelations of Christianity and the treasures of classical culture. But another important factor was the tension produced by the attractions of profane culture in men whose education was fundamentally Christian. We may smile at the thought of copies of Ovid being produced at Cluny, but it must be stressed that this kind of internal contradiction was a remarkable and lasting factor in the forging of European culture. The ramifications of all the labour expended in reconciling classical culture and revealed religion, or in proclaiming, for good or ill, their irreconcilable antagonism, have not been fully explored; but they have shown us its value as a spur. Perhaps it is to this that we modern Europeans owe the restless, questing spirit which gives us no respite in the search for progress.

BIBLIOGRAPHICAL HINTS

There can be no question here of providing a complete bibliography, or even of mentioning every work used in the preparation of this one. This is simply a list of works to which the author is most indebted, or those which seem most likely to interest a reader seeking further information.

GENERAL

For everything to do with the intellectual background and cultural geography of Europe there is a great deal to be found in LESNE, E., *Histoire de la propriété ecclésiastique en France*, vol. IV: *Les Livres, scriptoria et bibliothèques, du commencement du VIIIe à la fin du XIe siècle*, and vol. V: *Les écoles, de la fin du VIIIe siècle à la fin du XIIe* (Lille, 1938 and 1940). For the growth of writing, see BISCHOFF, B., *Paläographie* (Berlin, 2nd ed., 1957) and BISCHOFF, B., LIEFTINCK, G. I., and BATTELLI, G., *Nomenclature des écritures livresques du IXe au XVIe siècle* (Paris, 1954). There is a convenient summary by HIGOUNET, C., *L'écriture* (Paris 1955, Coll. *Que sais-je?*).

On monastic culture, secular education and literature: LECLERQ, J., *L'amour des lettres et le désir de Dieu* (Paris, 1957); SMALLEY, BERYL, *The Study of the Bible in the Middle Ages* (Oxford, 1941, 2nd ed., 1952); THOMPSON, J. W., *The Literacy of the Laity in the Middle Ages* (Berkeley, 1939); GHELLINCK, J. DE, *Littérature latine au Moyen âge* (Paris, 1939, 2 vols.); CURTIUS, E. R., *Europäische Literatur und Lateinisches Mittelalter* (Bern, 1948. French translation Paris 1956. English translation by W. R. Trask, 1953).

In philosophy, a major work is GILSON, É., *La Philosophie du Moyen âge* (Paris, 3rd ed., 1947; English translation 1955). Complementary to this: FOREST, A., VANSTEENBERGHEN, F., and GANDILHAC, M. DE, *Le Mouvement doctrinal du XIe au XIVe siècle* (Paris, 1951; vol. XIII of *The History of the Church*, ed. by A. FLICHE and V. MARTIN).

In science the bibliography for the period is very full – rather fuller in fact than its subject. There is a great deal of information in: SARTON, G., *Introduction to the History of Science* (Washington, 1927–31), vol. I and the beginning of vol. II. A good general view is to be found in CROMBIE, A. C., *Augustine to Galileo, the History of Science, A.D. 400–1650* (London, 1952). Also worth mention: THORNDIKE, LYNN, *History of Magic and Experimental Science* (New York, 1923), vols. I and II; HASKINS, C. H., *Studies in the History of Medieval Science* (Cambridge, Mass., 2nd ed. 1924); *Histoire générale des sciences*, dir. R. TATON, vol. I (Paris 1957).

On religious and philosophical opinions bound up with linguistic problems (such as the principal language, variety of dialect) there is a very full account in BORST, A., *Der Turmbau von Babel* (Stuttgart, 1957–59, vols. I and II, 3 vols.)

THE PERIOD OF ALCUIN

Quite indispensable is LAISTNER, M. L., *Thought and Letters in Western Europe, A.D. 500–900* (Ithaca–London, 2nd ed., 1957). Extremely valuable also: LEHMANN, PAUL, *Erforschung des Mittelalters* (Stuttgart, 1959–62, 5 vols; it is a collection of articles previously published individually).

The most up-to-date studies of Charlemagne are those by GANSHOF, F. L., 'Charlemagne', in *Speculum*, 1949, and 'Charlemagne et l'usage de l'écrit en matière administrative', in *Le Moyen âge*, 1951. Now, there is the collective work on *Karl der Grosse, Lebenswerk und Nachleben*, ed. by W. BRAUNFELS (Düsseldorf, 1965–7, 4 vols.)

For the preceding period, the most recent general study is RICHÉ, P., *Education et culture dans l'Occident barbare, VIe–VIIIe siècles* (Paris, 1962).

Of works on Alcuin, particularly worth mentioning are KLEIN-CLAUSZ, A., *Alcuin* (Paris, 1948); DUCKETT, ELEANOR S., *Alcuin, Friend of Charlemagne* (New York, 1951); WALLACH, L., *Alcuin and Charlemagne, Studies in Carolingian History and Literature* (Ithaca, 1959).

Biblical studies and exegesis can be found in BERGER, S., *Histoire de la Vulgate pendant les premiers siècles du Moyen âge* (Paris, 1893); GANSHOF, F. L. 'La revision de la Bible par Alcuin', in *Humanisme et Renaissance*, 1947; SCHÖNBACH, A. M., Über einige Evangelienkommentare des Mittelalters', in *Wiener Akademie, Philosophisch-historische Klasse, Sitzungsberichte*, 1903.

Lastly, some books on various other aspects: KLEINCLAUSZ, A., *Eginhard* (Paris, 1942); ARQUILLIÈRE, H. X., *L'Augustinisme politique, essai sur la formation des théories politiques au Moyen âge* (Paris, 1956); LOT, F., 'A quelle époque a-t-on cessé de parler latin?', in *Bulletin du Cange*, 1931; FARAL, E., 'Les conditions générales de la production littéraire en Europe occidentale pendant les IXe et Xe siècles', in *Settimane di Studio del Centro Italiano di Studi sull'alto Medioevo*, II, 1954 (Spoleto, 1955).

THE PERIOD OF GERBERT

An outstanding though unfortunately incomplete general study is FOCILLON, H., *L'An Mil* (Paris, 1952). Also useful is POGNON, E., *L'an mille, textes traduits et annotés* (Paris, 1947). Extremely stimulating are LOPEZ, R., 'Still another Renaissance?', in *American Historical Review*, 1951; Symposium on the Xth Century in *Medievalia et Humanistica*, 1955. Endlessly fascinating is the section devoted to the growth of mental attitudes in BLOCH, MARC, *La société féodale*, vol. I, *La formation des liens de dépendance* (Paris, 1939, English translation L. A. Manyon, 1961).

On Gerbert himself: PICAVET, F., *Gerbert, un pape philosophe, d'après l'histoire et d'après la légende* (Paris, 1897); OLWER, NICOLAU D', 'Gerbert i la cultura catalana del segle X', in *Estudis catalans*, 1910; MILLAS VALLICROSA, J. M., *Assaig d'historia de les idees fisiques i matemàtiques a la Catalunya medieval* (Barcelona, 1931) and *Estudios sobre historia de la ciencia española* (Barcelona, 1949), also very useful for the following chapter; LEFLON, J., *Gerbert, humanisme et chrétienté au Xe siècle* (St Wandrille, 1946); and finally the most recent chronological study: UHLIRZ, MATHILDE, *Untersuchungen über Inhalt und Datierung der Briefe Gerberts von Aurillac* (Göttingen, 1957).

On other individuals and regions: KURTH, G., *Notger et la civilisation au Xe siècle* (Paris, 1905, 2 vols); ROUSSET, P., 'Raoul Glàber, interprète de la pensée commune au XIe siècle', in *Revue d'Histoire de l'Église de France*, 1950; STENTON, FRANK, *Anglo-Saxon England, c. 550–1087* (Oxford, 2nd ed., 1947); LEMERLE, P., 'Problèmes de la première Renaissance byzantine au IXe siècle', in *Bulletin de l'Association Marc Bloch de Toulouse*, 1958–60.

THE PERIOD OF ABELARD

Deservedly the classic is still HASKINS, C. H., *The Renaissance of the XIIth Century* (Cambridge, Mass., 1933); a useful complement to this is PARÉ, G., BRUNET, A., and TREMBLAY, P., *La Renaissance du XIIe siècle, les écoles et l'enseignement* (Ottawa–Paris, 1933). A lively and stimulating little book by LE GOFF, J.: *Les intellectuels au Moyen âge* (Paris, 1957).

For literature, law and theology it is worth mentioning GHELLINCK, J. DE, *L'essor de la littérature latine au XIIe siècle* (Brussels–Paris, 1946); FOURNIER, PAUL, 'Un tournant de l'histoire du droit, 1060–1140', in *Nouvelle Revue historique de Droit*, 1917; FOURNIER, PAUL, and LE BRAS, G., *Histoire des collections canoniques en Occident, depuis les Fausses Décrétales jusqu'au Décret de Gratien* (Paris, 1931–32, 2 vols.); GHELLINCK, J. DE, *Le Mouvement théologique du XIIe siècle, études, recherches et documents* (Paris, 1914; 2nd ed., 1948). CHENU, M. D., *La théologie au XIIe siècle* (Paris, 1957).

This brings us to Abelard himself, and first of all to the admirable book by GILSON, E., *Héloise et Abélard, études sur le Moyen âge et l'Humanisme* (Paris, 1938); translated into English by L. K. Shook, 1960. There is much to be found in SIKES, J. G., *Peter Abailard* (Cambridge, 1932). It is also worth mentioning a few articles: COTTIAUX, J., 'La conception de la théologie chez Abélard', in *Revue d'histoire ecclésiastique*, 1932; GANDILHAC, M. DE, 'Sur quelques interprétations récentes d'Abélard', in *Cahiers de civilisation médiévale*, 1961. It would be easy to go on, but I cannot conclude this bibliography without saying how much I owe to my talk with Monsieur JEAN JOLIVET, maître-assistant of the Faculté des Lettres Paris-Nanterre, author of an article 'Sur quelques critiques de la théologie d'Abélard', in *Archives d'Histoire doctrinale et littéaire du Moyen age*, 1963; and of a thesis to be published on *Arts du langage et théologie chez Abélard*. I have tried to follow his advice, but he cannot be held responsible for any mistakes of mine.

On another central figure of the period: LECLERQ, J., *Pierre le Vénérable* (St Wandrille, 1946).

An approach to the Spanish background will be helped by MILLAS VALLICROSA, J. M., 'La corriente de las traducciones científicas de origén oriental hasta fines del siglo XIII', in *Cahiers d'Histoire mondiale*, 1954; and LEMAY, R., 'Dans l'Espagne du XIIe siècle, les traductions de l'arabe au latin', in *Annales E.S.C.*, 1963.

Finally, the older article by PIRENNE, H., 'L'instruction des marchands au Moyen âge', in *Annales d'Histoire économique et sociale*, 1929, is not without interest for our own subject.

MAPS

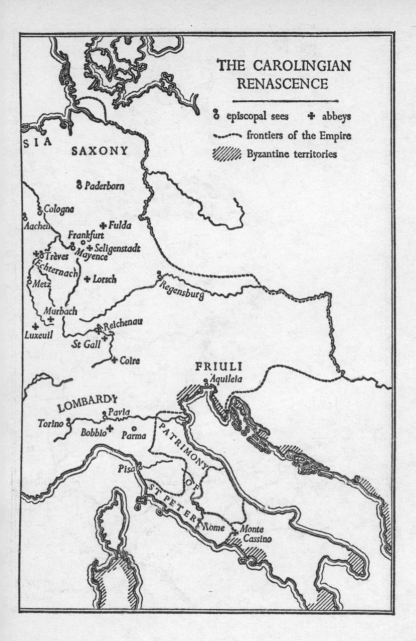

THE CAROLINGIAN RENASCENCE

ℰ episcopal sees   ✠ abbeys

⌁⌁⌁⌁ frontiers of the Empire

░░░░ Byzantine territories

SIA

SAXONY

ℰ Paderborn

ℰ Cologne

Aachen

✠ Fulda

Frankfurt

Mayence ✠ Seligenstadt

✠ Trèves

Echternach

ℰ Metz

✠ Lorsch

Regensburg

Murbach

✠ Reichenau

✠ Luxeuil

St Gall

✠ Coire

FRIULI

ℰ Aquileia

LOMBARDY

Torino   ℰ Pavia

Bobbio ✠   Parma

PATRIMONY OF ST PETER

Pisa

Rome ✠ Monte Cassino

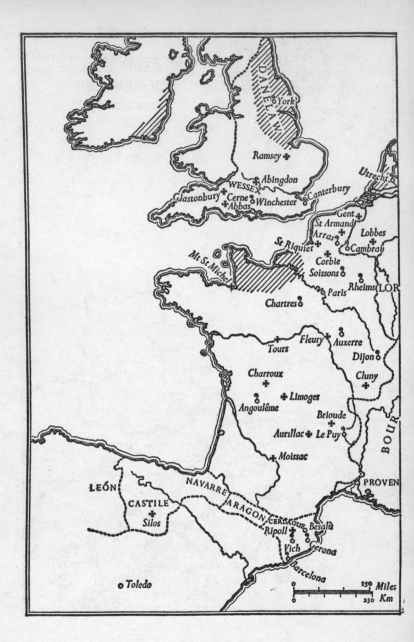

EUROPE IN THE AGE
OF GERBERT

episcopal towns ✳ abbeys
frontiers
frontiers of the Empire
regions occupied by
the Normans

DENMARK

Hamburg
R.Recknitz

SAXONY
Hildesheim
Herford ✳
Corvey ✳
Gandersheim ✳ Magdeburg
Cologne THURINGEN
Aachen
Liège Echternach
Trèves Mayence
Worms Wurzburg
RAINE FRANCONY
Gorze Speyer

POLAND

Fulda

Prague
BOHEMIA

Strasbourg

SWABIA BAVARIA
R.Lech
Reichenau ✳ St.Gall
Einsiedeln ✳

GOGNE

CARINTHIA HUNGARY

Vercelli Milano Verona
Cremona Venice
Bobbio ✳ via
Ravenna

CE

Garde
Freinet

Arezzo

ROME
Monte
Cassino
R.Garigliano Naples
Salerno

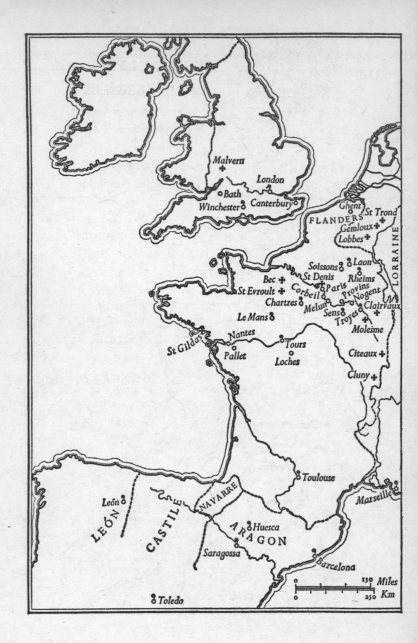

Malvern ✠

London
Bath ○
Winchester ○   ○ Canterbury

Ghent ○   ○ St Trond
FLANDERS   Gemloux ✠
Lobbes ✠

Soissons ○   ○ Laon
St Denis   ○ Rheims
Bec ✠   Paris ○
St Evroult ✠   Corbeil ○   Provins ○
Chartres ○   Melun ○   Nogent
Le Mans ○   Sens ○   Troyes ○   ○ Clairvaux
Molesme ○

Nantes ○   ○ Tours
St Gildas ○   Pallet ○   Loches ○   ○ Citeaux ✠
Cluny ✠

○ Toulouse

Marseille ○
León ○
L E Ó N   C A S T I L E   NAVARRE
A R A G O N   Huesca ○
Saragossa ○   Barcelona ○

Toledo ○

150   Miles
250   Km

EUROPE IN THE AGE
OF ABELARD

☧ episcopal sees   ✼ abbeys

SAXONY

POLAND

☧ Bamberg

☧ Worms

☧ Metz

☧ Freising

HUNGARY

☧ Milano
Pavia ☧
☧ Piacenza
Genoa ☧
Pisa ☧
☧ Bologna
Florence
Venice
Ravenna

☧ ROME
✼ Monte
Cassino
☧ Naples
☧ Salerno

INDEX

(Chief references are printed in bold type)

FOR THE BEST IN PAPERBACKS, LOOK FOR THE 🐧

In every corner of the world, on every subject under the sun, Penguins represent quality and variety – the very best in publishing today.

For complete information about books available from Penguin and how to order them, write to us at the appropriate address below. Please note that for copyright reasons the selection of books varies from country to country.

In the United Kingdom: For a complete list of books available from Penguin in the U.K., please write to *Dept EP, Penguin Books Ltd, Harmondsworth, Middlesex, UB7 0DA*

In the United States: For a complete list of books available from Penguin in the U.S., please write to *Dept BA, Viking Penguin, 299 Murray Hill Parkway, East Rutherford, New Jersey 07073*

In Canada: For a complete list of books available from Penguin in Canada, please write to *Penguin Books Canada Limited, 2801 John Street, Markham, Ontario L3R 1B4*

In Australia: For a complete list of books available from Penguin in Australia, please write to the *Marketing Department, Penguin Books Australia Ltd, P.O. Box 257, Ringwood, Victoria 3134*

In New Zealand: For a complete list of books available from Penguin in New Zealand, please write to the *Marketing Department, Penguin Books (N.Z.) Ltd, Private Bag, Takapuna, Auckland 9*

In India: For a complete list of books available from Penguin in India, please write to *Penguin Overseas Ltd, 706 Eros Apartments, 56 Nehru Place, New Delhi 110019*

Another Volume in
The Pelican History of European Thought

THE ENLIGHTENMENT

Norman Hampson

'I love that philosophy which raises up humanity,' wrote Diderot, and his words echo in all the intellectual achievements of the eighteenth century.

Armed with the insights of the scientific revolution, the men of the Enlightenment set out to free mankind from its age-old cocoon of pessimism and superstition and establish a more reasonable world of experiment and progress. Yet by the 1760s this optimism about man and society had almost evaporated. In the works of Rousseau, Kant and Goethe there was discernable a new inner voice, and an awareness of individual uniqueness which had eluded their more self-confident predecessors. The stage was set for the revolutionary crisis and the rise of Romanticism.

In this book Norman Hampson follows through certain dominant themes in the Enlightenment, and describes the contemporary social and political climate, in which ideas could travel from the salons of Paris to the court of Catherine the Great – but less easily from a master to his servant. On such vexed issues as the role of ideas in the 'rise of the middle class' he provides a new and realistic approach linking intellectual and social history.

FOR THE BEST IN PAPERBACKS, LOOK FOR THE 🐧

A CHOICE OF PENGUINS AND PELICANS

The French Revolution   Christopher Hibbert

'One of the best accounts of the Revolution that I know . . . Mr Hibbert is outstanding' – J. H. Plumb in the *Sunday Telegraph*

The Germans   Gordon A. Craig

An intimate study of a complex and fascinating nation by 'one of the ablest and most distinguished American historians of modern Germany' – Hugh Trevor-Roper

Ireland: A Positive Proposal   Kevin Boyle and Tom Hadden

A timely and realistic book on Northern Ireland which explains the historical context – and offers a practical and coherent set of proposals which could actually work.

A History of Venice   John Julius Norwich

'Lord Norwich has loved and understood Venice as well as any other Englishman has ever done' – Peter Levi in the *Sunday Times*

Montaillou: Cathars and Catholics in a French Village 1294–1324
Emmanuel Le Roy Ladurie

'A classic adventure in eavesdropping across time' – Michael Ratcliffe in *The Times*

Star Wars   E. P. Thompson and others

Is Star Wars a serious defence strategy or just a science fiction fantasy? This major book sets out all the arguments and makes an unanswerable case *against* Star Wars.

The Apartheid Handbook   Roger Omond

This book provides the essential hard information about how apartheid actually works from day to day and fills in the details behind the headlines.

The World Turned Upside Down   Christopher Hill

This classic study of radical ideas during the English Revolution 'will stand as a notable monument to . . . one of the finest historians of the present age' – *The Times Literary Supplement*

Islam in the World   Malise Ruthven

'His exposition of "the Qurenic world view" is the most convincing, and the most appealing, that I have read' – Edward Mortimer in *The Times*

The Knight, the Lady and the Priest   Georges Duby

'A very fine book' (Philippe Aries) that traces back to its medieval origin one of our most important institutions, modern marriage.

A Social History of England   New Edition   Asa Briggs

'A treasure house of scholarly knowledge . . . beautifully written and full of the author's love of his country, its people and its landscape' – John Keegan in the *Sunday Times*, Books of the Year

The Second World War   A. J. P. Taylor

A brilliant and detailed illustrated history, enlivened by all Professor Taylor's customary iconoclasm and wit.